WITHDRAWN

RAISING LAZARUS

ALSO BY BETH MACY

Dopesick
Truevine
Factory Man

RAISING LAZARUS

HOPE, JUSTICE, AND THE FUTURE OF AMERICA'S OVERDOSE CRISIS

Beth Macy

Little, Brown and Company
New York Boston London

Copyright © 2022 by Beth Macy

All photographs are by Josh Meltzer, with the exception of pages 150 and 279, by Beth Macy, and page 8 of the photo insert (Nikki King photo by Matt Eich, Mike Moore photo by Irina Rozovsky).

Hachette Book Group supports the right to free expression and the value of copyright. The purpose of copyright is to encourage writers and artists to produce the creative works that enrich our culture.

The scanning, uploading, and distribution of this book without permission is a theft of the author's intellectual property. If you would like permission to use material from the book (other than for review purposes), please contact permissions@hbgusa.com. Thank you for your support of the author's rights.

Little, Brown and Company
Hachette Book Group
1290 Avenue of the Americas, New York, NY 10104
littlebrown.com

First Edition: August 2022

Little, Brown and Company is a division of Hachette Book Group, Inc. The Little, Brown name and logo are trademarks of Hachette Book Group, Inc.

The publisher is not responsible for websites (or their content) that are not owned by the publisher.

The Hachette Speakers Bureau provides a wide range of authors for speaking events. To find out more, go to hachettespeakersbureau.com or call (866) 376-6591.

ISBN 9780316430227
Library of Congress Control Number: 2022936663

Printing 1, 2022

LSC-C

Printed in the United States of America

In loving memory of
Forrest "Frosty" Landon—
editor, uncle-in-law, friend,
and lifelong stone-roller.

In times like these you have to grow big enough
inside to hold both the loss and the hope.

—Ann Pancake,
Strange as this Weather Has Been

It's easier when fewer things go wrong in your
life to think you're smart or better than the
people who are always in the soup. But you're
not. You're just luckier.

—Robert Gipe

Contents

Contents

Tim Nolan initiates treatment outside a client's home, Icard, North Carolina.

Prologue
The Secret of Patient Care

On a chilly spring evening in 2021, nurse-practitioner Tim Nolan set up his portable exam room next to a McDonald's dumpster in Hickory, North Carolina, and he waited. His desk was the dusty dashboard of his gray Prius, his office this parking lot. It smelled like frying oil and fermented trash.

In the time it takes a drug user to pull up a shot of heroin, Tim can fashion a medical lab of test tubes and testing strips on the roof of his car. He's a practitioner on the move, delivering harm-reduction supplies, lifesaving prescriptions, and treatments for injection-related infections to patients who can't make it to his office because they don't have cars.

Or because the transmission on the one they were borrowing just blew.

Because they're not inclined.

Because the only thing they can think about is scoring drugs, so they won't end up on the toilet again, dopesick and in excruciating withdrawal.

A middle-aged factory worker named Sam, new to Tim's practice, was supposed to meet Tim in the parking lot at 5:30 p.m., but Sam had misplaced his cell phone and was running late. Also, he was super high.

Meanwhile, twenty minutes away, in a 1960s ranch that had morphed into a trap house—a home dedicated to the selling and partaking of drugs—a cluster of young and middle-aged men and women gathered, playing darts while they awaited their own appointments with Tim. When Tim first began delivering clean needles to the group two years ago, they were living in the garage. But the owner of the house—someone's grandmother—had recently moved to assisted living, and, for better or worse, the place was now all theirs.

Grandma's fussy cut-glass pitchers and doilies still dotted the interior. Out of respect for Tim, thirty-two-year-old Jordan Hayes had spent hours that afternoon cleaning the place up. A hairdresser in another life, she was tired of being the de facto house mom. "I'm trying to get me a car so I can live out of that," she said. It was Saint Patrick's Day, so Jordan ordered green Krispy Kreme doughnuts via DoorDash, trying for a festive mood that was maybe a stretch for a hepatitis C–testing party.

Soon, Tim would arrive at the now-tidy house in the Appalachian foothills toting his usual array of clean needles, hepatitis C–testing kits, and a couple of pizzas. But first, he waited for Sam. He had two important messages for his new patient.

One: You *can* get better.

And two: Don't disappear.

Prologue

*   *   *

The Centers for Disease Control and Prevention estimates that more than a million Americans have died from drug overdose since 1996, the largest factor by far in decreasing life expectancy for Americans. In the past two decades, overdose deaths have *quintupled*. If life-expectancy declines persist, experts predict it will take more than a century to recover.

Roughly six months into my reporting for this book, COVID-19 emerged in March 2020. Overdose deaths went up as the pandemic further isolated people with substance use disorders (SUDs). That community was already plagued by the poisoning of street drugs with fentanyl, a synthetic opioid 50 to 100 times more potent than heroin, and an environment that makes it far easier for people with addictions to use illicit drugs than to access treatment for addiction and their underlying mental health issues.

Within the first pandemic year, the overdose count was 29 percent higher than the year before, and the numbers kept climbing. By late 2021, it was clear that addiction had become the No. 1 destroyer of families in our time, with almost a third of Americans reporting it as a serious cause of family strife, and drug overdoses claiming the lives of more than 100,000 Americans in a year—more than from car crashes and guns combined.

And yet, after reporting on the issue for more than a decade, I have learned that whatever most people believe they know about drug addiction, unless they understand the issue firsthand—unless they know people like Tim and Sam—the reality of addiction is hard to fathom. In one small Appalachian city, EMS workers have tended the overdose deaths of more than a dozen of their former classmates, not counting the calls for addiction-related domestic violence and child abandonment. In a small Tennessee town, a thirty-two-year-old told me she'd already lost 27 percent of her high-school class to overdose.

As Tim waited for Sam, the United States Congress debated how to hold to account the Sackler family, sole owners of Purdue Pharma, whose OxyContin painkiller was the taproot of the opioid crisis. The Sacklers are just one node in a vast network of opioid lawsuits broadly acknowledged to be the most complicated in American history.

Under pressure from litigation against Purdue Pharma by 2,600 cities, counties, and Native American tribes, and to forestall further lawsuits against the Sackler family, the company filed for Chapter 11 bankruptcy in late 2019. The move was both cunning and literal, as it was preceded by a change of address that allowed the company's legal reckoning to be determined in the sleepy suburb of White Plains, New York.

White Plains has only one bankruptcy judge, Robert Drain. And Drain is known for favoring settlement deals that make economic sense and for trusting big law firms to get the details right. Judge shopping, the practice is called.

The Sackler family was nowhere near bankrupt—and had no meaningful connection to White Plains; it was simply piggyback- ing on Purdue's bankruptcy, offering to swap out the company and a smallish portion of its wealth in exchange for blanket civil immunity. Nonconsensual third-party releases, that controversial practice is called, and Drain was known to favor those, too.

If Drain confirmed the bankruptcy plan, the full extent of the Sacklers' role in the overdose crisis would never be known. The Sacklers would not admit wrongdoing. And they would never be held to account for their role in helping addict people like Sam, one of an estimated 3 million Americans with opioid use disorder, or OUD.

For a quarter century, the Sacklers masterminded and micro- managed a relentless marketing campaign for their killer drug, then surgically drained the company of $10 billion when they saw trouble on the horizon. The family socked much of that money away in family trusts and offshore accounts. But they needed a court's help to shield this money—permanently—from the company's creditors and other victims.

At the same time, any effort on the part of the government to rein in drug companies had long been dwarfed by the greed of private industry. Under Republican presidents before and after Barack Obama, career prosecutors who'd worked mightily to nail Purdue's owners and executives for fraud were twice thwarted by politically appointed superiors at the Department of Justice, thanks largely to repeat influence peddlers.

During the Obama years, lobbyists pushed legislators to pass into law a bill called the Ensuring Patient Access and Effective Drug Enforcement Act. It *sounded* good, but in actuality the law severely limited the Drug Enforcement Administration's ability to freeze suspicious narcotic shipments from drug distributors to pharmacies—setting the stage for more pills, more deaths, and more litigation. In recent years the opioid lobby has spent eight times more than the gun lobby to curry favor with lawmakers.

By the spring of 2021, the naming of President Joe Biden's new drug czar was bogged down in politics, as was the possibility of his appointing the acting commissioner of the Food and Drug Administration, Dr. Janet Woodcock, to the actual post. Earlier in her career, when OxyContin and many other potent painkillers were approved, Woodcock was supposed to have been the nation's "top drug cop." But for two decades, regulatory watchdogs stood by as pharmaceutical and health-products corporations plied lobbyists, political campaigns, and Capitol Hill politicians with $4.7 billion to smooth the pathway so they could sell, sell, sell.

How did the Sacklers get away with so much for so long? They surrounded themselves with sycophants hired to shield them from the consequences of their faulty product. They bought influence. As OxyContin scion Richard Sackler put it, "We can get virtually every senator and congressman we want to talk to on the phone in the next seventy-two hours."

America's 1 million overdose-death count is predicted to double by this decade's end. It is already as if a city the size of San Jose has vanished, and, by 2029, those deaths will be Houston-sized.

But such disappearances are quiet and geographically dispersed as the epidemic remains hidden in plain sight, buried in a fierce, century-old battle between shaming drug users as criminals or treating them as patients worthy of medical care.

At this point, too much attention is focused on stemming the oversupply of prescription opioids. A quarter century into the crisis, many people with OUD have long since transitioned from painkillers to heroin, methamphetamine, and fentanyl, the ultra-potent synthetic opioid. And we now have a generation of drug users that *started* with heroin and fentanyl.

As President Biden faced pressure to make up for the drug war sins he'd committed in the 1980s and '90s by championing punitive "tough on crime" laws that scapegoated Black and poor people, overdose deaths from fentanyl rose most among Black Americans, surging 38 percent in 2019. (Native Americans claimed the highest overdose-death rate in 2020, but no group has seen a larger increase than Black men.)

In American cities being slammed by illicit fentanyl and in much of rural America where the crisis initially took root, a disparate group of people who work outside the realm of mainstream bureaucracies has begun tackling what officials have failed for decades to do: keep people alive. While many government-run programs were initially hobbled by pandemic rules designed to protect workers, people like Tim simply masked up and carried on. They worked long hours from the trunks of their cars, under bridges, and in fast-food parking lots. Some risked arrest to deliver sterile needles, lifesaving addiction medications, or treatments for injection-related hepatitis C and HIV/AIDS. The most passionate among them were former drug users who now do outreach and are officially called "peers" (short for peer recovery specialists or peer coaches).

As the Reverend Michelle Mathis, who coordinates Tim's street outreach, described it: Those who get close enough to people who use drugs may get to personally witness the miracle of wellness—but only if they first answer the call. As with the disciples who unwrapped a raised-from-the-dead Lazarus at Jesus's command, Rev. Mathis explained, "it doesn't always smell like flowers, and you might get a little something on you. But the people who are willing to work at the face-to-face level get to see the miracle and look it in the eye."

As Tim worked nights visiting drug users, Judge Drain spent his days focused on buttoning up the bankruptcy. The Sackler family was on the verge of locking away most of its wealth even as overdose deaths kept breaking records.

In a country that spends five times more to incarcerate people with SUD than it does to treat their medical condition, progress was stagnant. In 2019, an estimated 18.9 million Americans in need of treatment didn't receive it. That's a treatment gap of roughly 90 percent. Among the lucky few who do get treatment, Black patients were far less likely than Whites to have access to lifesaving buprenorphine ("bupe"), a medicine that blocks opioid cravings, for their OUD.

When Americans fall into addiction, survival remains a luxury.

Just as it did when OxyContin first erupted in rural Virginia and Maine in the late 1990s, the national press mostly missed the out-of-the-way contours of the story. If you're addicted in, say, Boston, you're much more likely to access evidence-based care than if you live in one of the underserved areas where the crisis began. And even there, treatment is scattershot—"a drop of water in an ocean of misery," as one Boston doctor put it.

Death by drugs is now a national problem, but the crisis began as an epidemic of overprescribed painkillers in the distressed communities that were least likely to muster the resources to fight back. It erupted in rural fishing villages, coal communities, and mill towns—because Purdue's sales strategy was to convince doctors that the nation's injured miners and factory workers were better and more safely served by OxyContin than its weaker competitors. The company even maneuvered to convince the FDA to back this bogus claim.

As one early OxyContin user told me, puzzling over how Oxy had so quickly taken over her Virginia coal-mining town, "It was like the government was trying to get rid of the lowlifes." Richard Sackler understood from the beginning that the shame felt by most families of the addicted would cloak his family's role by blaming the very people OxyContin had helped to addict. "We have to hammer on the abusers in every way possible," he famously strategized.

From the stony patch of land next to a set of West Virginia railroad tracks to the smooth sidewalk in front of an LA Pottery Barn, the "lowlifes" and "abusers" were now everywhere. Many were neither voters nor campaign contributors, so the political apparatus felt free to look away from them.

In the Uneven States of America, stigma of one kind or another was always at the root.

The epidemic continues to shape-shift. When prescription pills grew harder to access in the aughts, drug cartels launched a second wave of the opioid crisis—heroin—understanding better than anyone that heroin and OxyContin are chemical cousins, and an opioid-addicted person's fear of withdrawal guaranteed repeat customers. A few years later, they pivoted to hyper-potent fentanyl to boost profit margins; fentanyl was both easier to manufacture—no expansive poppy fields were required—and it was both tinier and more potent, making it easier to smuggle. A third wave commenced as dealers mixed fentanyl into almost every street drug, including fake pain pills and fake benzos, cocaine, and methamphetamine. What we now refer to as the "overdose crisis" is really an epidemic of death by polysubstance.

Given that the US government was also trying to recover the $12 billion that Juaquin "El Chapo" Guzman had made in illicit heroin sales, why shouldn't it also redistribute the $12 billion made by the Sacklers to taxpayers harmed by OxyContin? "El Chapo got a life sentence, and he's going to forfeit $12 billion. The Sackler family through Purdue has three felony convictions, but no one's in jail, and it has its billion still," Rep. Peter Welch (D-VT) argued during one heated congressional hearing.

A theory began circulating among some public health experts and reporters that, to the extent that lawyers and politicians could convince the American people that it was Big Pharma's job to fix the crisis—and not the US government's—the Purdue bankruptcy and other opioid cases would let change-resistant bureaucracies off the hook. "The litigation probably sucks up more oxygen than it deserves," one public health lawyer told me.

Given the political fault lines rippling across the nation's heartland, could litigation soothe the families' pain and right the injustices and turn back an overdose crisis that only grew worse in the face of COVID-19? What was the *real* fix—not the easy hit or half measures that desperate users and wealthy companies alike had resorted to in place of real recovery?

If money alone can't swoop in to fill a leadership vacuum fueled by stigma and a racist War on Drugs that overrides the health of the most vulnerable Americans, what can?

Since the publication of my 2018 book, *Dopesick: Dealers, Doctors, and the Drug Company That Addicted America*, I have often been asked to explain why the crisis just keeps escalating.

A month before the COVID-19 pandemic broke out, a group

of Indiana sheriffs invited me to address them. When I explained the benefits of treating addiction in their jails—or, better yet, connecting arrestees to treatment *instead of* jail—they scoffed. I cited the example of the city of Burlington, Vermont, where police and civic leaders cut overdose deaths in half after becoming the first in the nation to assiduously track the addicted they had previously arrested or those who had been identified by social workers as suffering from acute addiction, then diverting them to medication-assisted treatment and social supports instead of jail. At the end of my remarks, only one of the ninety-two sheriffs in attendance *very slowly* clapped.

Reader, they stared nine-millimeter bullets at me.

In Charleston, West Virginia, complaints about vagrancy and needle litter outside the public health department's needle exchange led to its closure in 2018, sparking a *1,500 percent* increase in HIV. The national press, understandably busy with the pandemic, mostly looked the other way.

There are confirmed health benefits to decriminalizing drugs, as Portugal did in 2001, and states like Oregon began to follow suit by decriminalizing all drugs in 2020. But most American states, with a patchwork of jurisdictions and overlapping agencies run by elected prosecutors and law enforcement officials who win votes by being "tough on crime," were nowhere close to conceiving of legalization, to say nothing of making heroin available in government-run dispensaries, as Canada and some European countries have done successfully.

Drug treatment doesn't operate in a culturally homogenous bubble as much as some harm-reductionists wish it did. Oregon doesn't get to tell West Virginia what to do, even when the science solidly backs Oregon.

Networks of underground activists who distribute clean needles in West Virginia blamed the vitriol they received for helping drug users on "assholes who think they get to weaponize trauma." A local journalist believed the pushback was more about old-money forces refusing to loosen their clutch on power: "Rather than acknowledging that real problems exist and trying to solve them, they create new problems that they alone claim to have the solution to," he said, referring to exaggerated complaints of needle litter. A Charleston peer summed it up best of all: "We all need therapy."

A trickle of settled lawsuits won't "satisfy the populace because what people really thought they wanted was blood," said Johns Hopkins University bioethicist Travis Rieder. "What we really need is a whole new public health infrastructure."

If we're going to reverse America's declining life expectancy, we need to treat people with SUD the same way we treat other Americans with chronic illnesses. Medications for people with OUD should be as available as insulin is for diabetics or dialysis for people with kidney failure.

But in a nation whose leaders can't even implement a watered-down form of universal health care—as of this writing, twelve states have yet to pass the Medicaid expansion—Rieder's solution remains an empty wish, especially in the distressed communities first targeted by Purdue.

While the Sacklers' lawyers battled it out—Marshall Huebner, their chief counsel, billed at a rate of $1,790 *an hour*—I gravitated toward the people who weren't waiting around for justice. They were activists, volunteers, and outreach workers—people who regularly traversed the backroads and under the bridge encampments of America's Third World.

I followed them as they innovated treatment regimens on manila envelopes, broke rules when they needed to, and butted heads with bureaucrats who refused to humanely treat those who had been most neglected, over the longest time, simply because of the stigma that adheres to drug use.

One rural syringe-services provider leveled a stare at me and begged: "Whatever you write, just tell it like it is, okay? Nobody [with the county] really wants to put a drug user in their car and give 'em a ride to treatment."

I was kvetching to my friend, the Kentucky novelist and activist Robert Gipe, who reminded me of Martin Luther King Jr.'s criticism of white moderates who are "more devoted to 'order' than to justice." "It's important to respect people who are out there on the leading edge trying to get change going," Gipe said. "Those who are pushing less hard are probably better at getting people to accept moderate change, but it's a balance, and you need both. Either way, somebody's gonna get yelled at."

I didn't like getting yelled at, but I got better at it.

In 2018, I watched my friend Patricia Mehrmann, a key source from *Dopesick*, say goodbye to her heroin-addicted daughter. Twenty-eight-year-old Tess Henry was a young mother who'd flown from her home in Virginia to Las Vegas for her third rehab attempt. Months after Tess relapsed and fled the facility, her body was found at the bottom of a dumpster on Christmas Eve. The week of her murder, she had been trying to secure the paperwork necessary to fly back home to try treatment again. She had already applied for Medicaid and researched methadone clinic options in her hometown.

I spent much of the next year helping Patricia retrace Tess's final steps. It was sad and frustrating, as dark as the underground homeless encampments through which we walked, showing Tess's picture, looking for clues. But, ultimately, Tess Henry's saga of patient abandonment led to real change in her Virginia hometown—a small step toward what Tess imagined as "urgent care for the addicted."

Whether we realize it or not, most of us continue blaming the victims rather than the corporations, politicians, and impotent regulators who allowed the wealthy to poison our nation. Though half of Americans report believing addiction is a disease, 80 percent still say they'd prefer not to be friends, neighbors, coworkers, or in-laws with someone who has SUD.

People blame victims rather than corporations, but they're also more willing to blame corporations than do the hard work of moving forward and allocating the resources needed to actually fix this thing.

The Sacklers should be punished, but identifying the initial bad actors will only take the nation so far. Like all crises that persist rather than get resolved, the overdose crisis has created crises of its own.

In a nation where the treatment gap barely budges, many Americans who use drugs resort to theft, sex work, and selling drugs to avoid the pain of becoming dopesick. Many also use methamphetamine on top of heroin, for the same reasons my friend Tess did—so she could stay awake all night to avoid being robbed and raped, so she could muster enough hustle to get up and do it all over again.

Many get trapped in an endless cycle of jail, probation, and relapse—caught in a roughly $50 billion bureaucracy that employs millions and reelects tough-on-crime sheriffs but does little to help the victims of Big Pharma's crimes. When you peer into the country's most intractable problems—homelessness, disability, domestic violence, child neglect—you see the persistence of dopesickness everywhere.

"If we fix the opioid crisis, we fix America," one reader e-mailed me, envisioning a country where meaningful work, health care, and social supports become not only embedded into treatment protocols; they might one day serve as prevention strategies, too.

When my displaced factory-worker mom in Ohio asked me what my new book was about, I told her the overdose crisis. She was in her nineties, with advancing dementia, and so she asked me this question approximately eight times a day. Having spent much of her life surrounded by addiction, she always had the same response:

"I think you should write a love story instead," she said.

Shadowing Tim Nolan, the sixty-two-year-old nurse-practitioner, reminded me of a quote I'd first heard from an addiction doctor in Massachusetts. He said the solution to the epidemic could be summed up in a single quote from a Harvard physician in 1926: "The secret of the care of the patient is in caring for the patient."

Recently, Apple announced it would create three thousand jobs and a new East Coast campus in nearby Raleigh-Durham, part of North Carolina's so-called Research Triangle, about two hours east of where Tim works. But outside the Whole Foods–rich triangle (four and counting), little opportunity beckoned for Tim's patients, most of whom were thirsty, hungry, unhoused, and divorced from mainstream health care.

Tim's patients aren't well enough to make it to the clinic where he works during the day, let alone apply for Apple's jobs in machine learning, artificial intelligence, and software engineering. They have lived off-grid and in the shadows for too long. The state pledged $845 million in tax incentives, and the county $20 million. But for the people in Tim's practice, no such investment is being made.

Street medicine is low-tech and high-touch, the antithesis of Apple. But more than most of the programs I've witnessed in my decade of reporting on the overdose crisis, Tim's low-barrier approach works—not always the first time, and not for everyone, but, eventually, for many.

Sam was giddy by the time he arrived at McDonald's. He stood between the dumpster and his dented SUV, apologetically late and unapologetically glassy-eyed. He asked Tim to prescribe him something no other health care provider ever had during his decade of using drugs: affordable buprenorphine.

"I'm ready to get off that damn needle," Sam told him.

"Why do you want to?" Tim asked, gently.

Sam stalled and took a deep breath. His eyes welled. "Sorry, man," he stammered.

"Is that a hard question you don't want to answer?" Tim asked.

Sam shook his head and told his story: He'd been imprisoned twice, once for selling drugs and once for assaulting a police officer during a full-blown psychosis that Sam blamed on a forced withdrawal. A year earlier, his eighteen-year-old son had been murdered in a drug dispute, shot in the head with a crossbow. Though Sam considered himself "a functioning addict," he'd been fired from his last job driving a forklift after a drug-related fight. Standing next to the dumpster, he vowed to stop using heroin before he began his next job.

"I've never even said all this to anyone," he told Tim, wiping away tears.

"I appreciate it," Tim said. "That's how we're going to work together."

But Tim worried. Burke County remained an epicenter of heroin, fentanyl, and meth use. On Facebook, the sheriff's department regularly boasted about drug arrests—many beginning with traffic stops or the suspicion of an invalid driver's license—in social media posts featuring mugshots of arrestees standing in front of a height chart and clad in black-and-white-striped jail garb, like out of a Coen Brothers film (the women's uniforms are pink). A torrent of comments posted by the community reads like an updated version of Shirley Jackson's "The Lottery":

"I think she had a baby while in custody if I'm not mistaken."

"What is with her meth head—does she have mange?"

"What a waste, but most of that family is."

Tim didn't have time for Facebook. His social worker wife,

Amy, worried that he worked too many hours. He didn't drive as well at night as he once did. On street medicine nights, he slept in his brother-in-law's basement, hours from his Asheville home. Nights and weekends, there was rarely a time when a stranger wasn't sending him a text, usually beginning "Hi. A friend told me you can treat me."

"Treat you for what?" Tim always responded, careful not to presume.

For addiction, for hepatitis, for HIV came the replies.

And sometimes: *Because I want to kill myself.*

If the patients couldn't find a ride to the nearest truck stop or Burger King, Tim took his mobile clinic to them. Absent a cohesive system of care to treat the afflicted, he created his own.

The next day, Tim phoned in Sam's discount prescription for Suboxone to Walgreens.

"I'm forty-one years old, and with nothing to show for it," Sam had said at the end of his first visit. COVID was raging at the moment, but his face mask dangled from one ear, broken.

"Well, let's turn it around," Tim said. "I always tell people, just don't disappear on me. If next week is a worse week for you, we're not going to throw you out of the program. I'll text you and ask if we can meet at the Burger King that's closer to your house. We'll talk more and see how the week went. Is that fair?"

Sam nodded.

"Just *don't disappear*, okay?" Tim repeated.

They started to shake hands on it, then awkwardly bumped elbows instead.

Then Sam took off in his Jeep, and he disappeared.

PART ONE
Affliction

Messages of hope, Olive Branch Ministry, Hickory, North Carolina.

Chapter One

Stone-Rollers

Abbie Setzer (right) watches TV a day before leaving for treatment while Michelle Mathis prepares supplies for delivery at Olive Branch Ministry, Hickory, North Carolina.

In ancient Rome, when tormentors branded an enslaved person with a hot iron, the scar left behind was called a *stigma*. During the Middle Ages, the pluralized version of the word became *stig mata*, used to describe the wounds left on Jesus's body by his crucifixion. By the 1600s, the words were used interchangeably to signify a mark of shame, deeply worn patterns of thinking so culturally ingrained that they can be hard to tease apart from rational thought. It turns into a given, then, that stigmatized people are branded and judged as beyond redemption, as ruined. Drug-addicted people often react to stigma by excluding themselves

3

from public life. They do this, in part, because drugs feel good when the actual world doesn't. Drugs help them forget, set aside, and numb their feelings of shame in a looping effect that exacerbates the very behaviors society initially reproached them for. In this way social death can become literal death.

The Reverend Michelle Mathis was thinking of the time Jesus arrived to see his dear friend Lazarus only to learn that he'd died four days before. Jesus would pull off the miracle of raising Lazarus from the dead. But first, he needed to share his sorrow and grief with his friends, so, together, they wept. Then Jesus instructed his followers to roll away the stone from Lazarus's tomb, and he commanded Lazarus to come forth, telling the mourners to unbind him from his burial cloths.

Jesus had already performed the miracle; now, it was up to the community to do the stinky, messy work of pulling the burial shroud off Lazarus.

Mathis uses the story of Lazarus to help people check their blind spots. She tells the parable not to inspire miracle work but to challenge people to take down barriers for those who can't do it themselves.

As cofounder of Olive Branch Ministry, Mathis and her wife, Karen Lowe, created what they call the nation's only queer-and-biracial-founded harm-reduction ministry. Based in the former furniture belt of western North Carolina, a state that lost more than 250,000 factory jobs in the wake of globalization, Olive Branch started out offering food and hygiene supplies to the region's homeless from the back of their cars in 2009.

The operation has grown to include syringe services, counseling, and addiction triage in ten counties. In her late forties and with purple-tinted gray hair (though she uses other colors in rotation), Mathis has a flower tattoo on her forearm with the words *Acta Non Verba*, which is Latin, she told me, for "Do shit. Don't just talk about it."

Mathis vowed to meet drug users where they are—physically, spiritually, and emotionally. But working in the heart of the Bible Belt, she also knew she would have to build bridges before anyone could roll stones across them. She had to meet the rest of the community where it was, too, including the NIMBYs (Not in My Back Yard) and the naysayers and the so-called CAVEs—short for Citizens Against Virtually Everything.

It was bridge-building that allowed Olive Branch to operate three needle exchanges in one of the most conservative parts of the country, as well as to provide cutting-edge low-barrier bupe and hepatitis treatment in collaboration with Tim Nolan, the nurse-practitioner who worked nights from his Prius. It was Mathis who picks up the pizzas for Tim's hep C gatherings, and it is peers from her office who manage patient intake and figure out the logistics of where and how they will meet Tim. He carries each patient's information in a manila envelope on the front seat of his car, their cell phone numbers Sharpied on the front.

Not everyone welcomes Mathis's stone-rolling sermonettes. When we first met in early 2019 in another North Carolina community, Mathis had been invited to share her knowledge with church-goers and civic leaders in Mount Airy, located in a county that then claimed the second-highest overdose rate in the nation. Mathis encouraged the crowd to extend help to drug users rather than judgment—even if it meant helping them continue to use drugs safely by giving them clean needles and other supplies aimed at curbing the spread of HIV and hepatitis C. "For some, taking off the bandages means handing a person a box of hep C medication, right?" she explained. "For some, it's low-barrier Suboxone, and for some, it's abstinence-based treatment."

In Mathis's home base of Hickory, North Carolina, miracles were slowly and messily coming to light. Inside her grant-funded double-wide donated by a nearby Presbyterian church, a string of handmade prayer flags proclaimed, "I am a beautiful work in progress" and "I have a purpose" and "I do deserve JOY."

At night, a houseless man named Michael, who sleeps in a back room of the church, keeps an eye on the trailer in exchange for food, clothing, and whatever else he might need. Drug users are invited into the Olive Branch trailer not just for clean needles and sharps kits but also to do crafts and use the center's laptops to apply for jobs—with peers nearby to advise which employers hire people with felony records.

At a second syringe program that Olive Branch operates in nearby Gastonia, participants range from young and middle-aged white people who don't mind settling for cheaper methamphetamine when heroin can't be found, to a Black retiree who said she'd been a functioning heroin injector for forty years and needed only syringes. On the wall near a phone bank, peers posted talking points on Post-it notes, including "Your safety is my biggest priority today" and "You're shining bright; what can you do to keep shining?"

Mathis and Lowe had come a long way from 2012, when syringe exchange was illegal. Back then, the couple gave away needles on the sly, posing as a food pantry that operated from the back of their pickup truck. (Needle exchanges are now referred to as syringe service programs, or SSPs, because they offer more than just syringes—and the phrase is more palatable politically.)

"We'd have three or four cases of donated food, and we knew which ones we'd already doctored," Mathis recalled. Taped-up boxes signified the dry goods to which they had added clean needles, condoms, wound-care kits, and socks. "Ten syringes fit nicely in a box of Nature's Valley granola when you take out a few bars," she said. They'd tuck in business cards with their phone number, e-mail address, and the ministry's name—but no mention of needles in case a spouse or kid or parent found the card.

With her close-cropped afro, tennis shoes, and jeans, Karen Lowe managed outreach to addicted sex workers in Statesville and met people by appointment in convenience-store parking lots across the furniture belt to hand out needles and fentanyl-test strips (so users could test the potency of their drugs and gauge how much to inject or snort accordingly).

One gray afternoon in mid-2019, I watched a man slowly limp over from a nearby apartment complex to meet Lowe in a Dollar Tree parking lot. She didn't want my presence to jar him, so I stayed behind in the car while I watched her hand him a blue Walmart bag full of drug-injection supplies, Narcan, condoms, and socks—enough to supply him and the four others he lived with until she could return in a few weeks.

Asked afterwards if she felt her work was stopping the spread of hepatitis C, Lowe let me know that I had asked the wrong question: "I *know* I'm doing that," she said. "What's important is that he knows somebody cares; nobody's judging him. And it wasn't just a transaction; I asked him how his day was. I treated him like a human being."

The idea that drug users are worthy human beings—that they are, in fact, *equals*—is harm reduction in a nutshell. That attitude wasn't something I'd witnessed much before in the largely Southern, rural locales where I'd previously covered the opioid crisis, and where most people—myself included, if I'm being honest—took it as a given that the persistent use of illicit drugs was bad. Well, maybe not marijuana, but you get my drift.

If and when the man at Dollar Tree wanted to stop using drugs, he'd know how to reach out to Lowe. People who go to needle programs are five times more likely to enter treatment—because their needs are triaged by trusted workers who can help them enter treatment if and when they are ready. They're also three times more likely to reduce or stop IV drug use.

As we drove away, I couldn't help but think of my young friend Tess Henry, who would have loved the friendly vibe of Olive Branch. (She, too, liked to write inspirational poems and lyrics on her walls.) But SSPs didn't exist in her Virginia hometown when Tess lived there. And by the time she flew to Las Vegas for rehab, the closest one operated on that city's outskirts—in a politically acceptable working-class neighborhood, far from the tourists as well as the abandoned minivan Tess sometimes called home.

Olive Branch was beginning to shift the way officials treated people with SUD in western North Carolina's foothills. In 2016, Hickory named a new police chief just as syringe exchange became legal in the state. Years before, Mathis and Lowe trained local police to carry and use naloxone, the overdose antidote. At the same time, Black Lives Matter–led protests were drawing attention to the police killing of Keith Lamont Scott in nearby Charlotte, and Mathis was organizing Unity in the Community gatherings around the state to facilitate discussions between law enforcement and marginalized groups. Mathis told the new police chief that Olive Branch planned to expand services in light of the state's new needle exchange law. And he responded: "We're good. That's all I need to know."

Mathis prefers to use a personal, behind-the-scenes approach rather than in-your-face activism. She sees this as another version of meeting politicians, law enforcement, and the community of those who use drugs where they are—a nonjudgmental stance that, in my experience, most harm-reductionists often didn't extend to law enforcement. "Because police have been in charge historically, health professionals too often act like adolescents who are mad at their parents," explained Keith Humphreys, a Stanford University psychologist and addiction researcher. "The most interesting people doing this work are the ones who can hold on to both ideas rather than just giving simple and pious-sounding statements...like 'This is a health issue, not a crime.' When at the same time you have addicted people who are committing crimes, including violent crimes, you have to [deliver justice] for the woman whose [drug-using] boyfriend just broke her nose."

"I'm like the grandma that does syringe exchange and delivers biscuits. I make sure our space is homey, kind of Appalachian-y," Mathis explained. "I won't sit on a couch in a trap house because of possible needles, but in general I find trap houses to be safe," she said. She'd transported needles and participated in a die-in protest outside the capitol building in Charleston, West Virginia, after local politicians effectively outlawed syringe exchange in that city in 2018, and activists from across the East Coast showed up in solidarity.

Now on the brink of delivering low-cost buprenorphine and home-based hepatitis C treatments to people—via nurse-practitioner Tim Nolan—Mathis and Lowe were about to pull off a cutting-edge coup for a small town in a red state that hadn't expanded Medicaid. They would help their participants who wanted to start buprenorphine ("bupe") get low-barrier care.

In a decade, Olive Branch went from serving 100 people in three counties to 1,900 people in ten counties, many of them displaced factory workers and veterans initially addicted to prescription pain pills. Staffers had linked 83 percent of their clients to care—not just referrals to detox, rehab, and addiction medicines but also to basic harm-reduction services: sterile syringes, fentanyl test strips, and the like for those who weren't ready to stop using. If you took out clients who were still using drugs, albeit more safely, their success rate for getting people into recovery was closer to 25 percent, Mathis said. "You have to be careful when agencies start spouting numbers. I want them to tell me the stories, and don't just tell me the same one over and over again. I can tell you our successes, and also where we've failed horribly, and I share them equally because I can't remember one and forget the other."

She delivers everything from Narcan to Taco Bell and, when people look like they need it, basic human touch. Back when he was still using, Garry Dolin told me, he met Mathis at a Rose's department store to get needles, in the middle of a four-day binge. "I was wearing dirty-ass clothes and I know I stunk, but she said, 'Would you care if I gave you a hug?'" said Dolin, an Army National Guardsman who became addicted to prescribed OxyContin after being shot in the shoulder in Kuwait. When his military doctors cut him off, Dolin bought black-market pills and, later, heroin. Multiple jail stints hadn't convinced him to seek treatment; it took having a near-death experience. "Getting the living shit scared out of me's what it took," he said. "Overdosing in front of my wife and daughter, and my wife giving me four doses of Narcan and doing CPR for forty-seven minutes until the ambulance got there." It took knowing Mathis, a person he trusted, to help him stop using drugs.

By 2020 he was taking daily methadone to stave off cravings; he'd been sober for three years. I reached out to him after stumbling on a Facebook post about how proud he was to have revived an overdosed man in a McDonald's parking lot, using Narcan provided by Olive Branch.

He'd recently gotten his driver's license reissued so he could return to his truck-driving job—but only after Mathis helped him get his twenty-two addiction-related misdemeanors expunged. "Michelle has great relationships with law enforcement, and the DA likes her," Dolin said.

Her biscuits and pragmatism had won over the local cops. In time I would see just how far her grandmotherly influence might extend.

*   *   *

A few mountain ridges northeast of Hickory, Mount Airy and surrounding Surry County seemed like another universe. Not only did it not have a single syringe service—"That town is nowhere near ready," Mathis said, shaking her head—but the county jail was filled at almost double the capacity, largely by people with SUD. For every slot of publicly funded bupe treatment, an additional two slots went unused. Behavioral health officials claimed to have no idea why. Clearly, the need was there.

In the scores of cities and towns I'd visited across the country, there was a paucity of treatment compared to demand. But here in Mount Airy, where the overdose crisis was beyond dire, most treatment slots went unfilled.

Transportation was part of it. Many people literally couldn't find rides. Emily McPeak, who directed the area's largest outpatient addiction facility, had one client who walked five miles for her weekly appointments from a homeless shelter the next town over. But when she finally secured housing, it was too far away to walk—and she relapsed.

It was these gaps in basic patient care that spurred Mathis to introduce the gospel of harm reduction to Mount Airy's faith and community leaders in April 2019—to explore the notion that churches serving meals to the homeless or hosting support groups were doing a form of harm reduction; they just needed to expand it. In Hickory, she'd talked a local crafting circle that refused to help her hand out sterile needles into crocheting Narcan bags for drug users instead. At Mathis's request, the women even added reflective thread so users could see the bags better in flophouses and other low-light areas.

Unhoused recipients especially loved the crocheted bags—they reminded them of home. Harm-reduction activists might have dismissed the crochet circle for being uneducated and overly timid, but Mathis felt it best to meet the crafters where they were, too. The women now call themselves the Old Hookers Club.

But in Surry County, the middle ground between drug users and the power structure didn't exist—not yet, anyway. Few leaders cared to look inside the trailers and trap houses where the most severely addicted lived. The cops were more interested in turning low-level users into confidential informants still in the game than funneling them to treatment.

Civic leaders did not care to tour the jail, now so stuffed that the county spent $750,000 annually to house some forty to fifty inmates on the other side of the state. The deputies in charge refused to consider (or even read about) jail-based treatment data, clinging to the notion that they had no space to administer bupe.

As jail administrators led me on a tour, we walked past newly arrived inmates who were shivering and dopesick. Several lay on urine-soaked mats on the cement floor of the intake area, clutching jail-issued blankets and vomit buckets. They were young men in their twenties and thirties, mostly, mashed together so they could be monitored for dehydration and sickness, the deputies explained. Black mold permeated the place, several former inmates later told me. The only form of recreation was to empty the toilet of its water, then bend yourself into the bowl to talk to inmates in other cells—a hack widely known as "the chrome phone" or "toilet talk."

The jailers were happy to let me see the poor conditions, hopeful that it would buttress their argument for a bigger jail. When I asked about offering bupe or methadone in the facility, they reiterated that there wasn't space, even as they pointed out a small nurse's office where, to my eyes, it might have easily been dispensed.

Asked what most surprised them about their addicted

incarcerated population, the jailers cited a 600 percent increase in incarcerated women. "This has hit everybody—preachers' families, even well-off families. You can't say it's sorry, trashy people anymore," said Lieutenant Randy Shelton. "It's drugs, period, and they don't discriminate," added Captain Scott Hudson. "I went to high school with a lot of the people here."

At one community meeting Mathis attended several months before, a Mount Airy historic-district leader complained repeatedly that her neighborhood had been overtaken by people engaging in around-the-clock drug deals. "We need to tear down those houses and abolish the Fourth Amendment so police can do what they need to do," the woman said.

Mathis listened patiently to a range of stigma-inflected comments. But at the mention of abolishing the Fourth Amendment she stood, her swirl of purple hair bouncing as she tried to match the emotion of the day without further inciting the CAVEs: "Y'all, I just have to ask: Do you know the song, 'They Will Know We Are Christians by Our Love'? Well, I'm not feeling the love in this room right now."

Mathis reminded them that Jesus tended first to people's physical needs because he understood that folks who were tired, hungry, and hurting "wouldn't have ears for what he needed to say." When the civic leader persisted, Mathis politely suggested she fix her neighbors a casserole—people who use drugs sometimes forget to eat, she explained.

Take drug users a casserole?

By the meeting's end, Mathis thought she'd coaxed leaders from some of the county's 260 churches into forming a volunteer transportation network so available treatment slots could be filled. But when the group gathered again two months later, this time it was the local Kiwanis Club president who hijacked the meeting, repeatedly interrupting with questions about who would pay for gas, and what to do if someone overdosed in her car. When the

Kiwanis leader angrily vented, "I think when they relapse, we should let 'em die and take their organs!" all hope seemed lost.

After the meeting, a few pastors pledged to spread the word about the network among their congregations, but six weeks passed, and no one signed up.

Few here wanted to touch the body of Lazarus.

The neighbors in Mount Airy were not so different from working-class people across America. Politically disconnected and angry at those they perceived to be bilking the government, they were turning on each other rather than placing the blame on the exploitative pharmaceutical companies that seeded the epidemic and the power-hungry politicians who rolled out the red carpet for them while doing virtually nothing about growing inequality, poor health care coverage, and declining wages that affected everyone, whether they used drugs or not.

"The local elite sort of see themselves as, 'Yes, I'm Appalachian, but me and my family have picked ourselves up. We own property. We're pillars. And when outsiders stereotype Appalachians, I don't like the dirt from my poor neighbors splashing over onto me,'" said Lesly-Marie Buer, a Tennessee-based medical anthropologist and harm-reduction worker. In 2005, Buer attended the funeral of an old friend who'd overdosed—and noticed how poorly rural drug users were treated compared to those in Denver, where she then worked.

"Part of the divide is amongst ourselves, and it has to do both with class and race, as in, 'This county used to be so great, but then these *urban* problems came in.'" They wrongly blame immigrants for taking their jobs when it was greedy corporate executives beholden to greedy shareholders who offshored the jobs, keeping more profits for themselves and treating the working class like a coal seam in Appalachia—a resource to be mined, no matter the human or environmental cost.

Naysayers blame Black drug users for soaring heroin and fentanyl rates when studies show that White people use those drugs at far higher rates than Black people. They mistrust government and anything that smacks of "socialism," even those who are benefiting from food stamps, Medicaid, and Medicare. And the ones who complain loudest are far more likely to vote for tough-on-crime Republicans—if they vote at all. "People are saying, 'I take care of myself, and it's not easy, but I do it,'" Indiana University sociologist Jennifer M. Silva told me. "They start valuing the individual over the collective as a means of survival. They're all so worn out."

The discourse grew more toxic by the day as legacy media outlets waned, property crime soared, and the overdose deaths kept escalating. In hard-hit Charleston, West Virginia, the local police chief, supported by a group called Charleston Has Had Enough!, worked to shut down needle-exchange operations in 2018. Opponents doxed harm-reductionists and flew drones over homeless encampments to out drug users to police. "We are the heart of the heart of the heart of the crisis," said Joe Solomon, a Charleston harm-reduction worker who leads the group Solutions Oriented Addiction Response (SOAR), and begged me to draw national attention to his group's plight. "But when the world calls you hillbilly and hick and redneck, it's so easy to internalize that stigma and say, 'Who can I punch down to feel like I have worth? There's people injecting drugs and stealing my kids' bicycles—fuck 'em!'"

Two months into the COVID-19 pandemic, I reached out to Anne Case and Angus Deaton, the husband-and-wife economist duo who first reported America's declining life-expectancy trend and coined the term "deaths of despair" as an explanation for soaring opioid, alcohol, and suicide deaths (particularly among middle-aged White men and women who hadn't gone to college).

Back then, Mount Airy had very few reported COVID cases and zero COVID deaths. But overdoses in the county were up 29 percent from the previous year, with an uptick in methamphetamine, polysubstance, and alcohol-poisoning deaths. "We are thinking about whether people will buy back into the role that government could play and seems to play successfully in a lot of other countries," Case said. "And we're hopeful that the explosion of distrust in expertise in America will be reversed. It's all right to mock science and expertise—until you and your family start dying." Deaton told me about a friend at Princeton who was healthy and in her early thirties, and yet had nearly succumbed to COVID in the pandemic's early weeks. Despite their friend's connections and relative affluence, she could not access a COVID test when she got sick. "Economists know the free market doesn't respond to emergencies—you don't put out a bid when someone's drowning in the ocean," Deaton said.

The madness that was America's piss-poor response to the coronavirus was the same madness that had long imperiled addiction treatment, only literally *no one* was immune from COVID, not even then-President Trump.

"Illicit drugs can't get here from China now, but the ABC stores will deliver booze to your door!" a recovery leader told me. More people were overdosing from contaminated synthetics manufactured in basements and back rooms. In Kentucky, the neediest drug users had fallen to seeking a methamphetamine-like rush by injecting an insecticide, which they called "wasp dope." In nearby Shelby, North Carolina, in a single day during the summer of 2020, five people passed out in gas-station parking lots after taking "dirty thirties," fake thirty-milligram oxycodone pills that turned out to be pure fentanyl. The following spring, a veterinary tranquilizer called xylazine caused a spike in overdoses and particularly nasty ulcers.

But as the pandemic dragged on, drug deaths continued their

upward trajectory, in part due to the sheer stress of quarantine. More people were using drugs while alone (with no one to Narcan them), and even people in long-term recovery were relapsing at record rates due to pandemic-related job losses, anxiety, and depression.

Drinking and alcohol-poisoning deaths were also up. A friend of mine prepared to pick up her friend for their weekly AA meeting, only to learn that the woman had been lying dead on her floor for days, having overdosed on alcohol.

In a survey of addiction-treatment efforts, the National Association of County and Health Officials found that most innovations to treat rather than incarcerate drug users were forged by dynamic leaders like Mathis, people with a natural capacity to connect with others, even CAVEs. "You see so much change being thwarted by fearmongers who come to public meetings and complain about why it isn't the way it was twenty years ago," said Stacy Stanford, public health transformation director of the group.

In a politically divided landscape where law enforcement policies are set locally and county sheriffs remain the highest-elected law enforcement officers in the country, there is no federal magic wand to force sheriffs to offer addiction medicines in jail or police chiefs to permit needle exchange. Was it possible to convince leaders to look at innovations working elsewhere in select states, cities, and even small towns? Or did the wheel have to be reinvented in every single locality? Where leaders clung to take-their-organs rhetoric, could harm-reductionists ever wrest control?

"Baby steps are better than no steps, but what we really need is a public infrastructure that works for more than just the middle class," said historian Nancy D. Campbell, the author of *OD: Naloxone and the Politics of Overdose*. "Because we don't have one now that's nimble enough or really public health–oriented enough, it seems to come down to individual champions who have to convert enough other individuals before significant change does start to happen," she told me.

Elected officials spurred innovations in some communities. In 2017, after her region was so overrun by overdose deaths that the coroner had to rent refrigerated trailers to store bodies, the mayor of Dayton, Ohio, helped initiate a regional opioid task force whose work brought forth a 50 percent overdose-death reduction the following year. Nan Whaley had first been shocked into action after a beloved boy she used to babysit in her small Indiana hometown died of a heroin overdose at twenty-two. "My EMS runs were going through the roof," Whaley recalled, in 2015 and 2016. "It was so bad we were having to rely on mutual aid from suburban cities thirty miles away. The national media was calling us 'Ground Zero of the opioid crisis.'"

Driving around Dayton in those days, Montgomery County sheriff Rob Streck was reminded of the television show *The Walking Dead*. "When you were sitting around listening to the [scanner], it was just 'person down, person down, person down,'" he told me. "Our medics would run out of Narcan by ten in the morning."

Mayor Whaley reckoned it was best to address the spotlight head-on, which sometimes meant coaxing reluctant leaders not under her jurisdiction. She initially focused on large-scale Narcan distribution (equipping first responders, everyone from police officers to workers in low-rent motels), real-time data sharing between police and treatment providers, expansion of syringe service programs (the Dayton area opened three), and jail-based drug treatment with peer coaches to help the incarcerated with SUD navigate recovery upon their release. (When a person's SUD has not been treated in jail and they reuse upon reentry, drug users are then opioid-naïve and far more vulnerable to overdose death than they were at the time of arrest.)

Using EMS data, Daytonians who overdose now get visited by

peers who hand out Narcan and try, when people are open to it, to help them navigate treatment barriers. A phone app shows users and family members, in real time, which facilities have open beds.

When Whaley got tired of Dayton being the subject of addiction porn—like the *Time* magazine photo essay that featured disturbing images of Daytonians injecting or passing out mid-overdose behind the wheel of a car—public health staffers begged reporters to write more recovery-focused stories. They wanted to flip the narrative from "Dayton is Ground Zero" to "People in addiction *can* recover." (They also trained reporters to avoid using stigmatizing words like *addict*.) "Too often, people think that no one recovers from this disease, so if we don't highlight recovery stories, the perception is that the only end to this is jail or death, and that's simply not true," said Barb Marsh, Dayton's assistant public health commissioner.

Sheriff Streck's assessment wasn't quite as cheerful as Whaley's or Marsh's. Streck credited the overdose decline not just to the new programming but also to the fact that drug cartels got better at mixing fentanyl to avoid deadly batches that rob them of customers. That, plus the fact that so many people were already dead. "Some of the other sheriffs in Ohio think I'm crazy," Streck said. "They call what we do 'namby pamby jail.' I say it all the time: If it's legal and may help the inmates or the employees, we'll try it. I don't care what it is."

But Streck was rare among the law enforcement officials I met, most of whom thought treating the addicted in jails equated to "hug-a-thug." He allowed me to tour his jail with a peer recovery specialist who knew most of the women in the pod—she'd once used drugs with them.

The stone-rollers broke down into two categories: some had the built-in power to grant permission, while others acted first and asked for forgiveness later. The most passionate ones I encountered were those with lived experience—people in recovery or relatives of the dead who felt that their only recourse was to make meaning of their loved ones' deaths.

An OB-GYN who lost her sixteen-year-old son to overdose started a syringe exchange in Peoria, Illinois, that now provides referrals for low-barrier bupe to her own obstetrics practice. It was Dr. Tami Olt's first time treating men. When someone says they want addiction medication, Olt's goal is to get them on bupe within forty-eight hours. Peoria's fatal overdoses in the pandemic were up 40 percent.

Early on in COVID, staffers at Olt's harm-reduction center gave out food to needy neighborhood residents, not just drug users, after an area food pantry closed because of pandemic fears—a goodwill gesture they hoped would pay off politically down the road. They also upped their outreach to sex workers, hand-delivering condoms and lube, and coaxing them to Zoom with their clients. "People are more scared to engage in sex with strangers, so our girls are having to engage in riskier practices," said Kshe Bernard, a former sex worker and drug user who now does outreach work for JOLT.

"I can't imagine another disease on the planet where if some-body didn't get better, everybody in their life would abandon them," said Olt's program director, Chris Schaffner. "Imagine having cancer and chemo, and everyone in your family going, 'Fuck it.' The idea that you have to hit bottom [before you can get better]—that's medical malpractice."

Barnard, the outreach peer, was focusing on a new homeless encampment next to a Peoria bridge that had sprung up at the site of comedian Richard Pryor's childhood home. She was blanketing the area with Narcan and using an online sex worker site to reach out to women who needed help with housing and harm-reduction supplies.

Nationwide, all the efforts put into place to reduce the spread of COVID—mask-wearing, social distancing, sheltering in place—were forms of harm reduction, Schaffner pointed out. He admired Olt because she was unafraid to say hard things, even at the risk of professional alienation. "Her theory is: 'Until you've lost a kid, you don't have any say over what I do. If you're Brené Brown, but you're not here in the ring getting your ass kicked like I am, your opinion doesn't matter.'"

A northern Virginia woman who'd rushed home to find her twenty-one-year-old brother dead of a heroin overdose in 2013 created a nonprofit that grew to have what is now a $1.6 million budget and fifteen employees who connect released inmates to treatment and recovery housing in her brother's name. It's called The Chris Atwood Foundation—or The CAF, for short.

Ginny Atwood Lovitt almost singlehandedly pushed into being Virginia laws that made naloxone more available, protected drug users who called 911 from arrest when a friend overdosed, and pushed into being a law that made it so that police chiefs no longer had the authority to put the brakes on syringe services in Virginia. She's been changing state laws since she was barely old enough to drink.

As Lovitt described it: "I spent the entirety of my early twenties going around and blabbing to anyone who would listen, 'My brother should not have died,' and none of you with your fancy public health degrees sat back and thought, *Maybe we should make sure people can get naloxone?*

"But I can only deal with one set of ridiculous regulations and rules at a time," she said. She'd recently learned that Virginia governor Ralph Northam earmarked $1.6 million of his budget for naloxone, only for state staffers to wait too long to make the purchase. The opportunity evaporated because of internal procurement policies and inattention. "I could have bought 21,000 doses with that money," she snapped. "I was livid."

Procurement pipes were clogged across the nation. Though the 21st Century Cures Act awarded $1 billion in state grants to fight opioid addiction over a two-year period, more than $300 million—nearly a third of it—went unspent. Bureaucratic bungling, a paltry public health infrastructure, and the grants' two-year stop date combined to produce a slow drip of dollars that one expert likened to people starving to death while food and water were "stuck in an airport somewhere."

Lovitt invited me to follow the implementation of a program she was setting up with the Fairfax County Sheriff's Office, with protocols that promised to be the polar opposite of the chaos at the Surry County Jail. Inmates in resource-rich northern Virginia would not only be offered bupe in the jail—a rarity in the United States—but they would also have access to The CAF's harm-reduction services. On a video chat set up by the jail, peer-support specialists counsel incarcerated people with SUD, then literally pick them up from jail when they're released and drive them to housing.

Like the outreach workers in Peoria and other harm-reduction programs I followed, Lovitt's nonprofit continued operating full steam when COVID hit. In the beginning there were bureaucratic wrinkles to smooth out—communication snags when peers weren't notified in time of an inmate's pending release, for instance. "Once that window has closed, they *poof*—they disappear," Lovitt said. Before the jail-based bupe program, The CAF had two volunteers lose loved ones who were withdrawing in jails. "They were thrown in there and just told to 'sweat it out.'" One woman died from a seizure, likely from alcohol or benzodiazepine withdrawal, the other from suicide.

*　　*　　*

"I'm reminded of a line from a Michelle Shocked song about growing up in Texas, where 'they could not make room for a girl who had seen the ocean,'" said Methodist minister Rev. Ray Morgan. "We've got to get past the garbage politicians have been feeding us to get reelected and come up with real answers to actually solve the problem."

Morgan was new to Mount Airy in 2019, when he and a group of area pastors met with county judges to advocate for a drug court. Drug courts waive charges for low-level drug offenders if arrestees complete counseling and other intensive treatment protocols, including random drug testing and regular meetings with the judge. But Surry County's judges shot the idea down—even after a Bureau of Justice grant was written to pay for it. At a follow-up town hall, the ministerial network managed to attract 300 concerned citizens, but the chief judge sent a lower-level family court judge, who had little say in the matter, to participate. "We have treatment slots that go unfilled because we can't match the right population to those spots—partly because they're all in jail!" complained Dr. Jason Edsall, a local hospital administrator and EMS medical director who participated in the meeting.

Two to three people were overdosing in Mount Airy every day, though activists believed the number was much higher. In a sprawling county of just 72,000 people, around 4,000 of them were thought to have SUD. And yet Daymark, the county's largest mental health provider, was treating just twenty people for addiction, a rate of one-half of 1 percent.

Would the Surry County jailers, blinded to any approach other than the War on Drugs protocols they had pledged to abide by, continue walking past the dopesick men clutching buckets on their intake floors, just waiting for construction of their bigger, $45 million jail? Who, if anyone, would convince them to try another way?

"My dad in Wisconsin isn't going to listen to the surgeon general or know who he is, or care," Stanford, the public health analyst, told me. But when local people in positions of power are moved to act, especially those with lived experience, that matters. Across the country, officials who refuse to open SSPs or sheriffs who rail against jail-based treatment rarely change their minds until maybe a cousin or someone they grew up with helps them make the switch, Stanford said.

Heartache, not data, was the best prompter of public-policy change.

Chapter Two

Die-In

Trail of Truth, an annual march of remembrance and die-in, Binghamton, New York.

W hen a person dies from heroin or OxyContin, there's not a direct line from the drug to a stopped heart. An opioid overdose is sneakier and slower-moving. It begins by lulling the lungs into cozy submission—the hijacked opioid receptors cause a rush of pleasure that turns into respiratory distress. The lungs sleep so hard that, as the airways constrict, the person literally forgets to breathe. Death lingers first over the fingers and lips; they turn limp and blue. Gurgling noises dangerously sound like snoring but are actually death rattles. Once the oxygen starvation moves inward to vital organs like the heart and brain, a loved one or rescue worker has three to five precious minutes to jolt the receptors awake and reverse the overdose before brain damage occurs and then death.

Nan Goldin thought about her own overdose as she lay on the cold marble floor of the Guggenheim Museum while 8,000 slips of paper fell down on her like snowflakes. She clenched her fists inside the sleeves of her black winter coat. It was February 2019, late on a Saturday when museum admission is free or "pay what you wish." Amid the crowd of tourists, there was an extra hum of noise that rose beyond the buzz of Jackson Pollock or Frank Lloyd Wright; even the security guards seemed to be puzzling over it, scanning the crowd. Something felt different.

Megan Kapler, one of Goldin's assistants, had done her security-detail homework. She'd taught fellow protesters how to fold the banners, tucking them inside the bottom of their bags; how to respond if a guard tried to take a banner down. A seasoned activist had coached her: "If you tell a security guard they can't touch your property, for some reason they'll believe you." It worked.

Goldin and her team had plotted every moment of their pretend-death experience, down to the text-message all clear. They had orchestrated a die-in, a civil disobedience strategy employed to protest everything from the Vietnam War to the government's sluggish response to HIV/AIDS to, more recently, the police killings of Black people.

As Goldin gave the go-ahead, red banners unfurled in unison over the sides of the famous spiral-ramped atrium, reading "200 DEAD EACH DAY," "SHAME ON SACKLER," and "TAKE DOWN THEIR NAME."

"Just the sensation of being on the ground, it immobilizes you, and you think: This could happen to me," Goldin told me. Could happen to her *again*, that is. She had overdosed in 2017, when a dealer sold her heroin that turned out to be pure fentanyl. She was three years into opioid addiction then, having been pre-scribed OxyContin in Germany following wrist surgery. Within two months, she found herself taking twenty pills a day—buying them wherever she could, doing anything to avoid the agony of withdrawal, which she described as "a form of torture beyond words. You have no skin."

The psychic pain was even worse. "It's deep, deep, *deep* darkness," she told me.

Goldin had understood that she was already susceptible to OUD, having been a regular heroin user in the 1980s. But it had been more than three decades since she'd last used opioids, and she thought OxyContin was safer because it was prescribed.

After German police busted her for mail-ordering pills from her New York dealer, her studio assistants talked her into going back to the same Massachusetts doctor who'd helped her get off heroin in 1989. Goldin was only nine months out of rehab when she read Patrick Radden Keefe's groundbreaking October 2017 *New Yorker* exposé of the Sacklers in an airport and pledged on the spot to shame the Sacklers where they would feel it most—in the esteemed art world they'd spent millions buying their way into.

The little slips of paper were fake prescriptions that fell inside the six-story atrium, blanketing Goldin and her supporters in white. The "action," as they called it, was mesmerizing theater, a camera-ready call-out. Nan Goldin couldn't believe how beautiful it was.

It was in that moment that Goldin, a lifelong atheist whose curly red hair matched her temperament, decided that agitating for justice would become her higher power. "This is the power bigger than myself, and this will keep me sober," she remembers thinking.

Her goal was to provoke media coverage, and that media coverage was meant to degrade and discredit all the arts and intellectual institutions that had accepted Sackler millions in exchange for celebrating the Sackler name, from Harvard and Tufts Universities to the Smithsonian and the Louvre. Reporters with the *New York Times* and *The New Yorker* were there, having received a heads-up in embargoed press releases.

The falling prescription stunt was inspired by something Purdue owner Richard Sackler had said when he asked his sales reps to envision a scenario erupting across America thanks to the debut of his new miracle painkiller. The unveiling of OxyContin "will be followed by a blizzard of prescriptions that will bury the competition," he predicted. "The prescription blizzard will be so deep, dense, and white."

The incendiary quote was taken directly from unredacted Purdue documents that were unsealed by a Massachusetts Superior Court judge and released under the direction of that state's attorney general, Maura Healey, the first official to name Sackler individuals (rather than solely Purdue) in any opioid litigation.

Goldin's group had designed its own Sackler prescription, cheekily written out to Solomon R. Guggenheim. In the box where refills went, they drew an infinity sign, and at the top of the script they entered the Guggenheim's phone number. Her assistants had labored over every element of the faux prescriptions, using a favorite printer in Queens.

The eighty-milligram prescription also quoted a real-life warning from another Purdue exec. When Sackler pressed his lieutenants to lobby for over-the-counter status for OxyContin in Germany in 1997, one worried whether such lax German controls would lead to widespread abuse. To which Richard stunningly responded: "How substantially would it improve your sales?"

It would take time before those who weren't in on the stunt began to comprehend the enormity of Goldin's message. The whole country had fallen victim to the Sacklers' one-two messaging: *Opioids are perfectly good for you, only the "addicts" are bad.*

When Goldin rose from the overdose portion of the die-in, she'd been sober for two years. She was taking daily bupe, and she chain-smoked continually, alternating between cigarettes and vape pens.

At the center of the storied atrium, she led a staccato call-and-response:

We want their money
For safe-consumption sites,
For harm reduction,
For treatment.
It's time, Guggenheim!
To take down their names!

The Guggenheim had received more than $9 million from the family between 1995 and 2015, but it wasn't the only museum to accept Sackler money. A year earlier, inside the Sackler Wing of the Metropolitan Museum of Art, Goldin's team had lobbed fake OxyContin bottles into the reflecting pool in front of the 2,000-year-old Temple of Dendur, the most famous of the family's gifts. The Sacklers had donated $3.5 million to build the Met wing in 1974, but because the gift was paid out over 20 years, it wasn't enough to fully finance construction, and the City of New York had to chip in $1.4 million.

The orange pill bottles floated on the water like ice-cream sprinkles, the labels framed by a yellow warning that contained a single word: DEATH. Goldin settled onto the floor next to that spectacle, too, that time chanting, "Sacklers lie, people die."

A month later, at the Smithsonian Institution's Arthur M. Sackler Gallery on the National Mall in Washington, DC, Goldin's gravelly voice punctuated the Zen vibe near the Asian artwork that family patriarch Arthur Sackler had so revered, collecting it to the point of hoarding. Arthur's "mother's little helper" campaign had turned Valium into the country's first-ever billion-dollar drug. And his relatives used that same playbook to convince doctors that OxyContin was safe. (In the 1970s, Goldin had a years-long prescription Valium habit.)

On cue, she shouted, "Arthur's skill was marketing pills! Pills for profit! Addiction equals profit!"

Along with a handful of activists and pro bono lawyers, Goldin, sixty-five, had now spent two years plotting protests from the coffee table of her Brooklyn apartment. They marched and protested and made the media pay attention to stunts they pulled off inside Sackler-named museum wings, from the Smithsonian to the Louvre to the Temple of Dendur. She also sold limited-edition prints of her work to fund harm-reduction innovations, from a mass spectrometer to test the strength of illicit drugs in Greensboro, North Carolina, to a center that provided sterile syringes and low-barrier bupe in rural New York.

If the public understood how the Sacklers used philanthropy to cloak their villainy, she hoped, the family would be forced to pay for addiction treatment on demand. "My goal is public outrage," she told me in 2020. "I want them not to be invited to galas. I want people to shun them."

Known for her raw portraits of outcasts and intimates, including people who use drugs, Nan Goldin is considered a pioneer in color photography and one of the world's greatest American photographers, on a par with Sally Mann, Diane Arbus, Gordon Parks, and Robert Mapplethorpe. In early 2018, against stern warnings from her agent and others who worried that her newfound activism might tarnish her career, Goldin formed the group PAIN, which stands for Prescription Addiction Intervention Now, with the goal of doing for the opioid crisis what ACT UP had done for HIV/AIDS. "Back then, they were like, 'Why would you bite the hand that feeds you?'" recalled Goldin's lawyer, Mike Quinn. "But within eighteen months, you mentioned the Sacklers to anyone in the art world, and they wanted nothing to do with them," Quinn said.

As a volunteer, Quinn adopted Goldin's cause with a combination of linguistic fervor and bad-boy hijinks. His fiery legal pleadings would become legendary markers in Purdue's bankruptcy case.

Goldin's radical aesthetic punctured the country's slumbering indifference like none of the OxyContin protesters had done before her. It rang louder and garnered more press than the survivors of those who had fatally overdosed on heroin or fentanyl, many of them initially hooked by OxyContin.

After the Guggenheim action, museum director Richard Armstrong called up Goldin's gallery owner, Marianne Goodman, and pleaded with her to "make Nan stop." Goodman, who was ninety-two, said she didn't want to. "She says what she wants," Goldin explained.

That it had taken a famous artist, of all people, to finally get under the Sacklers' skin said as much about what captures Americans' attention as it does about corporate influence-peddling.

If you only remember one thing about Ed Bisch by the end of this book, let it be that the first time he heard the word OxyContin in 2001, his only son was dead from an overdose of the drug. For twenty-one years, he has refused to let the Sacklers forget that fact.

A salt-of-the-earth IT worker from Philadelphia, Bisch had never heard the name Nan Goldin until the activism surrounding the Purdue bankruptcy pushed them together. Bisch and other parents of the dead didn't even know back then that it was the Sackler family, as the sole owners of Purdue, who'd been the ones steering the drug's marketing blitz.

By design, most people didn't. Years ahead of the company's first guilty plea and settlement in 2007, the family had presciently stepped back from executive to board positions—securing a better angle from which to throw their loyal trinity of executive under-lings under the bus. The press largely missed that story, too.

"Nan's famous," Bisch said, chuckling with excitement, as he and several other parent-activist group leaders decided to join forces with her. Together they took the fight into the virtual courtroom, where the case was now being litigated, as the Ad Hoc Committee on Accountability, hoping it would get them heard in the press as well as inside the court.

Like Michelle Mathis's belief in meeting people where they are, the activists had to meet their targets in the courtroom, because the Sacklers didn't give a shit about what was happening inside the nation's emergency rooms or under its bridges. Back then, public outrage rarely penetrated the Purdue bankruptcy in White Plains. The proceedings were opaque, managed behind closed doors, with rulings issued in dry, technical legalese—and that was before COVID-19 forced the proceedings out of the courtroom and onto the Internet (the public could only listen in, with staticky telephonic access).

Much to their surprise (and mine, too), the Ad Hoc Com-mittee was eventually heard, thanks largely to Mike Quinn. At thirty-nine, Goldin's mop-haired lawyer took on the committee's representation. He spent large chunks of every day on his pro bono bankruptcy work—writing briefs that infuriated the Bank-ruptcy Boys Club (especially Judge Robert Drain), scheming with the group, and smoothly working his contacts on Capitol Hill and in the press. "I love journalists!" he said, working me, too. "I think you guys are literally the only defense this country has against corruption."

Goldin was the kind of famous that captures the attention of not just the wealthy and avant-garde but politicians, too. "We are deeply in your debt," Nancy Pelosi, then the House Minority Leader, told her at a press conference in support of opioid-epidemic funding in 2018.

*　　*　　*

When I first met with PAIN in December 2019, the group was at a crossroads. Confused by the morass of opioid litigation, they were puzzled about their next steps and even a little scared. Kapler, a slight blonde, had spotted someone surveilling the group outside of Goldin's apartment in Brooklyn. In the following weeks she saw him again twice, including outside her own apartment in another neighborhood. When her companion started videoing him, he fled. "He looked like a big old Staten Island guy," said Goldin, who sought advice from filmmaker Laura Poitras, whose national security reporting had won an Academy Award and who was working on a documentary about PAIN.

"It was very scary," Goldin said. "At one point, I went and stayed with somebody else." Quinn feared that the moment the Sacklers secured legal immunity, they would sue his clients. He, too, had been spooked by the presence of a man walking outside his family home in ten-degree weather with a flashlight—in New York's Hudson Valley, where he'd retreated when the pandemic hit. As the litigation came further into focus, I heard even more stories from the group—or was it paranoia?—as the activists and their pro bono lawyers switched from chatting on group text to a more secure messaging app.

The following year, I, too, took note of an unfamiliar van lurking in the alley behind my house. Richard Sackler's lawyer had mailed inflammatory and intimidating letters to lawyers for Hulu, which was filming *Dopesick*, a forthcoming television series inspired by my book. The letters were marked in bold, **"Confidential—not for publication or attribution."**

In the summer of 2019, the Louvre in Paris—the most visited museum in the world—took the Sackler name down from a wing devoted to Eastern antiquities, following a protest by PAIN. In a country where the government had anointed Goldin a Commandeur de l'Ordre des Arts et des Lettres, on par with Bono and Marcel Marceau, the Louvre's decision was a big win. (The museum president claimed the twenty-year naming agreement had, coincidentally, just expired.)

In November, PAIN stormed the Victoria and Albert Museum in London, where, clad in matching red-and-black "PAIN KILLERS" shirts, the group held another die-in atop the 11,000 handmade porcelain tiles that formed a Sackler-named courtyard. They strewed red-ink-spattered dollar bills with the words "The Overdose States of America" and "In Pharma We Trust." A circular "OC"-stamped OxyContin pill took the place of George Washington's head. The Tate and National Portrait Gallery promised to eschew future Sackler gifts.

In interviews with the British press, Goldin slammed the Sacklers' funding of "decadent architecture" over treatment and overdose-reversal meds. "If museums don't stand for the basic value of human life, what do they stand for?" she asked.

Recapping events over pizza inside Goldin's bohemian Clinton Hill apartment, the group held heated strategy sessions and hilarious debates. They grilled me about the bankruptcy. They begged me to speed along the Hulu show, over which I had very little control. They described their August 2019 trespassing arrest outside Governor Andrew Cuomo's New York City office, after they blocked his doors for refusing to grant the opening of a safe-injection pilot site in the city. When they asked me for treatment advocacy advice, I suggested they make Goldin the poster girl for low-barrier bupe. (They looked into it, briefly, but largely kept their lens trained on the Sacklers.)

They brainstormed how to heap yet more public shame upon Richard Sackler, reciting his recently released quote from a 1997 e-mail about wanting "to be feared as a tiger with claws, teeth and balls, and build some excitement with prescribers that OxyContin

Tablets is the way to go." "That man is the epitome of this whole thing, Richard Sackler," Goldin said.

Harry Cullen, Goldin's other assistant, had tried to stake out a property that was listed in Richard's name for a potential protest, "but the idea of going to a gated community and doing an action in front of a gate—it was not exciting," he said.

Other than Goldin's print sales, the group had almost no funding to support their travel; the latest donations from their website had come from a cheese society in Crown Heights ($93, via PayPal) and in memory of a recently deceased eighty-four-year-old whose adult children believed that opioids had led to her downfall ($50). Goldin had met a wealthy donor at a fundraiser for the Ms. Foundation for Women the night before. "She was talking about how they fund community organizations, and she was looking at me the whole time," Goldin said. "But when I went up to her afterwards, she just wanted a selfie!"

PAIN's reach extended further than they knew. By February 2020, the group had multiple lawyers giving them free legal advice. Former drug-prosecutor-turned-author Charlotte Bismuth had brought her preschooler's giant drawing pad to her first PAIN meeting that month to illustrate the many flanges of the White Plains bankruptcy. She broke down how it differed from the non-Purdue opioid cases against drug distributors, makers, and pharmacies that were being overseen as part of the Multidistrict Litigation (MDL) in Cleveland. (Purdue's lawsuits were initially part of the MDL until the company filed for bankruptcy in 2019.) Initially, Bismuth, too, wanted the author equivalent of a selfie from Goldin—a blurb for her forthcoming book, *Bad Medicine*. But she soon became the group's chief explainer and cheerleader, translating opaque legal briefs into common English and providing real-time commentary on Twitter during bankruptcy hearings, including via her own animated cartoons.

By the time COVID forced the group's actions indoors,

PAIN had created an offshoot devoted to bankruptcy activism—OxyJustice. Its members included parent support-group pioneer Joanne Peterson of Learn2Cope, Ed Bisch, and other relatives of the dead. They began holding Thursday night Zoom sessions, with occasional expert guests. The group aimed to educate the public about the proceedings, ensure that eligible creditors understood how to file their claims, and fight an unjust outcome.

The pixelated thumbnails on my computer screen could barely hold the boisterous lot of them, hailing from California to Kentucky to Cape Cod. They were an incongruent bunch—politically, economically, intergenerationally. But they were united in their pain and rage.

"I literally get so full of anxiety when I even just hear the Sackler name," Joanne Peterson told me, after one especially disappointing bankruptcy hearing in late 2020. She'd recently lost a niece to a fentanyl overdose. "And it's been seventeen years of funerals for me, and that's why I'm so mad. Because people still don't feel it, see it, know it. Because they're not on the streets like we are." In the early months of COVID, Peterson's group received so many calls from stressed-out parents that they had to design new telephone protocols. "The death calls are the worst," she said.

A man in her Massachusetts support network lost his father to COVID and, two weeks later, lost his son to overdose. "He said he wanted to crawl into the coffin with him," Peterson said. "These are the calls we get every day."

OxyJustice vowed to agitate their way onto the official docket in White Plains whether the judge wanted them there or not. They begged investigative journalists to ask probing questions about the process, but "getting the media to cover this is pulling teeth because you have to give them a dissertation on Bankruptcy 101," as Cullen put it. Many reporters who'd written about it earlier were too busy covering the pandemic. Goldin said she'd coaxed

Patrick Radden Keefe, the *New Yorker* writer who was now working on a book on the Sacklers, to publish an October 2020 article about the bankruptcy against the advice of his book publisher, who preferred that he save the material for his forthcoming book. "As an artist to another artist, I begged him, 'You don't hold back for your own career,' and he agreed," she told the group over Zoom. (Keefe told me he was already working on the piece when they spoke.)

Repeatedly, they hounded retired *New York Times* reporter Barry Meier to release a damning 120-page prosecution memo he'd obtained after his coverage of the 2007 settlement. They worried that Meier was holding the memo back for use in forthcoming Netflix and HBO projects based on his 2003 book, *Pain Killer*. But Meier declined, explaining that it contained confidential grand-jury testimony that was illegal to publish.

When Goldin described how she'd written Meier "a very strong e-mail in all caps," a California mom who'd lost a son to OxyContin overdose in 2005 started crying and abruptly left the Zoom. She was outraged by the thought of journalists—all of us—enriching ourselves at the expense of the group's dead kids.

The truth is, though, the roots of the crisis remained obscure to most Americans who hadn't bothered reading exhaustive multipart newspaper series or nonfiction exposés. The story would have had even less traction had it not been for sustained journalistic muckraking, from Meier's bulldogging of the company's earliest marketing maneuvers to Keefe's *Empire of Pain*. "PAIN and the press amplified each other," Goldin told me.

Yet all the ink spilled in the name of holding power accountable could very well add up to nothing more than one of the best-publicized examples of billionaire justice in America. "It's like Trump; he commits one crime after another and you think, 'Surely, this is gonna bring him down,' and then nothing does," Goldin said.

But PAIN kept yelling, trying to puncture the bankruptcy-court bubble. In the summer of 2020, Cullen, twenty-seven, successfully petitioned for an extension so that more victims could file personal-injury claims against Purdue. He spent months fielding questions like, "If I'm filing for my daughter who died and also for her kids and myself, who lost a daughter, and my brother-in-law, who's in prison—how do I file that claim?"

Strangers broke down crying on the phone to him. He worried about the claims that wouldn't get filed by families who were too ashamed and/or too heartsick to fill out the forms, or simply didn't know they could. "At the same time, we're trying to drum up hysteria and mud in the courtroom," Cullen said. "We're trying to throw everything but the kitchen sink. And then the kitchen sink."

It was anybody's guess whether a group that had so successfully enacted subversive stunts in art galleries could translate that energy into the courtroom, where the Sacklers had long held the upper hand.

But a lot would change in the coming months. Quinn warned me, "It's about to get ugly."

Chapter Three

Freeze Frame

Nostalgic reminders of The Andy Griffith Show. *Mount Airy, North Carolina.*

Opioid use disorder is a chronic, recurring acquired disease of brain structure and function, according to the prevailing theory on it. OUD resides largely in the brain's reward center and the parts of the prefrontal cortex involved in executive function and decision-making. So it doesn't really matter whether the opioid is legal or not: when a person takes heroin or OxyContin, his brain is flooded with far more opioids than his body can naturally produce. Biological tolerance can develop, for some as quickly as within five days. The opioid receptors then become desensitized, the body's own endorphin production slows dramatically, and, without the addition of external opioids, its natural opioids stop functioning. Powerful cravings for the euphoria produced by opioids will eventually lead to changes in the brain, skewing a person's actions. As the cravings further intensify, the drugs become even more irresistible.

Without external opioids, then, the brain is literally starved of its ability to feel normal. Withdrawal symptoms take over, causing crushing anxiety and crippling pain. A person becomes desperate to alleviate that starvation.

This desperation explains how a one-time honor student ends up doing sex work, or a homemaker finds herself living under a bridge in winter ("With about ten blankets, it's not so bad," an unhoused woman in Charleston told me). It's why small towns across America are now full of grandparents raising their grandchildren.

Some people "kick" or beat withdrawal symptoms, then relapse anyway, even after their physical dependence is largely resolved—which means that OUD isn't just a biological problem but can be a psychological one, too. Harmful behaviors associated with addiction have never meant that the addicted person doesn't love his family. It means that, by the time most people realize they have an opioid problem, it's often too late for them to fix it on their own. The desperation of being dopesick rules the day.

But because of entrenched stigma, most American communities remain likelier to arrest people for OUD-driven behaviors than to provide them with treatment. It's as inefficient and costly as it is inhumane.

We know, from the few cities that have begun treating and housing the addicted instead of just arresting them, that criminal recidivism can drop as much as 58 percent. While some critics point out that police officers shouldn't be the first point of contact for addicted people who've already suffered trauma at the hands of police—Black and Brown people in particular—the truth is, in most American cities and towns, they are.

We know, too, that recovery without the benefit of bupe or methadone can be dangerous; that treatment-seeking patients with OUD who only get counseling have extremely high rates of relapse, even after a very long and stable detox with good counseling support. Before he was found dead in an apartment with a heroin needle in his arm in 2014, the acclaimed actor Philip Seymour Hoffman had been mostly sober for more than two decades.

With fentanyl increasingly poisoning the drug supply—putting even casual drug users at risk of accidental overdose—opportunities for people to get better on their own aren't as possible as they once were, particularly in light of overdose deaths rising among people in their teens, twenties, and thirties. Which is another strong argument for making bupe more widely available, along with harm-reduction supports like clean needles and fentanyl test strips—especially in rural communities where stigma is most entrenched.

In Surry County, North Carolina, you can drive into town on Andy Griffith Parkway and eat a meat-and-three lunch at Aunt Bea's Barbecue restaurant. The tourism board will happily take your money for the privilege of letting you ride in Deputy Barney Fife's police cruiser. The town's water tower, the culture center next to the library—everywhere you look you see Sheriff Andy and his son, Opie, usually toting a fishing pole.

"It's classic, stick-to-your-own rural America," Michelle Mathis told me in 2019. "But more than that, it is literally Mayberry, so the stigma is higher than any other place we work." Even though it now claimed one of the highest overdose rates in the state, Surry County was nowhere close to teaching sex workers how to Zoom, or arranging reentry housing from the jail, or even passing out clean needles and Narcan.

Mount Airy had not only been the county's textile- and furniture-making hub; it was also the actor Andy Griffith's hometown, the setting for the long-running eponymous television show that celebrated the wholesomeness of small-town America. Not unlike Barney when he got his police-issued knickers in a knot, a stubborn streak hummed through the personality of the town. In its more prosperous decades, Mount Airy was peopled with the kind of feisty Scots-Irish descendants who could afford to call their own shots, many with small farm plots or orchards they owned outright and worked on the side.

When an outside company took over a long-standing Mount Airy furniture maker in the 1970s, its workers refused to abide by the new company's stricter—and borderline-abusive—protocols. "They are very independent mountain people who will just tell you to go to hell and walk out!" a former manager told me. But after most of the furniture and textile mill jobs moved to Mexico, then to Asia, the largest employers became the schools, the hospitals, and Walmart.

By 2019, only 52 percent of the working-age population had jobs at all, a rate 12 percent below the national average and 10 percent below the state's. In previous years, Surry County pharmacies sold *55 million* opioids between 2006 and 2014—enough for every man, woman, and child to annually consume 83 pills, a rate more than double that of the pharmacies located in surrounding counties.

Countywide, there were 500 job openings but a dire shortage of applicants who could pass a drug test. A local chicken processing plant was so hard up for employees that managers bused in immigrant workers from adjacent counties. During my three years of reporting on Surry County, things would get a lot worse before they would begin to turn around.

In working-class communities where pain medications were aggressively prescribed, job losses and the opioid crisis were perniciously entwined. One nearby factory owner told me it took five applicants to find one who could pass a drug test. That ratio continues to widen.

Countywide, the number of children in foster care went up 50 percent in a decade, more than half the county's kids lived in low-income homes, and addiction-related EMS calls soared by 350 percent. By early 2021, the number of job openings had more than doubled to 1,200. And that same chicken-plant manager had since resorted to flying workers in from Puerto Rico, housing them in nearby apartments for nine-month stints.

Princeton economist Alan Krueger calculated that, nationally, the rise in opioid prescriptions accounted for 43 percent of the decline in the country's male labor force participation rate. When he analyzed the correlation between low workforce participation and high opioid prescribing among the nation's 3,007 counties, Surry County ranked number ten.

"When I was growing up, Mount Airy was booming," said Wendy Odum, fifty-three. "Both parents worked, and I don't remember everybody being on food stamps because people worked and took pride in it. Then, everything—I mean socially, spiritually, physically—it just slowly imploded." Odum lost her nursing license after becoming addicted to prescribed painkillers—following a fall on Thanksgiving of 2003. She had been carrying a broccoli casserole down a flight of stairs and missed a step. She was in methadone treatment for a decade, including in 2007, when her mother died from a combination of oxycodone and Xanax. In 2018, Odum's thirty-year-old daughter died from a fentanyl and methamphetamine overdose. "Our foster system is so overrun that my husband and I are now raising our four grandchildren, and so are all the grandparents we know," Odum said. "All our kids are dead."

In Mount Airy, it felt like the town was trying to freeze-frame itself in a black-and-white postwar situation comedy. Which, in a way, it was. Google the words *Mount Airy,* and the town's web address—visitmayberry.com—told you everything its civic leaders wanted you to know.

But in furniture-making parlance, that image was a cracked veneer. Elected leaders couldn't own up to what was happening on the ground because then they'd have to admit their No. 1 marketing tool was a mirage.

Even those who'd lost loved ones to overdose bought into the lore, as if "thoughts and prayers" could erase the growing crime threatening their neighborhoods or bring back their dead children.

And harm reduction was an especially tough sell, not only because addiction has been entrenched here for decades but also because harm reduction isn't harm eradication. It demands new and even counterintuitive thinking that strays too far from the fictional nostalgia that townspeople most like to evoke. And yet by eschewing basic interventions that would make bupe, fentanyl test strips, and sterile syringes widely accessible, the mythos of Mayberry only slid further out of reach.

With some coaching from Mathis, Odum quietly began delivering Narcan to the trailer park in nearby Patrick County, Virginia, where her daughter died. She expanded to other nearby communities with the help of harm-reduction supplies donated by a coalition based out of nearby Winston-Salem and a small cavalry of people in long-term recovery who knew where the overdose hotspots were because they'd once used drugs there.

James Stroud, a forty-eight-year-old former banker in recovery after a decade of daily opioid and meth use, became Odum's right hand, zigzagging the county to drop off needles and Narcan. They counted forty-eight reported overdose reversals in their first three months, but the work felt minimal compared to the needs they witnessed.

Many users, skeptical of outsiders who might alert police, trusted Odum because they had known her daughter, Jessica. "Now it's like the Munchkins when the Wicked Witch leaves—they all start coming out when they see my car," Odum said. "I feel I am healthier and better able to raise my daughter's children if I'm coming from a place of love and common sense."

Odum had recently been called out to a gorgeous outdoor wedding to administer naloxone to a groomsman who'd over-dosed. She lived near the site and had previously Narcanned him on four occasions. (County EMS workers arrived after Odum administered his first dose, then they took him to the hospital when he kept overdosing—because the fentanyl was longer-lasting than the naloxone—and put him on a naloxone drip.)

"He was literally lying on the grass with people all around him," Odum said. "A young lady was giving him rescue breaths as I got there, while the mother of the bride was clutching her pearls. And I remember noticing that his shoes were so shiny and new." He'd taken enough care preparing for the wedding that his socks matched his wingtips, but, with the pandemic drug supply more erratic than usual, he couldn't gauge the level of fentanyl in his heroin.

"It was so surreal—this beautiful place with this brutal, ugly truth."

In the fall of 2020, Odum met with Michelle Mathis at Olive Branch and a new Methodist minister, Ray Morgan, to plot the opening of a syringe-exchange in Mount Airy—one that would operate initially out of the back of Odum's and Stroud's cars. Odum had already organized volunteers to meet (masked up, following COVID protocols) in the party room of the local Pizza Hut, where they packaged needles with wound care kits and toiletries. She filed a safety plan with local law enforcement officials, as required by state law, but she refused to wait around for their approval. Mathis worried that she should.

In my own adopted hometown of Roanoke, Virginia—where the police chief initially likened the opening of a syringe-services program to "handing out marijuana cigarettes to schoolchildren"—syringe services were mired in controversy for two years before one finally opened in 2019, and only after Ginny Lovitt lobbied to have Virginia's syringe law revised. Even then, after two years, the exchange was kicked out of its space because of NIMBY neighbors—a nearby florist was particularly peeved—and forced to operate from a van. Watching Odum as she packed her car with kits, I also counseled caution. If they weren't careful, all their good work could be waylaid.

But people were dying now—every day they were dying, some of them their friends—and it wasn't in Odum's nature to wait.

"Change has always been driven by people with boots on the ground," said Sam Snodgrass, a nationally known harm-reduction activist in Arkansas. "People who realize that saving lives is more important than getting arrested." Stroud and Odum were following a tradition started by Chicagoan Dan Bigg, the father of America's harm-reduction movement, who began an underground syringe exchange out of the trunk of his car as a response to HIV in the 1990s. Bigg believed in incremental steps, or as he put it: "Any positive change as a person defines it for him or herself is our definition of recovery." Bigg would continue to coach people like the Peoria obstetrician-turned-bupe-provider Tami Olt, sending her her first supply of Narcan in the mail.

"If you're a physician and you read the data, it's not about your opinion; it's irrefutable," said Olt, who had lost her teenage son to overdose, of the efficacy of buprenorphine. "The problem is getting people to read the research. To step away from their inherent biases and opinions, which are wrong." Most of Olt's bupe patients are covered by Medicaid, as Illinois was an early adopter of Obamacare—still the No. 1 tool for helping people with SUD access care.

But for six years, Olt funded Narcan distribution in her community out of her own pocket, hand-delivering kits to users. She gave tearful speeches at community meetings to get police and health department leaders to work with her.

"Being a doctor gave her the credibility to say hard things about the way we treat SUD," said Chris Schaffner, Olt's program director. "But the sympathies that came from being a grieving mother of a sixteen-year-old who'd just overdosed—that was the only thing that kept assholes from being full-on assholes to her."

In a town like Mount Airy, where the epidemic was now striking a third generation, could Odum and Stroud harness that same combination of credibility and empathy? I admired their pluck but had doubts. In a few liberal pockets of North Carolina, an anarchist bookstore had long distributed sterile needles and fentanyl test strips. In one nearby city, a needle program I visited quietly operated a restroom where addicted people could use intravenous drugs and be monitored, a practice known as "safe consumption," modeled after sites established in Canada in 2003 and in Europe in the 1980s. At another Southern SSP, "I'm going to the clothes closet and I need privacy" was code for: "I'm going into the back room to shoot up; please check on me if I don't come back out soon." In a small Appalachian town in one of the poorest counties in America, I met activists who allowed people to get sterile needles and inject drugs from their porch and inside their living room.

Advocates in inner-city Philadelphia, New York, Denver, and Seattle tried for years to open safe consumption sites but were repeatedly stalled by community opposition and federal lawsuit threats—which didn't mean safe injection wasn't happening in the United States; it was just happening underground. Then, finally, in the fall of 2021, Rhode Island announced that it would open the nation's first two-year pilot program after years of pushback, including an opposing politician who called it a "moral oxymoron." And New York City's health department also green-lighted the opening of two supervised injection sites, where, almost immediately, workers began saving lives. (In its first two weeks of operation, 330 people visited the sites, and the overdoses of 36 people were reversed.)

But giving out needles in a place that wouldn't even permit a drug court? "I didn't want to be Negative Nancy, but I kept saying, 'We have to approach this with a spirit of humility and invite law enforcement to be our partners. We have to meet the community where they are,'" Mathis warned.

There are more than 3,500 drug courts directed by judges across the nation, making them among the most politically palatable treatment options, the lowest of the low-hanging fruit. On a NIMBY scale, giving sterile needles to IV users who use them to inject illicit drugs is less controversial than safe consumption but far more politically contentious than opening a drug court—though there are more than 200 syringe programs in the United States, and even some conservative states (Kentucky, for instance) have dozens of needle exchanges.

It would fall to a former Marine and retired DEA agent to puncture the rigid criminal justice bureaucracy in Mayberry. In the three years I followed him, I lost track of how many times Mark Willis half threatened to quit his job. Was the low point when the Kiwanis Club president suggested harvesting organs from the overdosed dead? Or was it when Willis coaxed thirty pastors into lobbying the judges for a drug court, only to be told the faith community had to solve the county's housing and transportation problems first?

Three years earlier, at the age of fifty-seven, Willis retired to the nearby village of Lowgap with his wife, a retired ER nurse, and their three German shepherds. In his mid-twenties, he had purchased a sixty-acre tract of Surry County land after vacationing there with a fellow Marine Corps pilot and helping him bale hay. Willis fell hard for the place: the diner where farmers conducted business and swapped favors over breakfast; the pretty waitress who knew his order on the second day. Early in his career, there were a few lean years when he missed payments on the property, and the local farmer financing his loan allowed him just to pay what he could.

"Everybody helped everybody; that's the thing that got me," Willis said. "Coming from Southern California, I was so shocked that nobody here locked their cars, nobody locked their doors, and people even left their screen doors open because they wanted the breeze to come through."

By the time he returned to live full-time and build his dream house in 2010, the neighbors' doors were bolted shut. What was once the quiet village of Lowgap was now home to several known trap houses. As Odum described that neighborhood now, "You don't just roll up to a trap house anywhere near here without texting first—or they're likely to come out and shoot you." For protection, she carries a .38 pistol in her purse.

Willis didn't relate to Mathis's purple hair or understand Odum's raw emotion. He wore khakis and L. L. Bean fleece, and spent a lot of time creating massive, wall-length charts on a whiteboard. A systems guy, he honed his methods through decades of DEA work that culminated with him tracing a key heroin-making ingredient, acetic anhydride, in source labs ranging from Japan, Germany, and India to Kingsport, Tennessee. Drug cartels mislabeled the chemical, then surreptitiously diverted it to Afghanistan, where it was used in the making of 93 percent of the world's heroin. Willis said his mission to disrupt the heroin supply chain failed because

DEA regional directors worldwide got kudos for seizing kilos of heroin; they didn't get kudos for seizing a chemical, even when those seizures ultimately led to reduced trafficking. Because, in a word, politics.

Willis was employing a similar tracking strategy in Surry County—as an inside joke to himself, he gave it the same codename as the Afghanistan project: Operation Vital Links. Only the goal now was to reverse the demand for drugs rather than disrupt the supply. On a whiteboard spanning an entire wall of his office, he assiduously tracked overdose statistics, mapping out the barriers as well as the spots where links to treatment could be created. With the aid of color-coded charts that were nearly impenetrable to anyone but himself, Willis set out to convert majority-red items (political nonstarters) to green. One year into the job, he'd flipped zero opportunities into actual programs, and the whiteboard remained far more red than green. Because, in a word, politics.

"It's frustrating because it's like being a teacher where you can't move any faster than the ability of your slowest student to learn," he told me after our first meeting. "I have to simplify everything…walk people through the fact that this isn't a 2019 problem; it's a 1979 problem. It's related to NAFTA and jobs going south, and black tar heroin coming north, and pain becoming the 'fifth vital sign.'"

Before working for the county, Willis had come out of retirement to work as a civilian contractor to build policing operations in Afghanistan. For two years he advised American military generals and forged collaborations among the FBI, DEA, and the Counter Narcotics Police of Afghanistan, whose procedures he co-wrote. Buoyed by that success and bored in his backyard woodshop, he remembered showing his wife, Theresa, a newspaper ad for the county's brand-new opioid-response director job. If he could create better drug policy on the other side of the world, he told her, surely he could do it here. But small towns, she reminded him, had their own stubborn challenges.

They had met three decades earlier in the ER where she worked. Then a patrol officer in Fairfax County, Virginia, Willis had been chasing a child abuser on foot, over back fences, and through several backyards—when a dog bit him on the butt. It became a family joke that she met his best side first.

When the MDL opioid litigation settled, Surry County stood to gain $650,000 annually for roughly eighteen years (not counting the Purdue bankruptcy settlement funds), and Willis intended to make sure that all the litigation money, when it landed, was spent right.

A drug court had the potential to save the county $400,000 a year in incarceration costs, he'd recently calculated. But the elected sheriff was still set on building a new jail that would house twice the number of inmates. "We can't do [bupe] in the jail, despite the fact that 85 percent of the 250 in there have a drug problem, because there's 'no room.' So it's a hamster wheel. When do we get off this thing? In four years, when we build a bigger jail? Like my dad used to say, it's hard to remember your original objective was to drain the swamp when you're up to your ass in alligators."

Willis calculated that Otis, the fictional town drunk in *The Andy Griffith Show*, had appeared in 31 of the original 248 episodes. In all but one of those, he ended up in Sheriff Andy Taylor's jail. "At some point, they give him a key to the jail, and he locks himself in there to sleep it off, then the next day he lets himself out," Willis recalled.

"At no point did anyone, not Andy or his friends, go, 'Otis, you have a problem, and you can't keep doing this. You've been doing this for seven years. We need to take you over to Mount Pilot and get you some help!'"

On the other hand, Otis was never placed on probation, never struggled to pay his court fines. He was never forced into home-lessness or stealing or sex work or standing in unemployment lines. It's hard to recall an episode where the local furniture factory or textile mill cut wages and increased production quotas before bugging out for China or Indonesia.

Willis sighed. "I could've stayed up on the mountain and been very happy with my German shepherds and my woodshop," he recalled during a low point in 2020. That morning, Theresa Willis wished him luck as she left for work, shaking her head.

"'Bye, stupid," she said.

Willis turned to his favorite Marine Corps motto: "Improvise, adapt, and overcome." It would take the help of some unexpected allies to convince officials that evidence-based treatment actually worked. He taped a snapshot of a teenager who'd died of overdose, sent to him by a local mother, next to his whiteboard and added a Winston Churchill quote: "KEEP GOING."

"If my Marine Corps had kicked in, I'd've said, 'Purple hair—it ain't happening,'" he recalled, referring to Mathis. "But I picked up early that she knew what she was doing, and her singular focus was amazing." He felt the same way about pastor Ray Morgan, who'd been in marketing before being called to the ministry. "He retains that salesman's ability to make you believe that what he's saying is absolutely true."

Among the first items Willis secured in his Operation Vital Links was a federal grant to provide drivers and cars to take people to treatment. It would soon be permissible to drive people with OUD to their buprenorphine and counseling appointments—as long as it was in a county-approved vehicle. Until the kinks were ironed out, the driving was mostly being handled ad hoc by Odum and Stroud, who worked night and day in their fast-food-littered cars.

Efforts to link the addicted to treatment came too late to

save many, including the young man who'd overdosed at the Mount Airy wedding a few months before. Not long after Odum revived him, he was living with relatives in Charlotte. When he used again, no one was around to administer Narcan. His mother had worked hard to get him into a rehab program, but he'd never taken buprenorphine, the treatment that study after study showed best prevented opioid deaths. His only periods of abstinence had been during periodic stays in the overstuffed Surry County Jail.

Chapter Four

White Privilege

Incarceration remains America's fallback treatment, Fairfax County Jail, Virginia.

It is possible to draw a direct line from the present-day vomit buckets in the Surry County Jail to the Harrison Narcotics Tax Act of 1914, which outlawed the use of unprescribed opioids and coca products at a time when experts estimated that thousands of Americans were regularly using them. Our nation's tendency to treat substance use as a crime rather than a medical condition is more than a century old, and that history is steeped in racism as a tool for generating wealth.

Chinese laborers who smoked opium had long attracted the ire of anti-immigrant crusaders who believed that Asians were corrupting young Whites inside their amoral opium dens. A century before the Chinese landed to build the nation's railroads, Native Americans were encouraged by American settlers to drink liquor to pacify themselves while the colonists robbed them of their lands. Two centuries earlier, it was the growing of tobacco that saved Jamestown when the first enslaved Africans were forced to work Virginia's plantations.

In 1914, an era rife with Jim Crow laws and lynchings against newly emancipated Black people working menial labor jobs, a *New York Times* op-ed writer claimed that coke-crazed Black men were madly attacking Southern White women under the headline "Negro Cocaine Fiends Are a New Southern Menace." "Everywhere you looked, people were taking cocaine to dull the pain of crushing labor—not just stevedores in the South but also miners in the West and textile mill workers in the Northeast," writes physician and bioethicist Carl Erik Fisher in his eloquent and thought-provoking book, *The Urge: Our History of Addiction.* "But in the Jim Crow era, stories about deviant drug users played to the racist stereotypes of violent and sexually aggressive Black people as well as the racist notion that Black Americans were especially vulnerable to the drug."

And while doctors had for decades recommended cocaine and heroin for everything from hay fever to menstrual cramps for White patients—one could literally order hypodermic needles and Bayer-manufactured heroin from the Sears & Roebuck catalog—people without prescriptions who were dependent on those drugs were suddenly branded criminals in 1914, forced by the new law to seek their medicines-turned-illicit-drugs in chaotic and dangerous black markets.

The question of whose pain is legitimate and therefore deserving of public intervention has been a recurring political battle in the United States ever since, from early struggles over returning soldiers' benefits to the battle over the Affordable Care Act.

The Harrison Act became a mechanism for reinforcing racism as a means for holding on to wealth and political power. From reefer madness to "super predators," instead of crafting public health safety nets to combat problematic drug use, lawmakers found it easier and more politically expedient to respond with tough-on-crime laws based on fear-based dogma. By cloaking the drug war in race-neutral language, Whites opposed to racial progress could indirectly express their racism, whether they understood that's what they were doing or not, as Michelle Alexander and other scholars have pointed out.

"Prohibition policies have this incredibly long history of being useful ways to increase the state's capacity to police a group that you're worried about," University at Buffalo historian David Herzberg told me. The author of the 2020 book *White Market Drugs: Big Pharma and the Hidden History of Addiction in America*, Herzberg would join the fight to hold opioid makers accountable for their misdeeds. "When you're a small-government society where people are skeptical of the feds nosing in on their lives, and yet you want to be able to wield state power to do certain things, the drug war has an incredible utility," Herzberg said.

If the Harrison Act was the genesis of President Richard Nixon's War on Drugs, proclaimed in 1971, it was also Nixon's dog-whistle redux—another way of stoking racial fear among Whites. Even top aide John Ehrlichman admitted as much when he told a writer years later: "Getting the public to associate the hippies with marijuana and Blacks with heroin, and then criminalizing both heavily, we could disrupt those communities. We could arrest their leaders, raid their homes, break up their meetings, and vilify them night after night on the evening news. Did we know we were lying about the [dangers of the] drugs? Of course we did."

A decade later, Nancy Reagan matched Nixon's "public enemy number one" claim and upped it to "Just Say No," a marketing campaign designed to give the First Lady something to do that also helped her husband gin up support among White suburbanites.

The influential mothers egging her on worried not at all about the surging number of cocaine or heroin users in the inner cities but about their own pot-smoking kids. (By the way, Nancy Reagan habitually used prescribed sedatives, and Nixon reportedly did the same.)

As an added bonus, "Just Say No" became the nail in the coffin of Lyndon Johnson's and John F. Kennedy's therapeutic approaches, which viewed addiction as a symptom of society's failures—racism, alienation, inequality, and lack of opportunity. It was Ronald Reagan, after all, who in 1961 tried to block the precursor to Medicare for elderly Americans, decrying it as socialism. He framed his outrage as an attack on doctors' freedoms—while working as a spokesman for the American Medical Association, then run by Nancy Reagan's dad. The AMA remains an opponent of single-payer health care, or Medicare for All, even as it enjoys widespread public support today.

If Medicare were enacted, the future president warned, "you and I are going to spend our sunset years telling our children and our children's children what it was like when men were free."

What often gets lost in the criticism of the War on Drugs is the fact that Nixon began his version of the war using *treatment*, not incarceration, as his primary weapon, a little-known story recounted in journalist Michael Massing's 1998 book, *The Fix*. He did it by appointing a scientist who reported directly to the president's office. A crusty psychiatrist, Dr. Jerome Jaffe became the nation's first drug czar, and he didn't care about politics or pleasing his superiors. As Massing wrote, "Only someone unschooled in the ways of Washington could have acted so nervily in the face of so much brass."

Jaffe not only figured out how to minimize heroin addiction seeping into the United States with returning soldiers who'd regularly used the drug in Vietnam, but he also designed a highly regulated, national system of 300 stand-alone methadone clinics that offered free or low-cost treatment, counseling, and social services in the early 1970s. For the first time in American history, however briefly, the government made treatment available in clinics across the nation, and both heroin use and the crime related to it plunged.

It was an extraordinary moment. No one had to commit a crime because they couldn't access addiction services. Jaffe's work led to a drug-budget formula where far more funds (70 percent) went to treatment than to incarceration (30 percent). And it was all based on Jaffe's fundamental belief that law enforcement should be seen as an adjunct to rehabilitation, not the other way around. Nixon liked Jaffe's methadone program, too, not only because he saw it as "the best available answer" to addiction but also because it allowed him to put a more humane face on his drug war, especially among addicted veterans. Jaffe believed in treating heroin users with methadone as well as offering them wraparound services, including twelve-step support—they were all "treatment" to him.

Now in his nineties, Jaffe marveled recently that the best medical treatments in use today were developed under his supervision during the Nixon administration. With the power of the president behind him, he told me, it took all of "six or seven days" for him to develop the crux of it. "I'm not faulting anybody for not having some magic breakthrough in fifty years, but it's not easy to come up with something that's cost-efficient and easy to scale up, and is both acceptable to the public and to those people who have the problem," said Jaffe, who still does addiction research at the University of Maryland.

As I continued to report for this book over the next eighteen months, I kept coming back to Jaffe's words, which applied to so many of America's sore points today, from anti-vaxxers and Big Lie theorists to syringe-exchange opponents. When politics are driven by gut feelings, facts take a back seat.

*   *   *

Shortly before his abrupt Watergate-prompted departure, Nixon took a sharp turn to the right to curry tough-on-crime political points. It had the effect of marginalizing Jaffe while doubling down on incarceration, especially of Black, Brown, and poor people. The Reagans mirrored this credo, using marijuana as the villain. But when crack hit, a new and more powerful target came into play. Though Richard Pryor set himself on fire while freebasing cocaine in 1980, and John Belushi died in 1982 from speed-balling heroin and cocaine, Nancy Reagan and her cabal of marijuana-hating moms looked right past the nation's soaring hard-core drug use to push the narrative that abstinence and "zero tolerance" were the only acceptable goals.

Pot was the alleged enemy. But it was drug users of color who paid—and are still paying—the stiffest price for the politics of "Just Say No." When Black college basketball star Len Bias died of a cocaine overdose in 1986, false rumors of a crack frenzy stoked a nationwide panic that sent thousands of low-level drug offenders into prisons and jails. Designed to make politicians look tough on crime, mandatory-minimum sentencing laws were enacted later that year and disproportionately targeted crack cocaine users. Penalties were literally 100 times harsher for crack trafficking than for cocaine when, pharmacologically, the drugs are the same. By 1992, more Black men were in prison on drug-related charges than in college, with the odds of a Black man enrolling in higher education dropping 10 percent.

Prison budgets soared, and Nixon's once-progressive drug-budget formula flipped. At the same time, Reagan's government-is-bad ethos weakened the FDA, then under attack for being slow to approve lifesaving drugs for HIV/AIDS patients—and only approving them after sustained, formidable direct-action protest by the grassroots group ACT UP.

Over the next decade, the same loosened-approval mechanisms that allowed antiretroviral drugs to save so many with AIDS would end up hurting another marginalized class of people. Deregulation ultimately paved the way for a powerful pharmaceutical lobby to influence the FDA—65 percent of the FDA's drug-approval budget now comes from industry user fees. And Big Pharma, assisted by the largest lobbying industry in America, kept chipping away at consumer protections until FDA regulators resembled miracle-drug boosters more than guardians of the public health.

The inmates vomiting in those Surry County Jail buckets? Many were hooked on opioids because of the over-marketing of OxyContin and other opioids as harmless wonder drugs with the approval of an over-friendly FDA.

Lest you think the two weren't in bed together, Purdue Pharma executives literally rented a suite of hotel rooms down the road from the Rockville, Maryland, FDA headquarters in 1995—for the express purpose of collaborating with FDA officials to speed up the OxyContin medical review. In a revolving-door story that would become moustache-twirling fodder in books, documentaries, and television series, the drug's FDA approval officer, Dr. Curtis Wright, went to work for Purdue soon after, earning $379,000 a year.

And the cowed politicians who followed Nixon and Reagan—especially President Bill Clinton, with the help of then-Senator Joseph R. Biden—continued to amplify mass incarceration. It was a cynical attempt to claw back centrist White voters with the notion that Democrats could be tough on crime, too.

By 2007, policing and imprisonment had become what financial gurus were calling a "superb growth industry." Syndicated financial columnist Malcolm Berko encouraged his readers who dabbled in stocks to invest in private companies dedicated to incarceration. Without the slightest nod to the drug war's human toll, he wrote: "Imagine the tens and tens of thousands of people who would be unemployed if crime were to disappear: Drug Enforcement Administration and FBI folks, parole officers, deputy sheriffs, cops, corrections officers, judges, and lawyers would be out of work and searching the classifieds for jobs."

No truer words were written than the kicker of Berko's column: "Because it pays, crime is here to stay and prosper."

By 2018, just 36 percent of the federal drug budget went to treatment, while law enforcement received well over half. Nearly 300,000 people were being held in state and federal prisons in the United States for drug-law violations—twelve times more than during Jaffe's tenure. Drug offenders were also given significantly longer sentences, even though imprisonment has never been shown to deter drug misuse. (Herzberg speculates that addiction rates have quadrupled since the Harrison Act became law.)

"For generations now, we've been oriented around the idea that 'Drugs are bad, drug users are therefore bad, and their behavior amounts to crimes, and we must punish them,'" said epidemiologist Daniel Ciccarone, of the University of California–San Francisco School of Medicine. "We need to stop that. It doesn't work. Period. It's done nothing to curtail drug consumption, and secondly, it's racist—study after study shows that we have [used those methods to] disproportionately lock up people of color."

Structural racism propels bad policing, and hyped-up media stories about police raids and Mexican cartels further inflame racist views. "The stories of people who are harmed by drug use play on so many different cultural hot-button points because of the way participating in informal drug markets transforms people's lives and tends to involve crossing all these social boundaries that we construct so carefully—from suburbs to inner cities, cheerleaders to sex workers," Herzberg said. "Authorities invest enormous resources into dividing people into hierarchical categories that become important political building blocks. And drug users are like little meteors shooting right through those categories, and it freaks people out."

It's an indication of how advantageous systemic racism is that so few politicians can resist exploiting it, Herzberg said.

When Donald Trump became president in 2016, the United States was the world's most prolific jailer. More than 6.4 million citizens were under correctional supervision—more than were enslaved in antebellum America. Overdose deaths were now the No. 1 cause of accidental death for people under fifty-five, claiming more lives than all the wars since World War II combined. Following the lead of presidents before him—and inflaming the racism he shared with his base—Trump stoked racial animus when he proposed using the death penalty on drug dealers and building a wall along the Mexican border. He exploited a system that had already handed disproportionate power to rural Whites by way of gerrymandering and electoral-vote machinations. By pushing racist and anti-government rhetoric, Trump amplified the rage of those displaced by globalization and technology—while doing very little to help them join the knowledge economy. Billionaires got tax cuts at the same time that Trump tried to plunder Pell Grants, the government's bedrock program to help poor people go to college—of which I will forever be grateful to have been a full grantee.

If I hadn't gone to college, I could very well have ended up being a subject in a book like this.

Under Obama, drug czar Michael Botticelli had begun to steer the office toward a more public health–oriented approach. But Trump's handling of the opioid epidemic was more hype than substance. In two years, he proposed only $900,000 in additional funding to address the epidemic, less than one-tenth of what was needed. He created tumult at the Office of National Drug Control Policy (ONDCP)—the drug czar's office and flagship addiction agency—by trying to move most of its budget to the Department of Justice, then led by anti-drug hard-liner Jeff Sessions. The cut never happened because lawmakers fought back, citing surging overdoses at home. But Trump did manage to appoint two people with no drug policy experience to key roles: political aide Kellyanne Conway as his opioid point person and Jim Carroll to head the ONDCP. A 2019 Government Accountability Office report described the ONDCP during Trump's tenure as disorganized and ineffective.

Had the Substance Abuse and Mental Health Services Administration (SAMHSA) and/or the drug czar's office under Trump taken an active evidence-based stance to provide low-barrier bupe and other harm-reduction approaches—like reversing the federal ban on funding needles—many drug-related deaths could have been prevented, most experts believe.

"One way to think about this is that the Trump administration's approach to the drug crisis was a lot like its hands-off approach to COVID," said Dr. Joshua Sharfstein, associate dean at Johns Hopkins Bloomberg School of Public Health, and an expert on how the opioid-litigation money should be spent. "Some monies were made available, but the federal government largely deferred to states on how to spend the funds, and many states deferred to localities. And it was another massive patchwork."

Until the federal government takes ownership of the overdose crisis, experts believe, the litigation money will continue to be hijacked by politicians who are more interested in getting votes than following the science to fix the problem.

When the pandemic hit in the spring of 2020, overdose fatalities broke records, following a slight decline that Trump took credit for in 2018. Even people with many years of sobriety were relapsing under the stresses of isolation, financial despair, and sickness.

In search of a silver lining early in the pandemic, an addictions doctor in Tennessee gushed about the temporary easing of federal SAMHSA restrictions that now allowed him to see patients via telehealth. But within three months, he noticed, many of those same patients had lost their jobs and homes, and were talking to him from their cars, some with little kids doing remote school-work in the back seat. "Stable patients are destabilizing," said Dr. Steve Loyd, who is in long-term recovery himself. "Isolation is killing people."

In Mount Airy, one family lost two adult children to heroin overdose within the span of six weeks. In a homeless encampment in Ithaca, New York, a bupe patient approached his community health worker with a hatchet wound in his head. In Peoria, an addicted sex worker was beaten to death by her trafficker. A needle-exchange operator in my hometown mourned the recent loss of a twenty-seven-year-old friend to injection-related endo-carditis after she "flat out refused to return to the hospital, where they always treated her like shit," he said. In a Virginia suburb outside Washington, DC, a judge noticed a disturbing new trend: probationers openly nodding out in drug court.

"I feel like a tidal wave is crashing down on us!" one addiction counselor told me. For the twelve months ending in May 2020, a record-breaking 81,230 Americans died of drug overdose, an 18 percent increase from the previous year.

It was an epidemic within a pandemic.

How do you unwind a half century of bad policing policy when public health budgets have been slashed by a quarter and so many people's jobs are now dependent on the billions America spends to keep its War on Drugs going?

In our capitalistic society, it turns out, there's at least one policy maintenance drug for our drug-war addiction. A century after the Harrison Act was passed, the billion-dollar fortunes that the Sacklers and "El Chapo" Guzman raked in had begun to attract both sides of the hyper-partisan aisle. After being viewed almost as a joke for decades, the legalization of cannabis and other illicit drugs was now seen as both smart policy and an excellent source of revenue. In the words of Republican John A. Boehner, the former Speaker of the House and now chair of the National Cannabis Roundtable, "When cannabis is on the ballot, it wins." (A decade earlier, when Boehner staunchly opposed legalization, he called it *marijuana*, a word of Mexican-Spanish origin coined by narcotics agents in the 1930s who meant to evoke sinister associations.)

In the wake of the 2020 election, Boehner gushed about cannabis reform. Even red states like Montana and South Dakota were now among the fifteen states to legalize recreational marijuana, and thirty-five states passed laws legalizing medical marijuana. The state of Oregon had even borrowed an idea from Portugal to become the first state to vote in decriminalization of small amounts of heroin, cocaine, and methamphetamine.

Led by the Drug Policy Alliance, the new Oregon law called for setting up voluntary treatment triage centers—paid for largely by taxes on recreational cannabis, legalized six years earlier, to the tune of roughly $45 million a year. Even the proponents and campaign workers who worked on Oregon's Ballot 110 decriminalization campaign didn't believe the United States was ready for widespread decriminalization. "The idea is frightening to people, especially those who've lived through fifty years of the drug war," said Ted Lewis, human rights codirector of the Global Exchange. "Even if we haven't believed all the hype, it has still seeped into all of us somehow."

As campaign workers went door to door in rural parts of Oregon, they were surprised by how many families were desperate to see treatment options expanded—and by how very few households remained untouched. Many Oregonians responded to the DPA's main message that providing addiction treatment would cost roughly a third of what state taxpayers were already spending on incarceration.

But most Oregonians just wanted to know: How soon can you help me get treatment for my kid?

"We went into it thinking we'd run a decrim and criminal justice campaign, but we ended up running a treatment and behavioral health services campaign that also decriminalized drugs," Sami Alloy, the deputy campaign manager, told me.

With popular opinion beginning to turn, President Joe Biden pledged to put $125 billion toward the overdose epidemic over ten years. Broadly, his plan called for ending incarceration for drug use and diverting people to drug courts and treatment. Back then, there was no mention of heroin-assisted treatment or safe-consumption sites, both of which have substantially reduced overdose death in other countries. But three months into the Biden administration, the Department of Health and Human Services finally expanded some access to buprenorphine, allowing all doctors to prescribe bupe without the special training course—but limiting the number of patients to thirty.

It didn't go far enough for most advocates who wanted to "X the X waiver," as the movement to eliminate the DEA-required training waiver altogether is called. After all, doctors don't have to go through onerous training to prescribe addictive opioids; why should they be required to obtain special DEA approval, with caps on the number of patients, in order to prescribe the main cure for opioid addiction? (The current cap for experienced, waiver-trained providers is 275.) "There are very few medications that reduce death by 80 percent in a year!" said Dr. Arthur Robin Williams, a Columbia University psychiatrist who runs a company that provides bupe via telehealth.

Affordable versions of the medicine remained hardest for

minority communities and poor people to access, especially in rural areas. But the new bupe rule was a start—and a far cry from Trump's lack of plan or empathy, including his public mocking of Hunter Biden's addiction woes.

A decade ago, when our teenage son was arrested for smoking pot on a Blue Ridge Parkway overlook—a federal crime because it's federal property—I asked if he understood why he was able, ultimately, to walk away with probation and a small fine when many in the courtroom that day left with job-killing felony records. Like most privileged White people, he had no clue. While most of his fellow drug arrestees were represented by overworked public defenders, we had the resources and social capital to find a respected lawyer who pre-negotiated a lesser charge. When our son was arrested again a few years later—this time for an Adderall pill (unprescribed to him) that police found at a college party he was hosting—the process repeated itself.

But we live in a world where white-collar families operating in the world of black-market drugs have access to insurance and cash on hand to pay for a rehab stint, and our son's case was looked on favorably again by another judge who allowed him to walk away with a second misdemeanor that was also, ultimately, expunged. The majority-Black or Brown people in the Richmond courtroom that day left in handcuffs—and with felonies. Our son, now twenty-eight, is gainfully employed.

When I shared my son's drug war near misses with the historian Herzberg, he said, "You just described a system that prevented a young person being foolish from being screwed forever. Everybody should have that. You want the kind of society where young people can fuck up and still come out okay on the other side."

On the first Monday of November 2020, the day before a national election that resoundingly affirmed legalization of marijuana in many states, I sat on a General District Court grand jury in Roanoke. Marijuana wouldn't be legal in my home state for another year and a half. Grand-jury duty is the annual civic responsibility that I try and fail to get out of every year (thank you, Deputy Thompson).

By far the majority of indictments in my mid-sized Southern city were for drug offenses, most involving not heroin or opioids (as had been the case during my past years of service) but marijuana and methamphetamine. The drug arrests were largely confined to predominantly African American neighborhoods, in fact to a single ZIP code where 98 percent of school kids qualify for free or reduced lunch. Most were initiated by minor traffic stops—a brake light was allegedly out, a license plate broken, or someone drove "through a high-crime area" with overly tinted windows. In almost every case, when officers reported smelling marijuana, minor stops turned into vehicle searches, often followed by felony arrests.

Black people are four times more likely to be arrested for marijuana than their White counterparts, even though both groups use and sell drugs at a similar rate. As the Columbia University neuroscientist Carl Hart has written: "Not only is this wrong, but it has created a situation where law enforcement agencies suspect damn near every black person as a drug trafficker." Hart argues that police officers target alleged drug traffickers in poor neighborhoods because most can't afford lawyers to point out their case flaws, and out-of-touch judges rarely challenge the police version of events. In 2015, Sandra Bland committed suicide in her Waller County, Texas, jail cell after just such an encounter with a state trooper—he had initially pulled her over for failing to signal a lane change.

By July of 2021, thanks to Governor Ralph Northam's move to legalize simple possession of marijuana (three years sooner than originally planned), adult Virginians could now grow up to four plants. People I knew were hunting down seeds before the ink on the law was dry. And Northam, who also ended the state's death penalty and presided over the toppling of Confederate statues, redeemed himself after being shamed for appearing in blackface at a medical school party in 1986, ending his term as the state's most racially progressive governor since Reconstruction.

But in a country that clings to a hyper-partisan patchwork of jurisdictions—with thousands of overlapping law enforcement agencies and prosecutors independently operating at local, county, state, and federal levels—decriminalization will never be as efficacious as it is in countries with centralized policing and universal health care, including Portugal, Switzerland, Canada, and the Netherlands.

As the Nobel-winning economist Paul Krugman puts it, "I still run into people who are sure that we have the world's highest life expectancy, when we actually die a lot younger than people in other rich countries." Economists Anne Case and Angus Deaton frame the comparison more bluntly: "Other countries have a range of other ways of organizing healthcare, all have their strengths and weaknesses, but none are killing people. None are supporting the brazen subordination of human need to human profit."

It is uniquely American that making money has long been the main driver of our health systems, not compassion, including Reagan's early screed against Medicare. Before that, politicos worked to associate compulsory health insurance with Bolshevism (in fact, it was the Kaiser who created such a system in Germany) during World War I. American hospitals and clinics had been founded as acts of compassion by civic leaders and religious orders. National plans were floated to pay for it all but ultimately dismissed as socialism.

Masking as "liberty," the notion of letting the free market drive the health of our nation was cunningly employed throughout the twentieth century by pro-business politicians who continued to connect single-payer health care to socialism, knowing full well that companies and doctors alike profit more when people are forced to take personal responsibility for their health—as if the American bootstrap mythology could cure cancer.

Drawing upon the research he did for his magnificent book *The Hospital*, journalist Brian Alexander told me: "American medicine transmogrified into big business floating on a river of trillions of dollars in cash. People became 'consumers' left on their own to navigate it."

As the free market unleashed a tidal wave of addictive pills and Americans fell for the ginned-up promises of relief sold by executives and consultants, these "consumers" were perceived as criminals who deserved jail or death. Big Pharma's "only personal responsibility was to make money for shareholders and themselves," Alexander said.

In Sydney, Australia, a public radio interviewer shook his head after I recounted how the opioid crisis took advantage of our nation's failure to provide basic health care to our citizens. He brought up his love of *Breaking Bad*, and his appreciation for the tough place Bryan Cranston's character, a high-school chemistry teacher named Walter White, found himself in—making meth to pay for his cancer treatment and to ensure his family's solvency after his death.

"If Walter White had had access to universal health care, he could've gone back to teaching," the host said.

But the United States remains too insular and too divided to learn from other countries' policy successes—or even from the winning innovations taking place in some of our own cities and states, scattershot though they are. The American health care system now costs more than twice as much as those of other rich countries, which have relatively few deaths of despair. "Our health care system is just killing the low-wage labor market, literally as well as figuratively," Deaton told me. People without a bachelor's degree report suffering from extreme distress at rates three times higher than those with college degrees, and they are far more likely to succumb to overdose death.

But only 36 percent of Americans have bachelor's degrees, so the vast majority fail to thrive while a minority of us prosper, amping up what Case and Deaton call "the politics of despair." Less educated Whites tend to oppose universal health care, erroneously believing that it favors Black people at their expense, as if health care were a zero-sum game. They vote for candidates who are suspicious of a federal government that allowed hundreds of thousands of their jobs to move offshore and whose wealthy supporters perversely oppose tax hikes that would pay for programs like universal health.

For 150 years, there has never been a time when massive numbers of Americans haven't regularly used illegal drugs. Today, roughly one in five Americans uses illegal drugs—that's 57.2 million people, and that number is on the rise. "I wish we could just accept that people do drugs, that they have very serious risks, and then build a way to pragmatically make those risks as minimal as possible," Herzberg said.

Daniel Ciccarone, the epidemiologist, pointed out that Chinese emperors successfully taxed and regulated opium a thousand years ago. "I'm in full favor of low doses of everything, including opiates, as a solution," he said. "Someone needs to propose opium dens again!"

While proponents of legalization argue that most people who use drugs outgrow their use without treatment or long-term deleterious effects—70 to 90 percent, depending on the study—most experts believe drugs should be carefully regulated. "Some people think that the fact that 90 percent of people who use drugs don't become addicted is a good argument for legalization, but I'm like, 'Dude, 10 percent isn't good enough!'" Herzberg said. "I wouldn't buy a car where the brakes only worked 90 percent of the time."

By the time deadly fentanyl saturated the nation's drug supply, making its way to California from the East Coast in 2019, the margin of error had become even slimmer: being in that nebulous 10–30 percent range of people who were lucky enough to use drugs without it ruining their lives was now a life-or-death gamble. Fentanyl was present in more than 60 percent of the 2020 overdose deaths reported by the CDC, a quadrupling of the portion it accounted for in 2015. By June of 2021, mortality kept rising as fentanyl and other synthetics were involved in a whopping 87 percent of opioid deaths and 65 percent of all drug overdose deaths.

"We have to accept the fact that this foe is outrageously strong," Ciccarone said, of fentanyl. "And we also have to face the fact that none of our tools are sufficient in and of themselves to the task. Not bupe, not the treatment system, and certainly not the criminal justice system, which tends to make things worse."

As the opioid litigation tussled into its second half, scholars reminded us that the racist *overpunishing* of people who use illicit drugs had always paved the way for profit-seeking doctors and pharma companies to downplay the addictiveness of prescription drugs. By drawing such a bold line of demarcation between licit and illicit, policy makers demonized one group of drug users while medicalizing another without recognizing the overlap. "There was a failure to take the risk of addiction seriously in [the legal drug] markets because addiction had been coded" as something that only happened illicitly in poor and minority communities, Herzberg said. In other words, the mass incarceration of Black people who use drugs and the overpromotion of OxyContin for rural Whites were two sides of the same very racialized coin.

We're familiar with the terrible costs borne by the Black and Brown communities targeted by the War on Drugs. But the opioid crisis revealed that even the people for whom the system was built—people who had privileged access to medical care—paid an awful price, too. In the end, the harms weren't equal, but everyone paid for America's segregated drug policies.

Herzberg was used to debating the consequences of the drug war. What he didn't expect was for his scholarship to end up in the crosshairs of the battle to hold Purdue and the Sacklers accountable for the overdose crisis. In late 2020, bankruptcy judge Robert Drain praised Herzberg's book, *White Market Drugs,* calling it "the most comprehensive and up-to-date history." But Drain distorted one of Herzberg's main recommendations for solving the crisis—to substitute drug companies with state monopolies modeled on public utilities. (As an example, Herzberg cited the government's centralized planning of penicillin during World War II, using private companies with federal contracts.)

Drain trumpeted Herzberg's solution as an argument for his approval of the Department of Justice's late-2020 settlement for $8.3 billion, which named zero of Purdue's executives or owners for criminal wrongdoing and called for turning the company into a public benefit company (or PBC) while fining the Sackler family a paltry $225 million. "We can't get rid of human greed, but you can minimize it, and one way to minimize it is by having a charter that says greed doesn't come first," Drain said at the hearing.

The Sacklers would benefit the most from a PBC, critics claimed, because it was a classic form of whitewash: the Sacklers gave up Purdue as a way to serve the public interest. Of course, this also meant that privileged documents would probably remain secret, and their personal wealth would be protected—including the $10 billion they'd pulled out of the company in the years leading up to Purdue's bankruptcy.

*　　*　　*

The Sacklers hoped Drain would grant them blanket civil immunity, which would go a long way to protecting the family and its wealth. Drain couldn't protect them from criminal prosecution, but the Sacklers leveraged the social capital of former federal prosecutors on their legal teams, lobbying the DOJ for leniency not extended to other pharmaceutical executives. Earlier in 2020, John Kapoor, the founder of Insys—maker of the fentanyl lollipop—was sentenced to sixty-six months in prison for scheming to give doctors kick-backs to prescribe a dangerous fentanyl-based spray, not unlike the violations of anti-kickback statutes Purdue pleaded guilty to in its 2020 DOJ settlement. (Insys was maybe even more brazen in its sales practices than Purdue, though, at one point hiring as a sales rep a stripper who gave a doctor a lap dance as enticement for him to prescribe more of its products.)

By strategically moving the litigation to Drain's bankruptcy court, the Sacklers were benefiting from the same culture of impunity that had sent just one midlevel banker to prison after the 2008 financial crisis when so many others behaved far worse. It's the same culture that sends low-level urban user/dealers to prison while people with resources get off scot-free.

The PBC concept rankled attorneys general like Massachusetts's Maura Healey, who said they wanted to see the Sacklers punished along with bigger fines and called the DOJ settlement terms a "mirage" designed to protect the Sacklers' wealth.

And it infuriated Ad Hoc Committee on Accountability members like Nan Goldin and parents of the dead who argued that under no circumstance should the government be in the business of selling the very drug that had ruined a generation. "How perverted that they're gonna sell OxyContin to fund rehabs; that's sadistic to me," said Ed Bisch, who worried the Sacklers' friends and lawyers would still call the shots.

Though he was flattered to be cited by Drain, Herzberg fired off a nine-page rebuttal to the judge outlining why turning Purdue into a PBC was not just a misinterpretation of his scholarship, but also a terrible idea: too small a punishment, too late in the game. "Because Purdue's greatest misdeed was to pioneer the use of these unethical and illegal activities in the promotion of a powerful opioid, true abatement requires correcting these corrupt practices, not just changing Purdue's behavior," Herzberg and a colleague wrote. "Transforming Purdue will send the wrong message to other pharmaceutical companies that the profits to be earned from bad behavior will exceed even the worst punishments."

Still, in early 2021, most experts believed that the Sacklers' scorched-earth litigation tactics would prevail. The family's sycophantic phalanx of lawyers, consultants, and public relations toadies would make it so.

Legal scholars predicted that the family would receive full releases from civil liability from Drain, even though only half the states were prepared to accept the initial settlement offer, negotiated more than a year before. But even if the Sacklers raised their payout from their initial offer by another two or three billion, the family would still walk away with several billion dollars of wealth and no jail time even after the company they owned and clearly controlled pleaded guilty in federal court—in 2007 and again in 2020—to multiple acts of fraud.

Clever billionaires can do whatever they want—they just need to hire the right people to manage the legal heat. It didn't seem to matter, even, that opioids were among the largest drivers of life-expectancy decline in recent American history.

"The blame is just so disproportionate," said Corey S. Davis, director of the national Harm Reduction Legal Project. "I think advocates should push the notion that fat-cat billionaires who started this thing are getting off scot-free. But your cousin, or the guy you used to work with at Subway, is still sitting in jail over a ten-dollar bag of dope."

Goldin's lawyer, Mike Quinn—the lone attorney whose firm wasn't billing for the case—was working nights and weekends trying to shift blame to the Sacklers. Quinn still had his regular caseload to tend to between writing anti-Purdue filings and feeding the press stories. Before the bankruptcy, Quinn's most high-profile case had been to defend an investor who'd been rooked in 2017 by the Ponzi-scheming organizers of the ill-fated Fyre Festival in the Bahamas.

The law firm where he works, with twenty lawyers head-quartered in New York's Union Square, was supportive of his knight's quest for justice against the Sacklers, he said, though his colleagues had yet to read his fiery briefs, he was relieved to say. When he consulted one of his coworkers about the inner workings of bankruptcy law, the lawyer asked Quinn which client to bill for his time.

"I said, 'Paul, this is, like, social justice. We're not billing.'"

Quinn's home in the Hudson Valley, a 1790 Colonial, is where he grew up and where he now sat out the pandemic with his fian-cée. Their first date had been PAIN's action at the Guggenheim in 2019. "We got there an hour before it started, and we were walking through this Mapplethorpe exhibit, and she kept saying, 'You're very, very nervous.'

"And I kept saying, 'You have no idea what's about to happen.'"

Within minutes they were inside the atrium, lying on the ground, next to forty-odd other protesters, watching the fake prescriptions flutter all around them.

Afterward, they picked themselves up and went out for sushi. "It was a pretty nice first date," Quinn recalled.

In November 2020, scores of white-shoe lawyers, each billing thousands an hour, listened in to the telephonic court hearing when Quinn asked the court to reject the deal Purdue had struck with the DOJ. Quinn stressed how inappropriate it had been for the DOJ to ignore individual families by entering into an arrangement that would force the public, through the bankruptcy's re-creation of Purdue as a PBC, to sell the drug that had killed their children.

Judge Drain suddenly interrupted Quinn, saying he couldn't hear him because "there was some paper rattling."

"Sorry. It's not paper," Quinn said. "I'm sitting on a very old chair."

"Okay. Well, maybe you should stand up so it doesn't break," Drain said.

Quinn appreciated Drain's sudden flash of humor. He would later tell me that Drain's quip gave him hope that the Court was catching on to his tactics. In a later pleading, Quinn asserted that several DOJ attorneys protested the federal deal by removing their names from the Sackler settlement signature page. It was a fact no bankruptcy lawyer would ever notice, let alone include in a legal brief. Quinn even pasted a side-by-side image of two DOJ signature blocks to show the missing prosecutors' names.

"My strategy was to hold up a sort of funhouse mirror to highlight the most uncomfortable aspects of the case," he said. By doing it in such unorthodox ways, "I hoped the Court would figure out that something was rotten in Denmark."

But for more than a century, American corporations had grown so accustomed to profiting from health care that the Sackler bankruptcy solution came off looking fair and reasonable—as distorted as it was—to the Court.

PART TWO
Acta Non Verba

Front window of a home, Whitesville,
West Virginia.

Chapter Five

The Avengers

Coal company, Sylvester, West Virginia.

Rampant overprescribing of opioids was happening everywhere in the United States by the late 1990s. But the crisis was quieter in places where factory jobs remained somewhat plentiful. It turned out that Americans would always need the caskets and hospital beds that companies in Batesville, Indiana, had been churning out for more than a century. In a region founded by German Catholic farmers and furniture makers, Ripley County residents were known for putting family first, working hard, and muting their emotions. The county was so scenic and quintessentially heartland that it was the setting for the 1986 movie *Hoosiers*, about an underdog basketball team and its flawed, stoic coach, played by Gene Hackman. When Jimmy Chitwood hits the final shot for fictional Hickory High, it feels like a victory for small towns everywhere.

There's not even a Walmart in Ripley County, making it the rare rural community that's held on to its locally owned stores and restaurants. Republican state rep Cindy Ziemke owns the biggest restaurant, a German eatery called Brau Haus, where she holds court on the creek-side deck and recommends the sauerkraut balls. A recently renovated Tudor-style hotel called The Sherman honors the Union Army general, and pictures of local veterans hang from streetlamps. To an outsider, Batesville resembles Mayberry more than Mount Airy, North Carolina, does.

The overdose epidemic rolled stealthily into Ripley County—it was harder to discern, easier to dismiss. Between 2006 and 2014, area doctors prescribed fifty-seven pain pills per person per year—a huge number, but considerably fewer than in places where jobs were sent overseas. (Surry County's number, for instance, was eighty-three. In the wealthier, job-rich DC suburbs like Fairfax, Virginia, the painkiller figure was just fourteen.)

In the decade following the release of OxyContin, the epidemic's first wave, addicted Hoosiers hadn't yet resorted to stealing copper cemetery urns for drug money. Rural Indiana's 2.0 version of the crisis didn't surface in the county's public narrative until much later, after the switch from pills to heroin. In the late aughts, teenagers and twenty-somethings began routinely making the forty-five-minute drive east to Cincinnati (or north to Indianapolis) to buy heroin. And the county's probation officers soon found themselves taking pictures of probationers' arms—recording their track marks. Many had been arrested for buying dope, some trading their shoes or their kids' baby clothes for it, and hiding syringes in the bottom of diaper bags.

It wasn't until 2017, when a local woman overdosed in a Chuck E. Cheese bathroom as her five- and seven-year-olds played in the restaurant, that county leaders identified the opioid crisis as the most pressing problem facing the community. By then, they realized, the child abuse and neglect rate in the county had quintupled in just five years.

By 2019, even foster parents were having foster kids removed because they, too, were using drugs. Some foster families had ten kids. There was such a shortage of homes that some children were being placed as far away as Chicago. In a state with the second-highest child abuse and neglect rate in the nation, Ripley County's rate was six points higher than the state average.

Jail or a Batesville-made coffin—for most addicted parents, that was the de facto choice. The county claimed no drug-treatment centers or detox facilities, not a single full-time psychiatrist, and addiction medicines were just about impossible to get. In a state with a Republican supermajority, talk of opening a syringe exchange in Ripley County was heresy. In 2015, Governor Mike Pence had reluctantly approved opening a syringe-exchange program in nearby Scott County after a major outbreak of HIV caused by injected Opana, a powerful painkiller made of oxymorphone and hydrochloride. But by 2021, county commissioners voted to shut it down in a flurry of NIMBYism and antipathy toward people who use drugs. "A welfare program for addicts," one county commissioner called it.

"No one should have to come outside and find a syringe in their yard," countered Dr. William Cooke, a Scott County addiction doctor whose 2021 memoir, *Canary in the Coal Mine,* chronicled his efforts to turn treat people with OUD in his community. (He, too, was initially trained by the Chicago harm-reductionist Dan Bigg.) "But that doesn't mean that the SSP is the cause of that needle being discarded there," he told me.

Into this miry pit of need and politics barreled an outsider named Nikki King, a feisty Kentucky native fresh out of college who had the gall and sheer gumption to think she could fix things.

* * *

I first met Nikki in her hometown in central Appalachia. It was late 2016, and I'd heard good things about her work as a National Rural Health Association fellow at Margaret Mary Health, a community hospital in Batesville. Already making a name for herself among national addiction experts, the twenty-four-year-old graduate student had been the lead data cruncher on the hospital's task force to reduce opioid prescribing, resulting in a 60 percent prescribing decline at the facility.

Nikki understood what many policy makers and journalists still failed to grasp—that abruptly stopping opioid prescribing without also making treatment available for addiction and pain actually contributed to a more than doubling of overdose deaths as the untreated sought out illicit opioids of unknown strength in the form of heroin and fentanyl. Nikki knew, too, that law enforcement officials who paid steady lip service to "We can't arrest our way out of this" largely still jailed the dopesick and addicted for drug-related crimes. After tracking her story for four years, I wrote about her tenacious efforts to break that pattern for *The Atlantic* in May 2020. But she was just getting started.

Nikki was impatient by nature, a lightning-fast talker prone to tapping her foot if she had to explain something twice. "She's always got some plan to grow things bigger and do more, but sometimes it's hard to keep up with her thought process," said Lindsey Gessendorf, a therapist and hospital coworker. Nikki's mouth got her in trouble sometimes, but no one delved deeper into the weeds of policy, or worked harder, or slept less, or was better at distilling complex trends into an entertaining sound bite suitable for national TV.

When I asked Nikki to school me on the opioid crisis, she'd only been out of high school for seven years. But already she could tick off the names of twenty former classmates who were dead from suicide or drug- and alcohol-related car wrecks, disease, or overdose. She was rationing her vacation time to attend the funerals of former classmates. "At fourteen, I could've pointed out everybody who would be dead of overdose today, and I would've been right. If I can do that at fourteen, how are we letting them fall through the cracks?"

To see the immiseration for myself, she suggested in her mountain accent that we meet in Letcher County, Kentucky—at her papaw's body shop in "Wattsburg," as I wrote in my notes. It's spelled Whitesburg. (The number of pain pills per person per year there? A whopping eighty-five.)

Donald Trump had just been elected, and J. D. Vance's *Hillbilly Elegy* topped the nonfiction bestseller list. When I brought up either of those things, Nikki's cheerful demeanor turned in an instant, her accent thickened, and she spoke at a rapid-fire pace that most non-Appalachians—and Internet transcription services—find difficult to process. Among the staff at her Indiana hospital, these high-speed semi-rants became known as "Nikki's going all holler."

The epidemic had not been caused by a crisis of masculinity or lack of thrift, as Vance posed in his memoir. No, Nikki tied it directly to the rapacious behavior of coal companies and Big Pharma. The crisis was also presaged by Reagan-era changes to the Community and Mental Health Act, which had decommissioned most of the nation's mental health hospitals, and aided by liberals' over-reacting to *One Flew Over the Cuckoo's Nest*. As Nikki put it memorably, "Drugs didn't come outta nowhere. Drugs came outta Ronald Reagan's ass!"

Raised mostly by her grandparents, Nikki was schooled by her grandmother Sue King to believe that her safety and economic fortunes lay far away from Letcher County. She remembers the moment when people in her hometown went from sleeping with the screen door unlocked to buying new doors without glass panes that could be knocked out by burglars. In middle school at the time, Nikki had gone to a birthday party where her friend's mom stumbled, smashing the daughter's cake into the kitchen counter. Nikki later found the woman passed out on the toilet with her head leaning on a wall heater, surrounded by vomit and OxyContin bottles with someone else's name on them.

By high school, she had exactly one friend who was being raised by both parents rather than by relatives or was in foster care.

Leave, Sue King said repeatedly before her death in 2001. *Go away to college. And, above all, do not let anybody from the bigger, wider world think they're better than you.*

And leave she would, even though her recently widowed papaw, Curt King, wanted her to stay home. By day he taught vocational education at the high school in Whitesburg; by night, he ran an auto-body business. In his mind, Nikki should become a nurse, and the nearby community college would suffice. It didn't matter that she had a 4.0 GPA, and he had no reference point for her ACT score of 32 (the average is 21). "He didn't understand AP classes," she told me. "He thought [that meant] I was 'slow.'"

So Nikki literally ran away to college. One hot August night, she waited for Curt King to fall into a deep sleep. And she sucked up every ounce of courage and tiptoed out the back door, so nervous she was shaking. She'd been plotting the move her entire senior year, covertly applying for scholarships and state grants that would cover most of her tuition, saving $800 from working at the comic-book store in the county seat. She had never set foot on a college campus.

Nikki felt guilty about sneaking off, and she worried about her Papaw, who was then sixty-five and had never lived alone. When she imagined him waking up the next morning to an empty house, she had to pull over and vomit. Her shaking turned into deep, heaving sobs. Ugly crying, she calls it.

She considered turning back. But then she remembered one of

her last conversations with Mamaw Sue. Not long before her death, Sue King had forbidden Nikki from going to her friend Brittney's house. They had both noticed Brittney's mom slurring her words. Then came the news of the woman's arrest for illegal possession of narcotics. She'd become hooked on OxyContin prescribed for a back injury, and she was on probation when she relapsed on illicit pills. Fearful of losing custody of her kids for a failed drug screen, she drank Clorox because her pill dealer swore it would erase the OxyContin from the test. Instead, it killed her.

Sue King had always urged Nikki to go away so she could come back with college smarts and help Appalachia. But now she changed her tune.

"Just go," she told Nikki. "And don't come back."

Nikki didn't, except for brief visits. She couch-surfed with friends during her first year of college in 2009, then her papaw and student loans paid her tuition after that.

When we first met, Nikki's long-term goal was to work on the opioid crisis in Kentucky, but she was too young and too female to get anything done in Appalachia, she said. In the county where she grew up, the workforce participation rate was down to 44 percent. A quarter of the county was on disability.

"If you took 100 job applications right now, you might get ten people who could pass a drug test," a former mayor of Jenkins, Kentucky, told us during a driving tour that Curt King took us on one chilly winter morning. The ex-mayor himself was living out of a storage unit.

"I don't see any hope," he told her.

"I think we can beat it," Nikki shot back. "I just need somebody to start listening to me."

She framed her personal code next to her desk: "Don't be afraid to fail; be afraid not to try." Though she had spoken across the country and had the ear of Indiana politicians, no one in her home region returned her calls.

That would change as Nikki demonstrated to bureaucrats and politicians who weren't naturally inclined to take outsiders' advice the best ways to offer evidence-based addiction treatment. She traveled across Indiana mercilessly poaching the best therapists, psychologists, and nurse-practitioners. She talked her boss into letting her first design the optimum model she could muster, and *then* figure out how to pay for it—at a time when one in four rural hospitals was at risk of closure, and when the hospital he ran was then $3 million in the red. Her goal was to create a team even better than those at the elite Hazelden Betty Ford Centers but for marginalized rural people with high rates of childhood trauma and comorbidities. By 2021, she had dubbed her team the Avengers of Mental Health. It had grown so fast that she had to move her own desk into the supply closet.

Nikki and I shared similar backgrounds—we were both reared in rural areas, with relatives who struggled with addiction and mental health issues. I didn't live with my grandmother, but she lived next door and literally kept a roof over our heads. (She owned the house we lived in rent-free.)

We'd both struggled with the glories and the survivors' guilt of being the first in our families to go away for college and enter the professional class. Going home meant navigating not only the skeletons of childhood trauma but also resentments from some of our kin.

During the buildup to the 2016 election, when I casually asked my retired brother-in-law how he was doing, he deadpanned: "I'm deplorable." The day the 2020 presidential votes were announced, one of my sisters, who'd never talked politics to me before, immediately renounced the results—while our mother lay in hospice. Months later, she refused to get a COVID vaccine because she insisted it contained unsafe metals and particles from aborted fetuses.

Another relative, in his late forties and with severe diabetic complications, was on a hospital gurney en route to a long-awaited pancreas transplant when he asked if the donor had been vaccinated. When a nurse told him yes, he ended the procedure right there on the spot.

Nikki had similar conversations with her relatives and her patients, most of whom refused to wear masks at the height of a severe COVID outbreak in the county. Fewer than half of her fellow *hospital workers* were willing to be vaccinated.

As Indiana University sociologist Jennifer M. Silva explained it: People living in distressed rural communities are "so suspicious of government; they don't think anything's really going to help them, and generally they don't see their futures as being very bright."

And no wonder. Between 1999 and 2019, the gap between rural and urban death rates almost tripled, growing from 62 per 100,000 to 169.5. That death-rate disparity was bigger now than the death disparity between Black people and White people, which academics pinned not just to deaths of despair but also to poor nutrition, lack of exercise, smoking, and uneven access to quality medical care.

Whether they meant to or not, people were literally killing themselves as the hyper-polarized government they hated stood by, and politicians who professed to lead them were engulfed in culture wars about transgender bathroom rights, Stonewall Jackson statues, and critical race theory. "People are making a virtue of going it alone and not depending on anyone, almost as a kind of self-protection," Silva told me.

Or as Nikki put it: "Rigid thinking is what it is, and that's a trauma response."

Methamphetamine use amped up the paranoia among her patients who were already conspiracy-prone, making rigid thinking patterns even harder to shake. "Their belief systems are definitely impairing their treatment," said Gessendorf, Nikki's chief therapist. When patients refused to wear masks to their therapy appointments, she had to delay restarting in-person appointments, which contributed to more relapses.

"They disagree about basic facts," said Nikki's boss, Tim Putnam, the Margaret Mary CEO. He'd been appointed to serve on President Biden's COVID-19 Health Equity Task Force and therefore was deemed by many in town not to be trusted. "My relatives think they know more about rural health than I do. They get defensive when I say rural populations are declining. It's 'often wrong but never in doubt,' and when you correct them, you're seen as being learned and arrogant."

Before a recent family gathering, Gessendorf made a list of discussion topics that were off limits—"nothing about Trump, nothing about Biden smelling people because he's a pervert," she said.

It felt like the entire country was on the verge of an intrafamily, internecine war.

After four years of tracking Nikki's work, I was surprised to learn we had something else in common. After my mother's death in late 2020, I found a letter she'd mailed to my dad at a rehab in 1974, nine years before his death. I was ten at the time and knew about his alcoholism but had no memory of him ever going away for treatment. Mom's letter was posted from our western Ohio hometown and addressed to Theodore Macy Jr., in care of "Serenity Hall, Margaret Mary Community Hospital…Batesville, Indiana."

Nikki, of course, knew none of this. And yet a month before I found Mom's letter, she had renamed her department the Serenity Program in honor of the hospital's old rehab wing. It closed in the 1990s due to aggressive austerity on the part of managed-care companies and HMOs, a time when insurance spending on addiction declined by more than 70 percent.

The place where my dad spent a month drying out was the exact spot inside the hospital where the Avengers now work.

Elsewhere in the country, drug courts—which allow addicted offenders to enter a treatment program instead of going to jail—had been shown to reduce recidivism. But drug courts are expensive to operate, and many treatment decisions are made by elected local judges and prosecutors who may or may not understand addiction or be willing to concede treatment decisions to clinicians on their treatment teams. About half continue to funnel probationers into abstinence-only treatment, despite overwhelming evidence that it's not only less effective for OUD; it's very often deadly. Fewer than a third of residential rehabs allow participants to take buprenorphine or methadone.

"What too many don't yet realize is, there are things they can do that would be fairly easy and save lives, and they wouldn't have to feel emasculated," said Brandon del Pozo, a former Burlington, Vermont, police chief. "All we did basically was re-norm buprenorphine and make it acceptable." Now a Brown University postdoc researching police reform, he added, "It's not like we're asking cops to paint their nails pink."

Back in 2018, Ripley County's probation program offered only two hours of group therapy and opposed probationers taking OUD medicines. Nikki convinced her hospital's emergency department to make bupe referrals for those who overdosed, but no-shows were more common than not. So she pitched the pioneering idea of housing a drug-treatment program for probationers as a condition of their probation—inside the courthouse.

The program Nikki built mirrored Dr. Jerome Jaffe's groundbreaking work: It coordinated patients' access to bupe and primary care. It also offered intensive counseling and group therapy along with a menu of social supports, from helping patients find jobs to childcare. Most participants were in their twenties or thirties and had spent much of their adult lives cycling in and out of jail for addiction-related crimes. To usher the program into being, Nikki delivered breathless promises to everybody from state legislators to the state drug czar.

The most important promise she made was to her boss, Tim Putnam, and it was a biggie. Within six months, she swore, the program would pay for itself through Indiana's Medicaid expansion.

But a few months in, during a meeting at the hospital, one administrator mentioned, in an offhand way, that Medicaid was refusing to reimburse the hospital for the program because it was housed at the courthouse and not in a medical facility—*even though that had been the most groundbreaking aspect of it,* forging collaborations between health care and criminal justice, between bupe providers and traditional twelve-step recovery. The program worked, Nikki argued, because the liberal therapist was now friends with the conservative head of probation; and because the program had grown from the ground up, albeit via copious amounts of arm-twisting, compromising, and sweat equity. And now some damn bean counter in Indianapolis was on the verge of mucking it all up.

When a higher-up at the hospital suggested they shelve the program, Nikki lost it right there in front of her boss and the executives—most were at least two decades her senior—and she ugly cried. "Y'all, I've got no more rabbits to pull out of my sleeve," she said.

This made the middle-aged men, stoic Hoosiers who weren't accustomed to seeing tears in the workplace, very nervous. To stop her crying, they quickly suggested workarounds to the problem, like moving the program to another clinic the hospital owned.

Then out popped another rabbit.

"Why can't I just buy part of the courthouse?" Nikki asked.

The hospital would rent part of the courthouse for $25 a year, carving off part of the expansive conference room they were already using. The head of probation would oversee the renovation process himself, getting supplies donated, bringing in houseplants, and putting up an applique that said MAKE TODAY AMAZING above the door.

Beside the new office, a sign read: "Margaret Mary Health, Ripley County Courthouse, *Suite A.*"

Six months later, by the time the first cohort of the Courts Addiction & Drug Services (CADS program) graduated, not a single person had overdosed. Thirty-four out of fifty-one had completed the program with no issues; of the third that had relapsed, half reengaged immediately with treatment.

When Nikki presented the results to her doctoral dissertation committee, she noted that 97 percent of her patients had co-occurring mental illnesses and 76 percent had documented PTSD. Overprescribed benzos and opioid pills had been by far her patients' biggest gateways to heroin and meth use.

Their preferred mode of self-care was to do drugs, not go jogging. "We ask people to deal with things nobody should have to live with, sometimes alone and with a totally inadequate safety net," Nikki said. "In all the things I've seen, I've never seen anything that's as traumatic as poverty."

When Nikki asked the first CADS cohort to name a short-term goal, one man said he wanted a second pair of pants. Another wished to taste salmon for the first time. She was stunned by how common hunger was. "The first time we brought out a snack bowl, they jumped on it like a wounded baby antelope," Nikki said.

"A lot of SUD programs just tackle the SUD, but they don't do anything with the underlying trauma and co-occurring mental health disorders. So it becomes, 'Don't do drugs, don't do drugs.' Well, they already know that! Our program's focus is, how do we get you to a place where you can cope with the things in your life?"

The recidivism data she collected from the project, peer-reviewed by her dissertation panel, also showed that the program worked. Most participants were getting jobs, getting their children back, and not using drugs. And she'd paid for nearly all of it by leveraging Medicaid dollars and grant funds while scrambling to identify early reentry problems with childcare, employment, and food-insecurity issues.

"If you live in a state that doesn't have access to Medicaid, you're screwed," she told her committee. She didn't say that she often worked sixteen-hour days, though that was certainly one key to the program's success.

Nor did she mention the fist-pounding clashes that erupted over whether a probationer should be jailed again for relapsing—sometimes the therapy team won, sometimes probation. When I saw the title of her doctoral presentation, "Changing What's Possible," I thought of the late harm-reduction guru Dan Bigg, who would have said of the small-town culture wars: *Any positive change…*

Nikki King proved that, with enough community effort, recovery *was possible*. But barring a flat-out overhaul of the War on Drugs—wherein a significant chunk of the estimated $50 billion spent annually on enforcement and incarceration would be funneled into treatment instead—could a tiny program like Nikki's be replicated on a large-enough scale to objectively improve health outcomes?

"I ask myself that all the time," Putnam said.

The day *The Atlantic* magazine published my May 2020 profile of Nikki King was not an amazing day in Batesville. Putnam had ordered a big stack of the issue to give away—only to hide it in his office closet when many in town (including some community leaders) soured on the story.

It would take months before I understood the kerfuffle, but it boiled down to this: Criminal justice leaders thought I gave Nikki too much credit. They thought I had cast them as pink-nailed pushovers when, for instance, I described the time they deferred to Gessendorf to decide that a patient who had relapsed could skip jail and be allowed to reengage in treatment. (A fact-checker at the magazine had corroborated every detail of the piece, including the judge's and probation officers' quotes.) Reelections were coming up; jobs were on the line.

That's when I learned firsthand how tricky it is to shine a national spotlight on a small conservative town without it back-firing. Some saw me as an East Coast elite. Even though I'm from rural Ohio and have reported from a mid-sized Appalachian city for more than three decades, I was perceived as an outsider who'd swooped in to glorify Nikki, another outsider.

"You have to remember that there's no longer news in small towns other than what happened at the local basketball game; independent reporting has all but disappeared," Putnam said. More than a quarter of the nation's newspapers have closed since 2004, the bulk of them in rural communities. Those closures have created news deserts that leave citizens dependent on their social media echo chambers.

"Rural areas are descending into this really toxic groupthink that can lead to really bad decisions, and those who do disagree are afraid to even bring up different perspectives," Putnam said. In a county where 80 percent of the population voted for Trump in 2020, Putnam's participation in Biden's COVID task force ended up creating political trouble for him, too.

Never mind that CADS claimed recidivism rates 35 percent lower than the national average, or that it had zero overdose deaths (compared to demographically similar places, which averaged six deaths over the same period). Or that some participants were now gainfully employed for the first time in their adult lives.

Ever the pragmatist, Nikki focused on expanding the program

into neighboring counties, where it was welcomed. Gessendorf had worked in one of them as a jail counselor earlier in her career and had a good rapport with its probation team.

The work continued to be gratifying, messy, sleep-robbing. Sometimes Nikki became so overwhelmed that she spent entire weekends in bed. When her papaw died of a heart attack in March 2020 at the age of eighty-three, she could not get the image of him dying alone, in his favorite recliner, out of her head. A few months later, COVID stole the life of seventy-nine-year-old Tom Deters, a beloved counselor on her team. After battling his own SUD years earlier, he had left the veterinary field to become a counselor. At the same time, participants and graduates began re-lapsing because of pandemic isolation and stress. In March 2021, the program saw its first death—a young man with kids who died of fentanyl-laced heroin.

At the start of the pandemic, the counseling team quickly switched to telehealth, but that made group bonding harder and rule breaking easier. Some phoned in for therapy while getting their nails done or while test-driving a car. After the election of Joe Biden, patients increasingly gravitated toward QAnon and the Big Lie. "People are getting trapped into conspiracy theories, which ups their anxieties," Gessendorf told me in May 2021. "They won't get vaccinated. They won't wear masks. They don't think COVID's real, even the ones who've had it."

Occasionally, Nikki went all holler, such as when a COVID denier called her and her colleagues out in a local restaurant during one of my visits.

"What's with the masks? Are you girls ugly under there or something?" the man said as they passed his table.

Nikki turned abruptly and shot back, "Not as ugly as you."

"I doubt that," he said.

"Well, I can fix that for you," she said.

When local officials balked again at the continued media attention—including an all-holler interview she gave to PBS's *Amanpour & Company*—Nikki dug in harder. She wrote more grants and eventually tripled the size of her staff. A site in Brookville would house a new program she designed for children who weren't being raised by their parents.

Nikki now believed that the county needed to make available the same boatload of therapy and psychiatric services for the region's foster kids. Called GROW—no one could remember what the acronym stood for—it would be housed inside the Brookville facility, in an adjacent county. The idea came to her when a Serenity Program patient relapsed just before Christmas and voluntarily gave her children up for adoption because she knew she couldn't give them the life they deserved. (That patient had herself grown up in foster care.)

Though she had very few relatives in Kentucky she stayed in touch with—she and her father are estranged—Nikki found family among her coworkers. It said so on the coffee mug one had gifted her: "Dear Boss Lady. Thanks for being my boss. If I had a different boss, I would punch her in the face and go find you." She was twenty-eight.

Nikki collected parental figures the way men in rural America collect oversized, overloud trucks. At the top of that list was Cindy Ziemke, the state rep (and sauerkraut-ball master) who strategically talked a lobbyist friend into arranging nearly a half-million dollars in grants for Serenity from Purdue Pharma, of all companies. Quoting a character from *Hamilton*, Nikki told me, "It's the art of the compromise; hold your nose and close your eyes."

Nikki used Purdue's money to lure a full-time psychiatrist away from his practice in Indianapolis—even though, as fifty-three-year-old Dr. Christopher Dull recalls it, he had absolutely no interest in spending most of his week in an apartment ninety minutes from home. When I asked Dull how Nikki managed to persuade him to relocate to a factory town famous for coffins, Dull said he'd found himself powerless to say no to the force before him. "You have to work in mental health to fully understand that what she's done just doesn't exist," he said. "Most health systems are locked into being solely funded by insurance money, but she figures out other ways. And she's not afraid to go up against the old boys' club."

And so Nikki persisted in hounding Dull after hearing from multiple sources that he was the best psychiatrist in the state. Ripping a page from the pharma-bros' playbook, she offered to show up outside his medical practice with lunch. When that didn't work, she surreptitiously arranged for him to speak at a medical conference she was attending to woo him during a group dinner. The magic combo of words that finally broke his resolve was a complex patient story she told him about a fifty-year-old who suffered from bipolar disorder, or schizophrenia, and opioid addiction, and yet had never had access to psychiatric care.

By mid-2021, the Serenity Program operated at 320 percent capacity. Whereas, two years earlier, Nikki said she felt like the dog in a cartoon, sitting at a table and saying, "This is fine," while everything around him burned, she now felt like the dad from *Lion King*, running against a stampede of wildebeests to save his cub. And Dr. Dull, it turned out, in addition to being the best psychiatrist, was also among the most absent-minded. Staffers constantly had to remind him of meetings and appointments, but he was so brilliant with their most traumatized patients that they deemed him worth the trouble.

Lead therapist Gessendorf had a new patient, the child of drug users, who'd started using drugs at age ten. A medical assistant in the program lost five friends to overdose in the pandemic's first year.

Asked how they coped, Nikki said, "We just cry a lot."

Purdue Pharma would pay for most of GROW, including advanced training for staffers learning to use yoga as a recovery tool ("The issues live in the tissues," the teacher told me), play therapy, anger management, and other advanced trauma-informed care. "I had absolutely no training in medical school" to treat such high levels of trauma, said Dr. Richard Turner, the pediatrician who directs the program.

"I hate Purdue's role in the opioid crisis, but that horse is outta the barn," added Ziemke, Nikki's legislative cheerleader and the mother of two adult sons who'd been addicted to heroin. A proud Republican ("but Never Trumper!"), Ziemke was so disgusted by the latest state legislative session—in which mask mandates, birth control, and abortion were all under attack "by right-wing loons"—that she vowed not to run for office again.

Giving up wasn't in Nikki's nature. She still despised Purdue. But if she waited for litigation money to trickle down, she reasoned, law enforcement might usurp the Sacklers' offerings for more policing and bigger jails.

Best to get what she could from them while she could still control it.

Chapter Six

Good Criminals

Joe Solomon (center) handing out harm-reduction supplies, Charleston, West Virginia.

A s Purdue's bankruptcy case lumbered toward a seeming conclusion in late 2020, I trailed an underground needle exchange operator in the capital of West Virginia, the state with the highest overdose rate in the nation. By way of explaining the state's anti-government fervor and just how ruby red it is: West Virginia has just one abortion clinic, it posts the second-lowest voter turnout rate in the nation, and 73 percent of the state legislature is Republican—including one delegate who would soon participate in the January 6, 2021, storming of the US Capitol. When another Republican state delegate made national headlines for joking about how he'd drown his kids if they were gay, no punishment came of it.

All of which conspired to make harm-reduction work in the heart of Appalachia a much grittier enterprise than Nikki King's programmatic approach or Michelle Mathis's grandmotherly have-pizzas-will-travel. In many of the hardest-hit areas first targeted by Purdue, treatment of the sickest still fell mainly to volunteers, many operating illegally or in a quasi-legal netherworld. As COVID exacerbated the overdose crisis, the political gulf between addiction treatment and criminal justice seemed only to widen.

West Virginia's most prolific harm-reductionist was a thirty-year-old nonbinary person whose pronouns are they/them. Lill Prosperino wore camo and an oversized nose ring. A sticker on the front window of their mountain-hollow bungalow had a coat hanger that said, "Abortion: You Do You." A box on their front porch contained needles, bottled water, and abscess supplies in case people who use drugs stopped by when no one was home. At the moment, four counties in the state, including Kanawha (which contains Charleston, the state capital and county seat), had already adopted or were in the process of adopting draconian legislation that would outlaw needle exchange.

A former addictions counselor at a sliding-scale health center, Prosperino was raised in an eastern Kentucky coal-mining town—they and Nikki attended the same high school—and both grew up surrounded by many of Purdue's victims, an upbringing Prosperino described without bitterness or judgment. "My dad was always a drug user and dealer; he went to prison when I was young," they said in a lilting drawl. "I learned from a young age that there were things to help people, like Suboxone and methadone, but which were very stigmatized." At the age of ten, they were at an Applebee's with their dad and his girlfriend when the girlfriend passed out into her plate of pasta. Super embarrassed, Prosperino took her to the bathroom, where she conked out again.

It was a defining childhood moment, as well as a lesson about how easily children absorb stigma about drug use. Unpacking stigma that stems from War on Drugs propaganda is lifelong work, Prosperino explained.

"I think it comes down to, people are always going to use drugs, so we have to have harm reduction. I have my own maintenance things that help me not wanna get fucked up all the time." Before we left their house to do "distro"—shorthand for passing out needles and other harm-reduction supplies—they made an espresso and hit a vape pen.

Prosperino had recently purchased an abandoned house on the lot next door to their home—for thirty dollars at public auction—with the goal of housing people who use drugs in the community. They regularly mailed out Narcan kits to people across the state, funded by a national nonprofit called NEXT Distro. With uber-potent fentanyl infiltrating the drug supply, it now took three or four doses of naloxone to revive an overdosing person.

In the meantime, they were helping about 800 people who use drugs a month via mail, in their personal vehicle, and/or by letting neighbors inject inside their home. "I have ice water and a couch for them to sit on," they said. Prosperino also relies on a diverse cast of people in town who either help with needle distribution—and/or look the other way.

"The controversy around race and around harm reduction is very different in the state outside of Charleston," Prosperino said. In one community they don't care to name, needles get passed out from a Black-church van under the umbrella of a program designed to help Black sex workers.

Asked how to fix the opioid crisis, Prosperino said, "We won't have real harm reduction unless we defund the police." But in large rural swaths of the country where many decry universal health care as socialism and American flags hang upside down as a symbol of distress, I asked them the same question I'd been scratching my head about for years: Was it a worthy goal for police officers to shepherd people who use drugs into treatment instead of jail?

"It's hard for me to think about how to fix things within the system, to be honest with you," they said. "I'm not sure it can be done here—which is why I work around the system."

Sometimes they're accompanied by a thirteen-year-old boy from the community named Jagger, whose childhood reminds Prosperino of their own. Jagger helps them do distro and Narcan trainings (he pretends to be the person overdosing), and he introduces them to people who use drugs because he knows everyone in town.

Prosperino gently mentors him, constantly giving advice, encouraging him to go to school (which he doesn't love), narrating the injustices they witness.

"This rail is flimsy," Jagger said. We were getting pizza following a harm-reduction event in Charleston, and he was pointing out the instability of the outdoor dining rails.

Prosperino quietly said into Jagger's ear: "You know, they put up tents just so rich people can eat dinner, but they tear down homeless people's tents who don't have anywhere to sleep."

I followed Prosperino as they and another volunteer made the hourlong drive to Charleston from their home in a tiny southern West Virginia town. Under a West Virginia Turnpike underpass in downtown Charleston, a fifty-two-year-old woman explained how she'd become addicted to prescribed fentanyl patches and lollipops and OxyContin following back surgery in 2002. "I don't blame the doctor; he thought he was helping me," Kelli Keen said. She was married to a preacher and had kids back then—until she reinjured her back. "But had Pandora's box not been opened, I wouldn't be here today." With the exception of a few brief periods of sobriety, she'd been a mostly homeless heroin user ever since.

"I've overdosed and been Narcanned forty-two times," she said. She was angry when Charleston's public health department closed its needle exchange in 2018 over claims that it enabled drug use. Some 24,000 residents had used the exchange, and when it shut down overnight, the thing harm-reductionists and scientists had been warning politicians about for years actually happened: HIV cases went up 1,500 percent. The city's mayor told listeners of his radio talk show that the needle exchange, inconveniently for him located across the street from the city's downtown mall, had morphed into a "mini-mall for junkies." Despite ample evidence to the contrary, he preferred the SSP operated by a free clinic, which mandated "one for one" exchange—meaning, you can't get a new needle until you turn your old one in.

"People think if y'all don't hand out needles, we'll quit using," Keen told me. "But it doesn't matter if the rapture's coming at 8:00 tonight—if you use, you're gonna use."

A few blocks away, we stopped to help a middle-aged dread-locked woman wearing slippers. It was thirty-two degrees, and she was pulling her belongings in a small fold-up shopping cart. The harm-reductionists scanned the streets for police, then cheerfully handed the woman a blanket along with clean needles, injection cookers and ties, and food.

The woman had just been diagnosed with hepatitis C. She told us that a growing number of her Charleston friends now had HIV, and that she was very cold and very tired. Before the month was out, a CDC doctor pronounced the county's HIV outbreak the "most concerning in the nation."

"Thank you, we need more people like y'all out here," the woman said.

"I'm sorry to rush off, but we're being good criminals," Prosperino responded cheerfully, still monitoring the streets for police. "I'll be back next week."

In two hours, they had unloaded a trunk full of winter supplies and safe-use kits in various alleyways and out-of-the-way parking lots. Just one person among the couple dozen homeless people we met that afternoon declined their offer of needles, saying he didn't use drugs. But he did accept a tin of homemade medicinal "drawing-out salve" that Prosperino had concocted from herbs.

"I'm kind of a hill witch," they explained, chuckling. They sometimes traded the herbal medicine for the ingredients used to make it. Needle-exchange participants who hunt ginseng are happy to scour for bloodroot while they're already foraging in the mountains. Digging American ginseng—*sanging*, they call it—with the intention of selling it illegally to Asian markets is a centuries-old Appalachian hustle, not unlike moonshining or, more recently, selling OxyContin without the benefit of a pharmacist's license. "They all use drugs, and they want to take care of their own abscesses," Prosperino said. "So it's a whole weird circle of underground economies."

In the richest country in the world, treatment of the sickest, neediest people fell to volunteers risking arrest to give out homemade tinctures discovered in the Middle Ages.

For two chilly months in the winter of 2020–21, the camo-wearing harm-reduction worker made weekly treks to Charleston. By late January, though, a handful of volunteers from the local harm-reduction nonprofit that had been shut down mustered the courage to resume SSP operations in the parking lot of a Unitarian Universalist church—despite the threat of arrest. The organizers Sharpied the hill witch's phone number on their legs in case they ended up in jail.

"They'll kick down a door if you need them to," organizer Joe Solomon said, referring to Prosperino.

At four foot ten and 125 pounds, Prosperino has two black belts in martial arts and is as sinewy as a cheetah. Protesting the Unite the Right rally in Charlottesville in 2017, they'd found themselves in the thick of the melee, near a woman who was knocked into the air by the same car that killed protester Heather Heyer. A friend ended up with a broken leg after being trampled. Someone sprayed Prosperino with bear mace and speared their leg with a sharp Confederate flagpole. "There's nothing like getting in fistfights with big Nazi people," they said. And, rest assured, they got in some licks, too.

Living in Kentucky at the time, they were helping organize the opening of a syringe exchange in Whitesburg at night and working as a counselor for a buprenorphine program that operated out of a federally qualified health center (FQHC), that is, a federally funded sliding-scale clinic, during the day. When their patients tested positive for illicit substances—an offense that could get them kicked out of the program—Prosperino refused, on principle, to report it. The only person they dismissed from the program was a man whose arm-sleeve tattoos announced his dedication to White supremacy. "He would come to our group therapy class and be like, 'All gay people should die. All Black people are N-words.' And I was like, 'Motherfucker, you can't say that in here!'"

Like most Americans, I'd noticed a surge in the street population of my hometown, mostly in the form of people begging for money in the medians of busy intersections. Not all were people who use drugs, of course. But not until I spent a day trailing a pair of volunteers and stopped to help them did I understand that nearly all the homeless people in Charleston identified as people who use IV drugs.

"I don't give a shit if some people are just taking the needles to sell them," Prosperino said. "If somebody's getting a clean needle, that's all that matters to me. If a poor person makes a dollar, that's not the end of the world. They probably need that dollar."

Two decades in, America's overdose crisis was still buried in bureaucracy, from the Surry County vomit buckets to the arcane rules of bankruptcy court, which was not and could never be a forum where victims would be permitted to air their grievances: its purpose was to restructure a company's debt—not to deliver justice for a crying mother. After Judge Drain cut short a testimony of one mother who'd found her way to an accidentally unmuted phone line during a hearing that winter, author and former lawyer Charlotte Bismuth captured the scene in a tweeted cartoon:

"Your losses are not calendared for today," she wrote alongside her drawing.

David Herzberg, the historian, was hired to testify in several of the opioid lawsuits, and he remained astonished by the government's inability to hold the Sacklers accountable for their crimes. "If somebody's going to have a billion dollars, they should've done something awesome," Herzberg said.

But the Sacklers were nothing like the valiant West Virginia volunteers. They were not good criminals. "They are literally a crime family—the only thing they ever innovated was how to sell drugs more dangerously," Herzberg said.

He compared the family to oligarchs who cannot be voted out of power. "They're still going to have more money than God. And money is power—not just gold-plated sinks, but it means they're still going to wield power in the world. People who mean us ill. Why would we leave them with any power?" Herzberg said.

At seventy-five, Richard Sackler rejected that characterization. In a deposition taken in late 2020, he said he didn't perceive his family as being "fabulously" wealthy. "There are many people who are much wealthier than I am, thousands and thousands," Sackler said. "I consider myself very fortunate to be weathering the financial crisis caused by COVID. There are people who have suffered more than I have, even given the pursuit of me in the media, so I don't feel sorry for myself."

And yet the portrayal of his family as architects of the opioid crisis had caused him "severe depression for a long, long time," he said. "I don't believe that OxyContin or any narcotic was the proximate cause of the vast majority of the numbers that you have been proposing—not because I'm challenging the numbers, but it's a far more complicated issue than simply the vehicle with which they participated in some way in their own death."

Asked how Sackler seemed that day, Ryan Hampton, the recovery activist who co-chaired the bankruptcy's Unsecured Creditors Committee, said Sackler looked old and tired but also laid-back and smug. During one part of his deposition, he paused in a way that was "insultingly casual," Hampton recalled, to take a bite from his sandwich.

The victims finally had their losses calendared on December 17, 2020, if not exactly their day in court. Their archnemesis, Richard Sackler, was not in the building. He wasn't even on Zoom. If the family had its way, neither would former Purdue board members Kathe or David Sackler (Richard's cousin and son, respectively). But there the two sacrificial Sacklers sat, from their respective offices, while the bipartisan House Committee on Oversight and Reform grilled them hard. It was either that or, as New York congresswoman Carolyn Maloney threatened a few days earlier, be subpoenaed to testify.

Exactly twenty-five years since the OxyContin launch, this one day was the first time the Sacklers faced any sort of public accounting for their role in America's opioid crisis. Nan Goldin had been calling for the hearing for years, along with Congressman Elijah Cummings, the now-deceased committee chairman. Mike Quinn, Goldin's pro bono lawyer, had been phoning Maloney's office daily for weeks.

To the ragtag Ad Hoc Committee on Accountability, the virtual gathering was a reckoning, and it was delicious. Goldin kicked off the hearing with a one-minute video clip explaining that

OxyContin had stolen three years of her life, sidelined her career, destroyed her relationships, and sent her on a path of speaking for "500,000 Americans who no longer can."

For the next three and a half hours, the Sackler duo was verbally thrashed, as one elected official after another took turns describing the constituents they had lost to the opioid scourge. Maloney pointed out how the Sacklers had withdrawn $10 billion from the company in the wake of the 2007 guilty plea—"80 times [more] than what the family had received before"—as a way to shield their wealth from litigation.

When David Sackler denied doing so, Maloney quickly countered by reciting an e-mail he had written to other family members: "We're rich...[but] for how long?" David wrote, pleadingly. "Until which suits get through to the family?" She accused him of siphoning off company money before opioid victims could file litigation claims against Purdue, a strategy he vigorously denied.

An Illinois congressman displayed slides of David Sackler's sprawling homes in Bel Air and Manhattan. A Tennessee congressman derided David's question-dodging by quoting Upton Sinclair: "A man has difficulty understanding something if his salary depends on him not understanding it."

Massachusetts congresswoman Ayanna Pressley recited Richard Sackler's oft-quoted "hammer on the abusers" deflection and blamed him for predatory practices that decimated minority communities already strained by mass incarceration. "Your family's rhetoric fuels the stigma and harmful policies that have denied people in need of the resources they require to overcome their addiction. We do not need another failed war on drugs. What we need is a reckoning and accountability for drug companies who put profits over people and rob us of lives and the freedom of our loved ones."

California representative Katie Porter held up a bankruptcy textbook that she herself had written, citing a federal law defining fraudulent transfers and calling the case against the Sacklers "textbook." "Why should the family not transfer back the $10.4 billion dollars to be used to pay the creditors in this case, including victims of opioid abuse?" Porter wanted to know.

The two Sacklers, for their part, did their best to appear contrite—"to express my family's deep sadness about the opioid crisis," said David Sackler, who'd cleaned up for the hearing, no longer donning the hipster beard he'd worn in his *Vanity Fair* portrait the year before. They seemed well prepped by their guards—the best legal and consulting firms and PR consultants that money could buy—about what not to recall, what not to say, and how to deflect. Above all, they stressed repeatedly, they had always acted "legally and ethically." The duo blamed the press for blaming the Sacklers while acknowledging that OxyContin addiction had played a role in the opioid crisis.

But they stopped short of admitting anything other than wanting to help millions of Americans in pain. As a mother, Kathe Sackler said, her heart "breaks for the parents who have lost their children. I am so terribly sorry for your pain."

And yet, asked directly to apologize for her role in causing that pain, she said, "I have tried to figure out if there's anything I could have done differently knowing what I knew then, not what I know now. And I have to say I can't—there is nothing I can find that I would have done differently."

At that point in the testimony, Ryan Hampton texted me, saying he couldn't take any more; he had to step away. "Knowing how bad this settlement is going to be for victims. It fucking sucks…This whole thing has been a setup since day one."

But it felt to me like something had shifted a little. Without others there to deflect, complicate, and obscure, the Sackler story came more sharply into focus: the Sacklers had drained the company of $10 billion, then pushed it into bankruptcy. They were offering a small portion of the amount they retained to help abate the opioid crisis—but only if they got to walk away with their freedom and most of their wealth. It was that simple.

In a group Zoom immediately following the hearing, Goldin and the other activists were ebullient. "It seems like the shaming was a success, but will this be a springboard to anything meaningful in terms of action?" asked Pete Jackson, who'd lost his eighteen-year-old daughter, Emily, to a single OxyContin in 2006.

Barbara Van Rooyan, who'd also contributed a video on behalf of victims, said the holidays had always been hard since her son, Patrick, died of an OxyContin overdose in 2004. Van Rooyan had spent several years following his death petitioning and calling on the FDA to restrict OxyContin use to severe pain only, but her efforts were thwarted repeatedly. "Having to make that video really put me back into a funk," she told the group. "But today, for me at least, my soul feels like it's flying."

Flanked by her assistants (and with Laura Poitras's documentary crew filming from the sidelines), Nan Goldin watched the hearing in her apartment, frantically texting her cohorts every time an official landed a blow. "The world is hearing us, finally," she said.

Quinn encouraged them to emphasize to reporters they spoke with how "good it was that there was bipartisan hatred of the Sacklers." At the time, he doubted a Biden-run Department of Justice would go after the Sacklers criminally because the family might then pull out of the bankruptcy deal, prolonging the process and angering those states' attorneys general who were already counting on the Sacklers' money for abatement.

The Sackler guards had orchestrated a Sophie's Choice between justice and treatment. As winter turned to spring, they continued collecting legal, accounting, and consultancy fees from the shrinking settlement pot.

"It would be tough to prove criminal liability because of the statute of limitations," Quinn said. "But we'll see. The public opinion can sway anything."

Further complicating the case was a little-known "poison pill" provision written into the 2020 Department of Justice settlement with Purdue for $8.3 billion—money that would never see the light of day since Purdue no longer had that kind of money, and the Sackler portion of that settlement only amounted to $225 million in civil penalties. If the reorganization didn't go according to the company's plan, the DOJ could swoop in and claim a lion's share of the money. Temple University law professor Jonathan Lipson, who had sounded alarm bells about Purdue and the Sacklers as early as November 2018, became Quinn's bankruptcy whisperer. He predicted that the poison pill would force creditors to support the plan—or risk recovering nothing. It was hugely complicated and incredibly shrewd, Lipson explained. We hadn't seen all of the DOJ's moves yet, but this one could prove decisive.

Behind the scenes, Quinn nudged the Reporters Committee for Freedom of the Press, which successfully filed for the release of more damning documents. The trove uncovered conversations over the last decade between Sackler relatives who worried about protecting their fortunes, strategized about how to increase Oxy-Contin sales and how to deflect growing anti-Sackler sentiments brought forth in articles in *The New Yorker*, *Esquire*, and the *New York Times*—some of which featured Nan Goldin's group. In one round of WhatsApp conversations among Sackler relatives, Marissa Sackler trumpeted her museum connections: "I speak regularly with [the Dia Art Foundation] on all of this and they fully support us and think Nan Goldin is crazy," she wrote.

Psyched to have gotten under the Sacklers' skin, Goldin changed her twitter handle to @crazynangoldin.

In 2018, as litigation threats began to close in on the Sacklers, the newly released documents revealed that Richard Sackler's branch of the family had hired PR consultant Davidson

Goldin—no relation to Nan—to counter narratives the family viewed as "inaccurate, unfair, misleading."

Lipson had been on the receiving end of the PR firm's ire, having recently spent fourteen hours defending an op-ed he'd co-written with Gerald Posner for the *New York Times* about Purdue's poison pill against inaccuracy claims from Davidson Goldin, who demanded the paper retract Lipson's piece. While Goldin had garnered a handful of minor corrections from the *Times*, ABC, and NBC since his hiring in 2018, no changes were made to the Lipson/Posner piece. An opinion piece I wrote for the *Times* a few months later about Purdue's long-standing cozy relationship with the FDA went through a grueling fact-checking session that lasted four days and seemed to require the sign-off of every top editor on staff. Richard Sackler's lawyer sent another letter criticizing some (accurate!) statements I'd made a few months before in an MSNBC documentary, essentially telling the lawyers at Disney, who were legally backstopping a forthcoming Hulu series based on my book, that I was not to be trusted.

The guards' full-court press was meant to intimidate. And it did, to a point.

More documents were due to come out in early 2021, which increased pressure on Drain to slow the pace of the settlement—and on the Sacklers to pay more. But slowing things down also meant that it would take longer for abatement money to reach the victims, whose numbers were growing by the day.

"The bankruptcy is a shit show, but at least we're making it hard to make it easy" on Drain, said Charlotte Bismuth, the author–former lawyer advising Goldin's group. The night before the hearing, the group joked on Zoom about putting a hex on David and Kathe Sackler. The next morning, Bismuth summarized that sentiment by drawing a "Sackler Spell"—a cartoon of a candle with this incantation below it: "the fifth amendment shall not protect you; your lawyers shall suck; the committee shall expose you; and you will never know another day of praise or glory for your dirty $$."

Bisch, too, wanted blood. The twentieth anniversary of his eighteen-year-old son's death was looming. Eddie had now been dead longer than he lived. "I was more than thrilled with the tongue-lashing they got [from Congress], but a tongue-lashing without any teeth is nothing," he said.

The chief executives of Enron, WorldCom, and Refco had all served prison time, Professor Lipson pointed out, noting that Purdue's bankruptcy was the only one in recent history with allegations of serious misconduct in which principals were not charged. If enough outrage could be mustered, would a Biden-run Justice Department pursue prosecuting the Sacklers?

"Drain has been sent a very, very clear message that Congress thinks these people are manipulating the system and, by extension, him," Bismuth said. And it had all been orchestrated by a ragtag group of activists led by a pro bono lawyer squaring off against a phalanx of lawyers and consultants who were billing north of $50 million a month.

Lipson was cautiously optimistic. The Department of Justice had not agreed to resolve the Sacklers' criminal liability—at least not publicly, not yet. The OxyJustice group wanted Congress to pressure the DOJ into explaining how the Sacklers themselves were not charged when the corporation they controlled pleaded guilty—twice—to paying kickbacks to doctors and other crimes.

Congressman Gerry Connolly (D-Virginia), a committee member, told me that his takeaway from the hearing had been how "unrepentant and unremorseful" the Sackler family representatives were. It reminded him of the philosopher Hannah Arendt's theory of the banality of evil. "In history we look back at people and think they must have been towering figures who oozed malignancy and evil, but actually they're bureaucrats and businesspeople who are going about doing their jobs and running their businesses," Connolly said after the hearing.

Or as the comedian John Oliver had once put it: "If you want to do something evil, put it inside something boring."

A week before Merrick Garland became Biden's new attorney general, Connolly vowed to personally press for federal criminal charges against the Sacklers.

While Joe Biden was being sworn in as the forty-sixth president of the United States, Judge Drain was on the verge of approving the release of seventeen new documents, called for by a press committee lawyer who said they'd been improperly sealed. But an opposing lawyer spoke up before he could: the Sacklers had recently received death threats that, they believed, had been fueled by recent press coverage, which stopped Drain in his tracks. Drain said he'd need another month to ponder the safety implications of releasing more material. (The next month, Drain did approve the release of those documents after hours of back-and-forth among the lawyers.)

Meanwhile, Bloomberg News reported, the Sacklers hit the brakes on upping their cash contribution beyond $4 billion, reiterating through their attorneys that they'd personally broken no laws and were still counting on the bankruptcy to resolve all civil litigation against them. Roughly half the state attorneys general were holding firm to wanting more than $5 billion to beef up addiction treatment and police budgets—in a mediation that one bankruptcy-court veteran referred to as a "high-stakes game of chicken."

But with the Sackler sideshow finally gaining traction among politicians, reporters, and Hollywood producers, Goldin, Quinn, and their friends had already gotten further than they'd imagined, as had harm-reduction activists and supporters of decriminalization. And they were not resting now.

But neither were the criminals, good or bad.

Chapter Seven

Weaponizing Addiction

Trail of Truth, Binghamton, New York.

For the pandemic, we saw civic center parking lots turned into mass vaccination clinics, and hotels turned into respite centers. We saw specialists who hadn't done primary care in decades stepping in to take care of COVID patients. We saw companies accustomed to letting China produce most of America's goods suddenly whir into action to make personal protective equipment—PPE.

But for an overdose crisis that had killed more people than COVID—it killed far more, actually, when you factored in all the addiction-adjacent hepatitis, endocarditis, and suicide deaths—America's corporate and governmental leadership was only capable of minor tweaks.

This lack of urgency frustrated Mississippi lawyer Mike Moore, who understood better than most of the opioid-litigation lawyers just how deadly the crisis was. He was the only one among the mass-tort players who had personally hauled a 250-pound relative, numbed into unconsciousness by an opioid maker's product, to a rural Mississippi emergency room in the back of his car. And he'd been fighting Purdue longer than just about anyone.

Not only that, but Moore also had a cautionary tale about litigation abatement funds.

When the potential opioid-litigation settlement money finally landed, from all the various cases against manufacturers, distributors, and pharmacies, as well as the Purdue bankruptcy deal, it would probably only amount to 20 percent of what was needed to turn the death count around. The first time we met, in late 2020, Moore had put the amount at $50 billion, but the delays—that is, the escalating legal fees resulting from the delays—kept draining the settlement pot, and the Sackler portion would be relatively small, Moore figured, less than a fourth of the total.

Moore represented hard-hit Ohio, some counties and cities, and several other mostly Republican-led states in the litigation. He'd negotiated the term sheet for the initial Sackler deal in 2019—the one they carried into bankruptcy court, in which they agreed to relinquish the company and give up roughly $3 billion in cash. Since then, Moore and his colleagues had continued to wrangle with the remaining defendants over a separate, much larger settlement with opioid distributors. And he was furious about how long the negotiations were taking. "The money should be out there saving people's lives right now," said Moore.

No matter what, he told me, "we're going to be very dependent on federal and state governments to continue to see this as an important issue." With the number of overdoses skyrocketing during COVID-19, Moore lamented the lack of urgency at all levels of government, fueled by the fact that elected officials couldn't count on fixing the opioid crisis as a political win. If they could, Moore said, "you'd see politicians standing on every street corner demanding that something occur."

In the annals of mass-tort litigation, Moore was something of a legend. In the mid 1990s, as attorney general of Mississippi, he had quarterbacked the "Big Tobacco" settlement, which had cigarette makers paying out $246 billion over twenty-five years and which has remained the largest corporate comeuppance in American history. When filmmakers set out to cast his character in the 1999 movie *The Insider*, about the whistleblowing bravery of a tobacco-company scientist played by Russell Crowe, Moore raised his hand and played himself.

By the mid-2000s, he was the most popular politician in the state. His name was floated for governor, US attorney general, and even the nation's drug czar. But Moore "just set aside that political stuff and went back home," said Curtis Wilkie, a Mississippi journalist who has chronicled Moore's career.

He's what we journalists call "a good talker" because he can condense complicated things into lines that are as memorable as they are gutting. As he told *60 Minutes* in 2018: "If you've got walking-around sense and you care, you're gonna check before you send nine million pills to a little bitty county in West Virginia or Mississippi or Louisiana or Ohio. You're gonna check—if you care."

The tobacco settlement negotiations, Moore reminded me repeatedly, had taken him just three months.

And yet their implementation had been a bust, a serious blemish on his historic coup. While smoking declined notably in their wake thanks to the hefty funding of anti-smoking campaigns, less than 3 percent of the tobacco money had gone toward efforts to curb smoking and nicotine-related disease. In an era of billionaire tax cuts and public-service austerity, the rest was usurped by cash-strapped state governments for the fixing of potholes and other things that are customarily funded with tax revenues. In suburban New York, tobacco settlement money built a jail and a golf course; in Alaska, a new system of shipping docks; and in North Carolina, in the ultimate irony, it upgraded the marketing and production of tobacco. Big Tobacco's owners remained fabulously rich, having made up most of the profit losses by simply raising the price of cigarettes.

Moore was working as a private attorney based in Jackson, Mississippi, when he and a law partner set out to lead negotiations for a settlement that would repair the damage created by the 2010 *Deepwater Horizon* oil spill, one of the worst environmental disasters in American history. Ultimately, British Petroleum paid $20 billion to compensate 100,000 people and businesses. And Moore became wealthy enough that he could afford to donate whatever money he made from the opioid litigation, after expenses, to addiction prevention—a pledge he made publicly on *60 Minutes*. (He was leaning toward donating the money to Boys and Girls Clubs and other prevention groups.)

He was half frenetic show horse and half Southern good ol' boy, but Mike Moore cared. Now in the waning years of his career, he was trying to get the details right this time, for professional and personal reasons alike. He christened what Purdue did to America as "a pill spill."

Back in late 2020, Moore believed he was well beyond the phase of waking up to 3:00 a.m. phone calls, or of hauling ass to his nephew's house and pouring ice down the front of his pants—the DIY version of overdose reversal when Narcan isn't on hand. Moore was so proud of Damian Sutherland's recovery, he talked about it in the national press. He even bought him a new Honda CRV.

At thirty-seven, Damian seemed to be back to his old self—

working in a factory, meditating and doing yoga, taking long daily walks along the Mississippi Gulf Coast. He was dating a woman who didn't drink or use drugs. He'd been sober for three years.

Moore had more understanding of addiction than the rest of his extended family. A voracious reader, he was constantly going back to books on addiction that he'd previously read to see what he could learn in light of new data and trends.

Most of the family saw Damian's repeated relapses as a weakness rather than as a medical problem. "What I have found through all of this is, you really can't tell people how they ought to handle this stuff, especially folks who are not as sophisticated," Moore said. "Everybody's used to doing things their own way, which in most families means nobody really wants to talk about it."

Not talking about it usually translates into not reading up on the brain science, or blindly accepting historically entrenched notions such as jail is the best place for people addicted to drugs—"They're clean when they leave *my* jail!" one of the Indiana sheriffs scolded me—or that OxyContin is safe for all but "less than 1 percent" of patients. Not only have Americans been culturally indoctrinated for decades to believe those mistaken theories, but corporations and law enforcement agencies alike continue raking in billions off voters' willful ignorance.

An American now dies a death of despair—from opioids, alcohol, or suicide—every two and a half minutes. During the pandemic, every time the CDC released its updated annual overdose-death counts, the numbers rose significantly.

As the lawyers pressed for more money and stacked delay upon delay, addiction experts were hopeful that a Biden administration would take a more proactive role, akin to what President Nixon had done in his early years. "I think President Biden needs to be in charge of [the drug czar's office], because right now nobody is," said Brandon del Pozo, the former Burlington, Vermont, police chief, speaking about the Office of National Drug Control Policy.

"If he radically reenvisions the role of the ONDCP, then he could generate national leadership to quarterback all the fragmented efforts among the fifty states and reduce the death toll.

"The truth is, when we come out of COVID, we'll realize that the opioid crisis is worse than ever."

And yet jail, not treatment, remained our country's default solution for problems related to mental health and substance use. As the Brennan Center for Justice puts it: "Holding hands, Americans with arrest records could circle the earth three times." But here's the reality that undergirds those alarming stats: When addiction-related behaviors cross the line, it's still police officers who show up when friends and family members have long since departed.

When Mike Moore first took his nephew to the doctor in 2005, he recognized Purdue's talking points immediately. Damian was struggling to manage the pain inflicted from an accidental gunshot wound earlier that year. A police officer at the time of the accident, Damian had been cleaning his .45 pistol after work (and, he admitted, having a few after-work drinks) when he accidentally put a bullet through the subclavian artery near his heart. He was on life support for weeks, followed by multiple surgeries and a pain-management regimen that combined multiple high-strength opioids with multiple benzodiazepines, plus meds for sleep and opiate-related constipation.

Within months, Damian was running out of his meds before his refills were due. In his late twenties at the time, he reached out to Moore, who had long been a father figure to him, and confessed that he was not taking his meds as prescribed. He begged his uncle to go to his doctor with him—to say what Damian himself could not.

Moore didn't hesitate: "It's ridiculous the amount of medication you've got him on," he told the doctor. The doctor's response didn't surprise Moore.

But it was eerie how perfectly it matched the same spiel Moore had first gotten from longtime Purdue Pharma lawyer Howard Udell. In 2004, Moore was looking into a potential case against Purdue on behalf of Mississippi when he first sat down with Purdue executives. If an injured patient reported pain to the point of problematic use, it wasn't that the patient was addicted, Udell told Moore; that patient was actually *pseudoaddicted*.

"What?" Moore replied, stunned. "I know what the word *pseudo* means, and I know the word *addiction*. Are you saying they think they're addicted but they're really not?"

"Exactly," Udell said.

All doctors had to do was get the number of milligrams correct— if their patients were currently on ten milligrams but were still feeling pain, they should try prescribing twenty. If they were taking twenty, they should up the dose to forty. "Once their pain is taken care of, the problem will solve itself," Moore recalled Udell saying.

Pseudoaddiction, it turned out, was first invented by Dr. J. David Haddox, a dentist who grabbed the attention of Richard Sackler with a 1989 article he'd coauthored on the topic. Haddox coined the term based on a study of just one patient he'd documented for the medical journal *Pain*. The patient was a seventeen-year-old with cancer—an appropriate candidate for pain-relieving opioids. A decade later, casting about for experts to convince doctors of the curative powers of OxyContin, Purdue hired Haddox to serve on its speakers' bureau and eventually to be a full-time medical director with the goal of overturning physicians' century-long skepticism of opioids for all kinds of pain, not just severe pain, cancer, and end-of-life.

Pseudoaddiction was bunk, of course. But for two decades it was referenced in legitimate medical journals and in the popular press, despite having no empirical evidence to back it up. When Purdue sales reps came calling toting shoddy science (along with tickets to a doctor's favorite sports team or musical act), busy physicians—especially family doctors, who hadn't received much training on addiction or pain—tended to believe them. It was all from the marketing playbook of Richard Sackler's uncle Arthur Sackler, the one who'd spun valium into "mother's little helper" in the 1960s—and eventually the nation's first billion-dollar drug.

"Purdue told me to my face that I was just wrong about the addictive nature of OxyContin," Moore recalled. "They said my problem was, I was just interviewing 'drug addicts' and all these other folks, and those people are *lawbreakers*. And it's really just the criminals who are the problem."

And now, Moore was hearing the very same spiel from his own nephew's doctor.

"No, there ain't another term for it," Moore told the doctor. "He's *addicted!*"

For the next several weeks, Moore held Damian's meds at his own home, slowly weaning him. But Damian grew tired of driving to his uncle's house in another town every day, and, after a few weeks, he determined to quit on his own. The cravings soon returned, along with the desperation and dopesickness. Too ashamed to return to his uncle for help, Damian quietly sought out pain pills and fentanyl patches from street dealers. By 2015, he was injecting the crushed-up pills, even the so-called abuse-resistant versions of Opana and OxyContin, which he quickly figured out how to manipulate. "You give me any pill out there and about three minutes, and I've got you a shot," he recalled.

"I was living like a double life," he said—working at a car factory, visiting family. As long as his supply remained steady, he could hide what he was doing, even from his mom and Uncle Mike.

*   *   *

A year into the pandemic, isolation-fueled opioid overdoses hit an all-time record, the CDC announced in early 2021. But the niggling over legal fees and payout schedules dragged on, placing the proposed $26 billion settlement with three major distributors and Johnson & Johnson that Moore was working on in a kind of abatement purgatory. Moore compared the impasse over how to split $1.6 billion between lawyers for cities and counties to a food fight. "Makes zero sense, but that's how crazy this thing has gotten.

"There's so many people out here not in it to solve the problems; they're in it to make money," he said, at the Washington, DC–based Truth Initiative, the nonprofit established by the tobacco settlement monies designed to fight teenage nicotine use (Moore is the board chair). "The state AGs and the cities and the counties, none of them can agree, either. There's a lot of greed. These are my complicating factors."

Because of his tobacco litigation experience, Moore was initially recruited to help sue Purdue by the high-profile litigator Paul Hanly of the Manhattan law firm Simmons Hanly Conroy. Also a repeat player in the mass-tort universe, Hanly represented more than 200 cities and counties in the litigation against opioid makers and distributors, and had been birddogging Purdue since 2002. (I interviewed Hanly twice in 2020; soon after, he was diagnosed with an aggressive form of thyroid cancer and died at age seventy in May 2021.)

With the exception of well-funded states like New York and Massachusetts and their firebrand attorneys general Letitia James and Maura Healey, respectively, most states involved in the present opioid litigation relied on private lawyers who work on contingency, just as the tobacco litigation did. But Hanly told me his legal team was the first to crack open the cruel world of Purdue Pharma—proving how even the most harmless insiders at the company were hurt by Richard Sackler's edict to "hammer the abusers."

In 2004, Hanly deposed Howard Udell's former legal secretary, Maureen Sara. In 1999, Udell had asked Sara to monitor drug-use chat rooms, and she found them abuzz with information on snorting and crushing the pills. When she submitted her report to higher-ups, Udell scolded her to "get rid of" the evidence. Later that year, when Sara learned of Purdue's plans to launch a 160-milligram version of the pill, she e-mailed her boss, "They are killing themselves with the 80s. Why would we come out with a 160?"

Udell furiously ordered her to destroy the e-mail, saying, "If this comes out in discovery, we are screwed."

Sara had been an award-winning employee at Purdue, but she was forced to resign after getting addicted to OxyContin, following a car accident, according to the sworn deposition she gave to Hanly in 2004. Her description of the company's inner workings would become crucial in the federal government's 2007 misbranding case against Purdue, in that she unpacked how Purdue and the Sacklers had known almost from the very beginning that addiction to their drug was widespread—and exactly how they'd endeavored to cover it up.

Sara laid out the particulars of a patent application owned by Udell and the Sacklers' longtime lawyer, Stuart Baker. Their so-called Self-Destructing Email Messaging system was a *Mission Impossible*-esque bit of programming subterfuge, though Hanly told me it never really worked. "It was proof that there was this total culture of fear and secrecy in the company," he said, referring to Udell as the Sackler family *consigliere* and "the Tom Hagen of modern pharmaceutical lawyering."

But as they did with other OxyContin-addicted people who sued Purdue, the company's lawyers weaponized Sara's addiction. During the deposition, a Purdue lawyer grilled the former secretary about her misuse: "Would you agree with me if a medication such as OxyContin isn't giving you the relief you wanted, the solution wasn't to crush it and snort it?"

"Well, I would—yes," Sara answered. "But in the frame of mind I was in at the time, I wasn't thinking logically or rationally. I just did whatever it took to get instant relief."

In a civil litigation separate from the federal case, Hanly went on to win a $75 million settlement from Purdue in 2007, on behalf of 5,000 clients who'd become addicted after taking the medicine as prescribed. Sara, though, got little more than a $100,000 one-time payout from Purdue when she was forced to resign (or else be fired) and escorted out of company headquarters by security. Hanly said Sara was dismissed from testifying before the grand jury in the first federal case against Purdue when she became incapable of proceeding with it. "It was very sad," he said.

Sara died in November 2021, at the age of sixty-two. It was another premature death that received little public notice. After her death, her sister reached out to me and Danny Strong, Hulu's *Dopesick* creator, to thank us, saying the show's portrayal helped her see Maureen in a different light—"not as a drug addict, but as a victim as well as a person who did a good job trying to help people."

When Hanly first threw down the gauntlet against Purdue in 2002, advertising on national television that he was suing the company for downplaying the addictive nature of OxyContin, Purdue's lawyers threatened to have him disbarred. "Their defense was, 'It's a great drug. Nobody will get addicted as long as they follow their doctors' directions, and therefore your claims are worthless,'" he recalled.

Working with Moore to recruit more litigants, Hanly eventually turned over more than 6 million pages of documents to federal investigators working on the first federal case against Purdue. In the 2007 settlement that resulted, Purdue and its top three executives pled guilty to criminally misbranding the drug and agreed to pay $634.5 million in fines—a pittance, compared to the $35 billion Purdue would end up making. The federal judge who approved the settlement did so without the benefit of having seen the damning, 120-page prosecution memo—the one that OxyJustice members were still fighting to get released. The memo had been buried by Purdue influence peddlers, including then–presidential candidate Rudy Giuliani, who lobbied Main Justice under the administration of George W. Bush.

To inspire him in the Cleveland-based Multidistrict Litigation and for use as props, Hanly displayed several Purdue marketing items in his Manhattan office—an OxyContin plush gorilla, a small calculator flogging Purdue's record-breaking sales figures, and Maureen Sara's Employee of the Year award—for her diligent work at Purdue on Y2K preparedness. He also held on to the memory of deposing Richard Sackler. "I've taken 500 depositions in my career, and I have never deposed a person whose ability to exhibit empathy is zero," Hanly told me. "Compared to Sackler, Donald Trump looks like Jesus Christ."

When the Sackler family finalized its first offering to Mike Moore and his co-counsel in the fall of 2019, it pledged $3 billion to 4.5 billion of their cash to the settlement and agreed to relinquish Purdue to a creditor trust—an offer estimated at roughly $10 billion over several years, the bulk of it from future sales of both OxyContin and anti-addiction drugs.

It wasn't a gift. It was an exchange: the family wanted to be released, fully and forever, from all litigation claims. Even though the Sacklers—who were nowhere near bankrupt—weren't the ones filing for Chapter 11, their lawyers had found precedent for the judicial end run. There would be no admission of guilt. And if the family's two-decade playbook held, many previously squelched documents could very well remain under seal.

To Moore, third-generation scion David Sackler seemed reasonable and eager to turn the narrative from "our family is killing people" to "our family wants to be part of solving the opioid crisis." And as a seasoned negotiator, Moore banked on the belief that the settlement value would only increase over the life of the bankruptcy case.

Hanly and Moore both predicted that Judge Drain would approve the plan to release the Sacklers from liability once Purdue hit the right number. "Because it increases the money that will go to the claimants, many of whom are deserving of money," Hanly told me.

"The real difficulty is that most of the Sacklers' money is abroad, and the money that's overseas is nearly impossible" to claw back, Hanly said. "Right now the judge is only looking at how much the Sacklers are willing to contribute, and is that number sufficient in his mind to justify the granting of a permanent injunction, letting them live the rest of their lives without being subject to further [civil] litigation?"

"Global peace" is what the Purdue and Sackler lawyers like to call it. They don't mean a world without war, or even the reign of God's love—for them, the everlasting sanctity of the Sacklers' international empire is just as good, or even better.

But the relatives of the dead weren't just feeling betrayed; they were disgusted. Funding treatment for Oxy-created addiction with future sales of Oxy? It wasn't just bad optics. It was utterly shameless. They needed to get their voices heard in bankruptcy court.

In February of 2021, Mike Quinn thought he'd scored a major win when his work appeared in a lengthy *Wall Street Journal* story outlining how Purdue's lawyers had a secret agreement with the Sacklers' lawyers that they'd failed to disclose in the Chapter 11 proceedings. Quinn had discovered the impropriety while scanning the firms' billing records—Purdue's legal bills were about to reach $380 million. The law firm Skadden, Arps, Slate, Meagher & Flom LLP and another firm working for Purdue hadn't divulged the preexisting deal they had with the

Sackler family's lawyers to share confidential information and legal defense strategies. Failing to disclose the deal was a no-no in bankruptcy court.

"It's the whole case, the whole corruption," Quinn enthused. "The fact that two of the biggest law firms in the world are pretending to represent adversaries when they're really working together in secret—to me, it's so big, but the court did nothing about the collusion!"

Quinn had beseeched the US Trustee—the bankruptcy court's watchdog—to look into the potential of conflict of interest and, hearing nothing back, he went to the press. But the *Journal*'s story suffered from John Oliver's quip about evil: it was not only bogged down by too much legalese; it was boring.

Eventually, people who mattered *would* care about Quinn's obsession. But back then, COVID soaked up most of the media's attention, and pandemic-related setbacks in the MDL case against pharmacies and distributors were giving defendants opportunities for repeated delays, much to the detriment of needy places like West Virginia, desperate to recoup costs stemming from the opioid crisis. The drug companies will "pull every trick in the book to delay because there's this opioid fatigue, and people are getting tired of hearing about it," West Virginia journalist Eric Eyre told me.

COVID was to the opioid defendants exactly what 9/11 had been to Purdue in 2001: The enormity of the fallen Twin Towers had taken the OxyContin crisis off the front page. "You saw right then how heartless the company was," a former sales rep told me. "They were willing to put profits ahead of human life."

Judge Drain's ivory tower of impermeability began to show some wear and tear when journalist Gerald Posner predicted in a *New York Times* op-ed that Drain would allow the Sacklers to walk away from negotiations with their secrets buried and their wealth intact. The judge lost his temper in open court, calling Posner a "numbskull." He did not want to "hear some idiot reporter or some bloggist quoted to me again on this case."

How *dare* a lowly journalist question the judgment of an Ivy League–trained federal judge?

If public shaming didn't sit so well with the prickly judge, Quinn predicted it would at least impact the Sacklers. "By 2023, how are the Sacklers going to hide from what they've done?" he said. "They're gonna be next to Easter Island, in a small boat. They'll have different names. It'll be like, 'Table for three, *Seckler.*'"

The eight Sacklers named in the litigation were estimated to be worth $13 billion—investigators were still trying to tally the family's offshore assets. They owned multiple homes on multiple continents, including a sprawling $7.4 million Florida mansion where David Sackler had recently retreated, knowing that the state constitution allows families to retain a principal residence (and up to 160 acres of property) against creditors' claims. Critics railed when David and his wife, Joss, fled their $6.5 million Manhattan apartment on the Upper East Side. As David complained to *Vanity Fair* writer Bethany McLean: "My four-year-old came home from nursery school and asked, 'Why are my friends telling me that our family's work is killing people?'"

The irony was not lost on South Floridians when the couple set up house in Palm Beach County, once the epicenter of an OxyContin-fueled pill-mill industry. It was now the relapse capital of America, a place where rehab-patient brokering and insurance-fraud schemes took advantage of desperate families of the dopesick and addicted. In 2019, the region counted more rehabs and sober-living homes than it had elementary schools.

"I, for one, do not welcome the Sacklers to my county," wrote Palm Beach County Commissioner Melissa McKinlay. "I wish they'd hide elsewhere, like a jail cell."

*   *   *

The shaming reminded Moore of the talks he had led between attorneys general and the Big Four tobacco-company CEOs in the mid 1990s. The first two things they traded were promises that the R. J. Reynolds Tobacco Company would kill Joe Camel—if Philip Morris agreed to get rid of the Marlboro Man, two of the biggest advertising icons in world history. The execs disappeared for an hour to talk among themselves, and when they gathered again, they agreed. The billboard mascots would go.

Then Moore looked the men in the eyes and asked: What would it take for you to funnel your billions into prevention and treatment?

Their answer surprised him. Above all, they craved the ability to go to cocktail parties and live their lives and not be mocked as "merchants of death," as one CEO framed it. Moore nodded politely and smiled, as if the attorney general of Mississippi personally had the authority to wave away vilification.

In late 2020, Moore learned just how dangerous protracted delays could be. After being sober for three years, his nephew, Damian Sutherland, relapsed. "It started at the beginning of this COVID mess, and I guess I just wanted a temporary release from reality," Damian told me. He started drinking, which led to black-market pill-seeking, which led to crossing paths with fentanyl-laced pills and, eventually, fentanyl-cut heroin. "The next thing I knew I had firemen and EMS in my face, and I was sitting on a syringe."

He entered a ninety-day, abstinence-based Christian rehab called Home of Grace, knowing he would not be allowed to take buprenorphine. Two weeks later, he was kicked out of the rehab and on his way to yet another relapse.

"Unbeknownst to me, he'd sold the brand-new car I'd bought him and probably spent half the money on drugs," Moore said. Damian bought a truck with the other half, then ended up wrecking the truck and selling it for scrap. It was exactly the kind of recurring relapse story that Moore had been hearing from families since OxyContin's early days.

During an intervention led by Moore over the telephone, the family told Damian he had to return to rehab, or they would have him involuntarily committed, which is possible for SUD in Mississippi but not all US states. There were no state beds available in his Mississippi county at the time, it turned out, so commitment actually meant that Damian would have to go to jail until one became available.

"His family, they were just so tired of the lies; it does hurt 'em," Moore said. "And they don't want to see that he's got a problem. They want to see it as a weakness, that he 'ought to straighten up.' No matter how much you try to educate people, it's just so ingrained that drug and alcohol abuse, 'That's just a failing; they're weaker than other people,' and it's hard to get past that."

Moore had addiction in his family going back generations, including a grandfather with severe alcoholism who went on to become a nationally known AA speaker. "That's why I know you never give up on 'em," he said.

Moore was hopeful that "something would click this time" when his nephew chose to go back to the Christian rehab rather than face jail or go into outpatient treatment. Still, every time his phone rang late at night, Moore cringed.

No one, including Moore's nephew, should have to decide between a jail cell and a rehab that had already failed to work. Mississippi has not expanded Medicaid under the Affordable Care Act—the nation's No. 1 tool for providing access for OUD treatment for the uninsured. The state consistently ranked either dead last or next to last on all health rankings, and it had cumbersome access barriers for people seeking methadone and buprenorphine treatment, including in rehab centers.

As Moore put it, "You ought to be able to go to the ER, just like if I broke my leg and they fix it up. Well, this is the same thing. It's a disease, and people ought to be able to go somewhere and be treated for it," whether it's a rehab bed or outpatient counseling with bupe. "Arresting somebody to get 'em help? That's crazy."

When he graduated from the rehab in mid-February of 2021, Damian proudly sent me a picture of the ceremony. Now forty, he didn't have a job so he moved in with his mom and stepdad, who agreed to house him for two weeks. (His girlfriend had broken up with him during his second rehab stay.) His goal then, he said, was to become an addiction counselor. Sober this time for three and a half months, he was hopeful, attending Celebrate Recovery meetings, meditating, and spending time outside.

During Damian's second rehab stint, four of his friends died of fentanyl overdose. In one week alone, two friends he'd met in rehab had overdosed and died within twenty-four hours of leaving Home of Grace.

Gently, I reiterated that people on bupe or methadone had much better outcomes. But Damian's mind was made up: those medicines weren't the right fit for him—partly, he said, because he'd had a harder time weaning himself off buprenorphine, after one brief foray into MOUD (medicines for opioid use disorder) treatment, than he had had with heroin. "It's either you choose one or the other. There's no difference, except for [on buprenorphine] you're not strung out and on the streets."

Damian believed wholeheartedly that his renewed focus on spirituality and meditation was the answer. In a follow-up text, he told me: "Quantum physics is revealing astounding information of man's ability to communicate with his intelligence, therefore making the possibility for mankind to heal himself from addiction and unwanted behaviors, suffering, etc., without the use of other drugs or expensive treatments."

In November 2021, the CDC announced another grim

milestone: between April 2020 and April 2021, we'd exceeded 100,000 deaths. Paul Hanly had warned me about the financial impossibility of turning back the opioid crisis: "The bottom line is, there just isn't that money in the whole Purdue-Sackler world." States had estimated it would take $2.2 trillion to address the harms of OxyContin.

Even if we could get close, would any of this settlement money reach the right recipients?

Most experts worried that the settlement monies would be wrongly funneled into abstinence-only treatment and incarceration-first modalities, entrenched holdovers from a decades-long War on Drugs embodied in Nancy Reagan's "Just Say No."

"You watch, the rehabs will suck it all up, when rehabs are particularly worthless" for people with opioid use disorder, said Sam Snodgrass, an Arkansas activist. Some 70 percent of people with OUD return to substance use in the first year after residential treatment, up to 35 percent will be readmitted within a year, and nearly half will be readmitted within two to five years.

A Virginia treatment activist who runs a rehab held a different opinion, of course: "When Purdue settled in 2007, the money all went to police radios, guns, and cars. Right now, politicians are already deciding how to spend the money behind closed doors and being directed by special interests," John Shinholser told me. "They never include the authentic recovery community."

Harm-reductionists demanded gritty cures that met the addicted where many of them were relegated to living: in trailers and homeless encampments, in jails, and under bridges and in the woods. They clamored for evidence-based treatment that differed vastly from Damian's and Shinholser's views.

Both camps relied on so-called evidence, of course, but if you drew a Venn diagram of their two ways of thinking, they would not even appear on the same page.

Chapter Eight

Peer Pressure

Sheriff Stacey Kincaid, peer recovery specialist training, Fairfax County Jail, Virginia.

Most people wait for their neighbor or friend to adopt a new idea before they do—and not just any neighbor or friend but someone whom they most trust. Social change typically starts on the periphery and picks up steam by way of close ties—not via chance encounters or geographic proximity but through what University of Pennsylvania sociologist Damon Centola calls "complex contagions." It can take decades before an idea eventually gathers enough support to cause a full-throated shift in social norm. But when that shift finally takes place, it often seems to have occurred overnight. Think of the acceptance of same-sex marriage or growing support for Black Lives Matter—both movements took years before change-makers mustered enough support for their ideas to become mainstream.

Centola has calculated that ideas reach such a critical mass not when a majority or 51 percent of minds are changed—as economic theorists had long claimed—but when just 25 percent of people are committed to changing the status quo. "You can give top-down information, or you can try to shame people into changing their views, and you can share all the best medical advice," Centola told me. "None of that matters if social norms are still blocking a fundamental shift from taking place. But if you can generate change within someone's own social network, that can be much more effective" in reaching the critical 25 percent mark.

In 2015, Shelly Young's thoughts about addiction were so far out on the periphery, they were moons orbiting a distant planet. The northern Virginia mom was not obsessing about social-movement theories but rather about something that would bring her comfort: casseroles.

Back then the notion of treating addiction as a medical problem was beginning to be discussed in the press but hovered nowhere near Centola's 25 percent mark, judging from the reactions of friends who watched Young struggle with her twenty-one-year-old son's repeated relapses and urged her to "kick him out." Young herself had spent the past three years waffling between being sympathetic to Mitch and believing that he just needed to muster the willpower to Stop. Using. Drugs.

At the same time, Young's best friend, Lisa, had a fourteen-year-old daughter, Amelia, who was in and out of the hospital for brain tumor treatments. Young couldn't help but notice how their mutual friends showered Lisa's family with casseroles, prayer chains, and constant support. Young herself led a cancer awareness campaign for a local Girl Scout troop on Amelia's behalf. Yet she knew that her friend's pain and her own pain were not dissimilar. Either one of their kids could die at any moment.

That winter, when Mitch was hospitalized for a life-threatening seizure from Xanax withdrawal, Young realized he'd been at risk both for death and permanent brain damage. If he didn't get the proper treatment, it was possible that she would end up caring for him for the rest of her life. She and I both knew parents that this had happened to.

Lisa had not been told to let her daughter "hit rock bottom" before taking her to an oncologist. The girl's doctors did not use eighty-five-year-old ideologies as an excuse to withhold the evidence-based medicines recommended to treat Amelia's cancer or suggest that one day Amelia would simply "age out of" having a tumor on her brain. No one suggested to Lisa that she simply lock Amelia up as the treatment for her disease. The Internet was not full of ads for $30,000 rehabilitation centers at which Amelia could be healed by the aid of therapy horses.

Something clicked in the hospital that day. "I told myself, 'I'm going to treat Mitch just like Lisa treats Amelia.' And then I asked everyone I could think of to help me do that. As opposed to me walking around with this bleeding child in my arms saying, 'Help me. My kid is bleeding,' there was no place where you could go for help," Young recalled. "So families are crowdsourcing this on Google and Facebook. And it's terrible information that's out there, most of it. Terrible! It's so dangerous, and so harsh, and, as a mother, it just didn't feel right to me."

So Young created her own rules, based on the principles of harm reduction—though, because that concept was still on the edge of the periphery, she didn't yet know the term. She read everything she could find about brain science, addiction, and attachment theory, then used it to repurpose the medical language she heard being used in Amelia's treatment protocols.

Like Michelle Mathis and Nikki King had done, lacking a

framework she could rely on for help, she made one up. It began with eschewing the tough-love tactics she'd been taught in certain twelve-step meetings like Al-Anon. She insisted that her family banish the word *addict* from their vocabulary and use humanizing language instead. At extended-family holiday gatherings, no alcohol was served in her home (and she gave up drinking herself).

When Mitch was high, she let him be and didn't engage. If he came home from a Xanax or opioid binge, she gave him food and water, and told him to sleep. When he was sober, she reiterated that he was scaring her and that she wanted to take him to a counseling professional for help. After much debate and research, they landed on a seven-month treatment program with a years-long after-care regimen that Mitch still follows to this day.

Six years later (and not all of them smooth), both Mitch and Amelia are considered NED—no evidence of disease. And Shelly Young's one regret? That she didn't view Mitch's addiction as a health condition—as life-threatening as brain cancer—sooner than she did.

I first met Young at a 2018 Google conference on addiction in Washington, DC. The company had invited addiction and technology experts to offer advice to the search-engine platform so it could disseminate the best information to the addicted and their stressed-out loved ones, rather than leave such life-or-death matters to a random search. Facebook, Twitter, Instagram—the social media giants all sent executives and top programmers to the daylong event. The goal was to build wider bridges among influencers, to take various ideas from various edges of the periphery, then build bridges among the disparate though like-minded groups.

I described how family, medical, and societal abandonment had led to the deaths of so many of the mostly young, addicted people I'd profiled in *Dopesick*. I talked about how twenty-two-year-old

Tess Henry had diagnosed her own opioid use disorder the first time she felt the agony of withdrawal. "How did you know you were dopesick?" I had asked her in 2015, the first time we met. "I put my symptoms into Google and said, 'Holy crap, I'm probably addicted,'" she said.

Tess went on to use Google, Facebook, and other websites to find sex work and arrange drug deals that further fueled her addiction. Her relatives Googled to find what they later realized was exactly the worst kind of treatment for her—a rehab bed in faraway Nevada that forbade addiction medicines and didn't even bother notifying her mother when Tess relapsed and checked herself out AMA—against medical advice. She was then homeless and on the streets of Las Vegas, vulnerable to traffickers and dealers alike, her only connection to friends and relatives at home via Facebook Messenger...when she could borrow a pimp's phone.

Instagram regularly targets us with ads that hit the pleasure centers of our brains and that spookily pick up on verbal conversations we have while our phones are in our pockets, I argued. If technology can be harnessed for profit, why can't it also be harnessed for good?

When it was Young's turn to speak, she attacked the prevailing stigma and shoddy treatment centers. She asked Google to end the parroting of dangerous advice heard at many twelve-step meetings, which was to cut off contact and let their loved ones "hit rock bottom." As Tess's mom had put it in the wake of Tess's 2017 murder: "Rock bottom has a basement, and the basement has a trap door."

In an era of fentanyl, Young told the group, rock bottom too often means death.

Young's words went on to influence how Google curated and monitored information around treatment in the United States. But the northern Virginia mother's DIY harm-reduction notions remained on a periphery that was equal parts geographic and philosophical.

A few years earlier, a therapist had introduced her to Ginny Lovitt, who runs the Chris Atwood Foundation. Lovitt lobbied to blanket the state with Narcan, to fix Virginia's syringe-exchange laws, and to strengthen the state's Good Samaritan Law that made it so people who call 911 for an overdose wouldn't be arrested. Lovitt did all of this in honor of her late brother, Chris, who had died of heroin overdose in 2013. In the northern Virginia and Washington, DC, region, The Chris Atwood Foundation ("The CAF," as Lovitt's harm-reduction group is known), had touched so many lives that it became, in Centola's parlance, its own complex contagion.

The CAF's sphere coalesced around the idea of treating substance users—including those arrested for breaking laws—as people worthy of medical care. Young joined The CAF's board and, together, they began to infiltrate the region's jails, courts, and pretty much anywhere else they found people who use drugs. I came to think of The CAF as the heretofore missing link between the streets and a jail cell, between bureaucracies that in most localities still weren't talking to each other, and, most important, between the realms of sickness and health.

Like most of the change I observed, innovation rippled out from individuals like Ginny Lovitt, Michelle Mathis, and Shelly Young—people who'd managed to find the Venn diagram in their own spheres.

It seemed to me the spaces overlapped best when women were in charge.

At the Fairfax County Adult Detention Center, it's hard to describe how differently incarceration of addicted people looks compared to the vomit buckets and overcrowded cells I witnessed in so many other American jails. It's as if Fairfax were a law enforcement realm unto itself, a place where committed volunteers and public servants replaced Nancy Reagan's mantra with Shelly Young's.

When a person entering the Fairfax County Jail is booked, they're screened for OUD using tools approved by the National Institute on Drug Abuse. Opioid-addicted inmates who are willing are funneled into the jail's buprenorphine program, which is managed by the jail's medical staff. They're also visited regularly by therapists who are employees of the local government-funded mental health agency (in Virginia, they're called community services boards, or CSBs), where they work full-time not in some faraway office, as is typical, but *inside the jail.*

There, people are referred to as "individuals" or "members" instead of "inmates," a subtle shift in tone meant to lessen stigma and create buy-in and trust. I overheard one CSB counselor wrapping up a session with a tearful woman she was counseling through a tiny jail-cell window by kindly saying, "Thank you for speaking to me."

Contrast that to Surry County, where there was no counseling at all, and where jailers walked past a familiarly positioned inmate crouched on the floor, his knees curled up in a fetal position, a dirty blanket and balled-up Kleenex surrounding him. (Surry also had, per capita, more than three times as many people in jail as Fairfax.)

Jail counseling in Fairfax is augmented by The CAF's peer-support specialists who have themselves battled addiction and often the criminal charges that accompany it. Most are women in their thirties and forties, with the exception of a sixty-year-old recent parolee who'd spent half his lifetime using heroin and crack—and had no idea how to use computers and cell phones, to say nothing of Zoom, following his thirty-year prison stint. (Not realizing that others could see him, he cut his toenails during videoconference meetings until his coworkers gently clued him in.) But Daniel Adams could quote from the Bible to Brené Brown, whose work had inspired him to stop using drugs twenty-five years into a prison sentence for killing his wife in a crack-fueled rage.

All CAF peers have been trained to counsel addicted inmates and to coordinate reentry housing from jails to sober-living homes and treatment centers in a "warm handoff" that facilitates continuing their bupe.

Navigating such a handoff defies any simple job description. CAF peers drive people directly from jail to their next homes. They manage snags with drug court. They find wheelchairs for people who can't walk because of injection-related abscesses, and they've been known on occasion to babysit a drug dealer's dog. (After filling her car's cup holder with water for the dog, peer Kristy Howard transported it to an animal shelter while driving another client to detox.) They tell their stories—emphasizing that *recovery really is possible*—over and over again, every single day.

"We're unique because many therapists [aren't allowed] to share, but we can," Howard told me, unleashing her own rap sheet of talking points: "I can say, 'When I was on probation I was pulled over eleven times and had two DUIs,' or 'I've been in trouble in four counties.' And that relationship definitely builds from there. Now I can also say, 'I'm forty, and I'm finally on my own for the first time, and I just brought a brand-new car.'"

Howard was arrested in 2014 in what was then the region's largest heroin and prescription pill bust, called Operation Dragon Slayer. In her jailhouse mugshot, she's rail-thin, her eyes brimming with tears. Five friends from her jail pod later died from heroin-fentanyl overdose—one while four months pregnant, another while on work release at a Burger King.

"I'm not a felon, but that's only because we spent $10,000 on a lawyer," said Howard, whose mother refinanced the family home to pay for it. And then she said something that resonated not just with the hundreds of interviews I've conducted on this topic but also with my own family experience: "Everyone knows it: You pay for your deal."

When they're not working in the jail or with the recently released, CAF peers crisscross suburban and metro DC, trying to get Narcan and sterile needles into the hands of as many people who use drugs as possible as a way to tamp down the spread of hepatitis C and HIV and the looming threat of overdose. Working in pairs, they hang out in methadone clinic foyers in the predawn. Later in the day they circulate among probation drug-testing sites and cheap hotels. They know these places because they are spots where they, too, had used drugs.

Every day—sometimes every *hour*—veers from sitcom to tragedy, from getting stuck with a dog to the time Howard tracked down a pregnant woman declared missing by police. "I found her through Facebook Messenger, using numbers I'd previously talked to her on," Howard said. "She did end up going back home to her family and had the baby shortly after. She was doing good for a bit and even got a job, but she has returned to use recently."

Because people with addiction are vulnerable to relapse, the glue doesn't always hold. But the peers persist, focusing on the hope that something, eventually, will stick.

The Fairfax model of integrating harm reduction and bupe is rare for a jail setting, some of which provide twelve-step and other abstinence-only approaches, while many offer nothing at all. Starting in 2020, multiple agencies in the county began collaborating not only across bureaucratic boundaries but also with nonprofits like The CAF. Just to get approval for their peers to work inside the jail (and over Zoom, during COVID), decades-old detention rules had to be loosened, like the one that says people working in the jail must pass rigorous background checks. That's because all The CAF's peers have served jail and/or prison time.

Best practices from other communities were studied and used to buttress arguments, like the fact that Rhode Island's prisons, after implementing buprenorphine protocols, saw a 61 percent drop in opioid overdose deaths within a year of release, contributing to a 12 percent drop in statewide deaths overall. Like the fact that detainees on addiction medications are three times less likely to have disciplinary issues inside the jail than those who are forced to go through withdrawal.

Resistance among the jail staff was initially high.

"We definitely heard our share of 'hug-a-thug,'" Sheriff Stacey Ann Kincaid told me, referring to deputies who found the program to be too coddling of inmates. After all, the vast majority of state prison systems, jails, and drug courts categorically still refuse to allow addiction medicines. Even though two-thirds of the people in jail nationally meet the psychiatric criteria for a drug-related disorder, Surry County's jail practices remained the norm more than the outlier.

Hearing about the new bupe regimens in an early training session, one Black deputy in the jail was skeptical and said, "You guys are all White and you're experimenting on us because most of the people in jail are Black." When the consultant tried to counter her concern with data, she interrupted him: "Maybe you've heard of Tuskegee?"

Physician assistant Scott Haga, one of the trainers, was taken aback. But the deputy softened when Haga explained that most wealthy (White) people with OUD had had buprenorphine treatment available to them for many years. He thanked her for sharing her historically grounded concerns about racial experimentation, rather than walking away and bad-mouthing the topic to her colleagues. "Once she expressed it and we talked, she was open to it," Haga said.

Less open, he added, were the drug court judge and prosecutor in a Michigan county, who were so incensed by the idea of treating the jailed population with buprenorphine—a drug that people were constantly being arrested for diverting and selling—"that they were preparing to assault me!" (Most diverted bupe is used informally for therapeutic reasons.)

When I told him about my slow-clapping Indiana sheriffs, he said, "I promise you, it was scarier than that. My guys had guns!"

Mine did, too.

We were all getting yelled at.

The medical point person at the Fairfax jail is Laura Yager, a can-do former addiction counselor whose mantra is "Ask for forgiveness rather than permission." Before bupe protocols were established and the funding spigots fully engaged, Yager used her company credit card to buy buprenorphine for inmates upon release. When she couldn't get newly released inmates transported to an outpatient clinic to continue their medications, she set up an Uber account to fill the gap.

She felt like she was building a plane and flying it at the same time. When naysayers complained about hugging thugs, she shot back: "I don't care if you don't understand this; this is what we're doing; this is what the sheriff wants."

"We got rid of a few," Kincaid said, referring to employees who flat out refused to implement the new procedures.

"It was too radical a shift for some," Yager explained.

In a county of nearly 1.2 million people, Kincaid had been the first female sheriff. It was the only place she'd ever worked, having risen from a college intern to the top elected law enforcement official in what was by far the largest county, population-wise, in the state. A Democratic stronghold, Fairfax County is younger, wealthier, and bluer than its rural counterparts; it's also better educated and more diverse. Its demography is the main reason that Virginia flipped for a time from deep red to a solid blue state with the election of President Barack Obama in 2008.

"You don't need bigger jails, and I've told the past two governors that," said Kincaid, the county's sheriff since 2013. "What you need are places where people can go and get their lives back."

Kincaid and Yager recruited in-house allies where they could, including the sheriff's legal counsel, Casey Lingan, a former prosecutor who well knew that most drug dealers in jail were there for selling to support their own habits. The jail's medical staffers were easily won over by the near-immediate results of using bupe to treat OUD. Most inmates had never had daily access to it before, only intermittently and via illicit channels. "To see them come in here, and they are so sick and in withdrawal, and then to see them stabilizing on their treatment, they're just so thankful," nurse practitioner Janet Wurie said. Asked what he would say to the naysaying sheriffs elsewhere, the jail's director of nursing, Tomas Navarro, said: "I would say that opioid addiction, like any other ailment, is something that can and should be treated with medication, exactly like diabetes."

When The CAF peers received their own security badges to go in and out of the jail at will, a psychological shift took place among jail employees that was almost audible, like the clunking of a cell key being turned.

"That's when you really felt the power of the sheriff," said Marissa Farina-Morse, a CSB manager. "She just kept telling us, 'Let's figure out how to get to yes.'"

Across the nation, getting anywhere near yes was still a slog. Just 11 percent of the people in the nation's jails and prisons were able to access SUD treatment, and fewer still were offered bupe—when the risk of opioid overdose death for people shortly after leaving incarceration is 129 times that of the general population. But while bupe is a critical first step—scientifically proven time and again to be a crucial act of mercy in reducing overdose deaths—it isn't a guaranteed guard against relapse, particularly for many who need substantial mental health treatment, including trauma-informed care, and help with basic needs like housing and food. What bupe does best is to create a window of reprieve from the daily hustle of avoiding dopesickness, thereby allowing people the chance to engage in all the equally difficult next steps of trying to build back their lives without drugs.

But most law enforcement divisions aren't accustomed to such gray areas—or of connecting people who break the law to housing and social supports—let alone providing critical linkages to care from inside the jail or at the point of release. So criminal-justice innovations remain slow and siloed. Treatment barriers aren't determined by a state or federal mandate but by a patchwork of local jurisdictions responding to the crisis in thematic fits and starts, often driven by elected politicians and judges, and the business leaders who fund their campaigns.

Change happened by way of one forward-thinking sheriff, one frazzled peer, one grieving mother at a time. It came by way of a purple-haired minister obsessed with doing shit rather than talking about it, and a lone practitioner in a dusty Prius.

"Ultimately, we have to remember that human beings are swayed by the group," said Jennifer Potter, a psychologist at the University of Texas at San Antonio and an expert witness in the opioid-abatement litigation. Naysaying officials were best approached, in her view, by talking about what matters most to their particular communities—whether it's promoting tourism, reducing crime, or maintaining a healthy workforce to attract more jobs. Potter cited a Corpus Christi judge who led efforts to force hospital, homeless shelter, and EMS staffs to work together to funnel addicted people into treatment. "I don't think she actually gets up every day wondering about helping someone with SUDs. She's motivated to make her community thrive and prosper because she wants people like me to go to Corpus Christi and vacation there and enjoy the fine dining experience—but her solution to that is to work on" addiction issues.

Nationwide, Potter credited the persistence of grassroots activists who, above all, were nimble. "If I can't implement change with the sheriff, I go to the fire departments," Potter added. "If the fire department isn't interested, I go to the preachers. If the preachers don't want to help, I find the parent who secretly has the kid struggling, and we work with them."

Citing Canada, where harm reduction comes in the forms of safe-consumption sites and treatment of OUD with pharmaceutically dispensed heroin, one researcher credited middle- and upper-middle-class influencers with forging change in Vancouver—predominantly mothers. Yale School of Medicine's Ryan McNeil cited the Vancouver Area Network of Drug Users for its work in opening North America's first supervised drug injection site, Insite, in 2003.

VANDU cofounder Ann Livingston wasn't a drug user herself—or even a relative of one—but she'd experienced marginalization as the mother of a disabled child, and she lived just two blocks away from Vancouver's open-air drug market. More important, Livingston's mother had been a lifelong community organizer who understood that problems didn't get fixed until the people who were most affected became intimately involved in correcting them.

"Revolution begins when the people who are labeled as the problem redefine the problem," Livingston told me. "It's exactly like people who used to think gay men were the problem with HIV. No. It's unsafe sex that causes HIV, not gay men. So there's this sense that 'junkies' are the problem when it's actually the War on Drugs that's caused the problem and abandonment that continues it."

Livingston realized early on that she needed to be able to recite the latest death, disease, and overdose statistics loudly and publicly, then she bombarded local officials with that information in daily phone calls. "They got so fucking tired of me," she said. To lend respectability to the work, she strategically invited academicians in to do interviews with people who use drugs because she understood that people in power tended to trust academics—even when those academics got their data from Livingston (who got them from drug users!).

Livingston became such a stalwart, showing up for public meetings in her floral dresses and combat boots, that some nicknamed the group ANN-DU instead of VANDU.

Twenty-five years into her advocacy for people with OUD, Livingston was now trying to open a safe-injection site in a wealthy community along Vancouver's edge—and getting the same kind of pushback as the West Virginia needle exchange operators. A drop-in center she started for homeless people who use drugs in a former tea shop hit a snag when the landlord suddenly evicted them, amid suspicions that city officials were actually behind the ousting.

"It's just a horrible struggle, and you have to do it locally—one community at a time. We started two new groups out in the hostile fucking burbs, but the work has never really changed. It's just spreading geographically.

"Academics can endlessly discuss it, but you won't get actual change until you eye-gouge, bite, and scratch."

Chapter Nine

The Moral Arc

*Ed Bisch (right), organizing the December 2021
DOJ rally, Washington, DC.*

As I walked the halls of the Fairfax County Jail and nearby methadone clinics in March 2021, the Ad Hoc Committee brainstormed ways to stop the Sacklers from winning their precious releases. Joined by other grassroots groups, they also lobbied the Biden administration against promoting Janet Woodcock to be the permanent FDA commissioner. As longtime director of the FDA's Center for Drug Evaluation and Research—the nation's so-called top drug cop—she had presided over the blank-check approval of OxyContin and other opioids from 1994 to 2004 and again from 2007 to 2021.

Painkiller prescriptions had quadrupled under Woodcock's watch, an explosion that former FDA Commissioner David Kessler referred to as "the worst mistake in modern medicine." Woodcock continued approving powerful painkillers long after opioid-related crime and addiction were well established—and even when members of her own advisory committees voted overwhelmingly *against* approval, citing safety concerns.

Fresh off the twentieth anniversary of his son's death from OxyContin, Ed Bisch was plotting with the artist Fernando Luis Alvarez to erect a two-story-tall curtain that said "DR. JANET WOODCOCK MUST GO" in front of Purdue's Stamford, Connecticut, headquarters. Nan Goldin's group wanted no part in Alvarez's stunt due to bad blood over an earlier action—but Bisch didn't care and showed up anyway. The only political conservative in the OxyJustice group, when political divisions arose at weekly Zoom meetings, Bisch was pragmatic enough to keep his mouth shut.

I spoke with Bisch multiple times most weeks, often before 8:00 a.m. (He works the graveyard shift at his IT job outside Philly.) I know how he takes his coffee, that he calls sub sandwiches *hoagies*, that he pronounces the word *huge* "yu-u-uge"—as in, "Judge Drain said he fears this bankruptcy scam might be challenged on appeal. This is *yu-u-uge*."

In March 2021, shortly before the bankruptcy settlement proposal was filed, the Sacklers' lawyers announced a deal-sweetening addition of roughly another billion dollars, bringing the family's offer up to $4.275 billion in cash—about a third of what the family had made off OxyContin.

But the gobsmacking news came a few days later, when Congresswoman Maloney announced that the Committee on Oversight and Reform was introducing a bill that could prevent the Sacklers from using the Purdue bankruptcy to hoard most of their wealth.

Maloney called the bill, designed to close a bankruptcy loophole, Stop Shielding Assets from Corporate Known Liability by Eliminating Non-Debtor Releases Act.

Aka the SACKLER Act.

The title was hilarious, given the family's decades-long history of plastering its name on the world's best museums and medical schools in exchange for Upper East Side swagger and, of course, tax credits.

Mike Quinn and Goldin texted each other celebratory videos of themselves dancing.

"It was the first time in ten years I've been this happy," Quinn said.

"How many cocktails did it take to turn SACKLER into an acronym?" chortled former California congresswoman Mary Bono, who'd been fighting to hold opioid-makers accountable since 2008, when a family member became addicted to OxyContin. "I used to cut out newspaper clippings [about overdoses] for my committee and hand them to my colleagues," said Bono, who'd replaced her late husband, the entertainer-turned-congressman Sonny Bono, after his death in office. "And they would always just get slid over to the side in favor of other issues."

The Palm Springs, California, Republican lost reelection in 2012 in part, she believes, because Big Pharma contributed mightily to her opponent. "I was painted as the 'hysterical mother,'" Bono recalled—while many of her fellow congressional representatives signed off on Big Pharma's playbook in exchange for direct and indirect campaign contributions. Between 2006 and 2015, Purdue and other opioid-makers spent nearly a billion dollars on lobbying and political contributions—eight times what the gun lobby spent during the same period.

"We are now losing 80,000 people a year," Bono said, though that number had ballooned to 96,801 predicted overdose deaths six months after we spoke, and for months thereafter the climb continued. "I know some families that haven't been impacted by it, but they're now the exception rather than the rule. And it's absolutely unconscionable that a family gets to keep the kind of money they made while so many people are dying."

Mary Bono had scared Purdue honchos because "she had their number way before" the public caught on to their role in the crisis, recalled Nancy Camp, a former Purdue secretary. Camp recounted all-hands-on-deck damage-control meetings at Purdue whenever a prominent person died who was addicted to OxyContin—Michael Jackson, for instance. "The Sacklers were so wealthy, they didn't know how to interact with people that weren't like them," Camp added. As an administrative assistant, Camp marveled that she'd made a hefty $95,000 annually at Purdue. "Have I made that much since? No! They kept people there; they kept people's mouths shut, right?"

Richard Sackler referred to the entirety of Appalachia as "West Virginia," Camp said, not bothering to discern one troubled state from the next. She recalled an angry mother of someone who died from OxyContin mailing in a photo of her child, and an executive admonishing her, "Don't ever show me that stuff again."

"They just didn't want to hear about it," she said.

But the stories were finally coming home to roost. No amount of subterfuge or lobbying could keep them from wearing the deaths.

Their name might even be written into bankruptcy law.

Quinn worked hard to amplify the growing anti-Sackler sentiment. With Bisch's help, he spent most of the weekend designing a write-your-representative website to increase support for the SACKLER Act. He'd never created a website before, but he knew how to Google, and he wanted to make sure that Congress saw it Monday morning first thing. He also posted a scathing objection on Judge Drain's docket, featuring a recently released 2002 e-mail from a friend of Richard Sackler's: "I hate to say this, but you could become the Pablo Escobar of the new millennium," warned the doctor friend. Back then, teenagers at a nearby private high school had been approaching classmates with offers to buy OxyContin; one told the doctor it was "a designer drug and sort of like heroin."

In his objection, Quinn expounded on the comparison: "When the Colombian government finally made a show of enforcement against Escobar, that country's judiciary oversaw a special arrangement, in which the drug dealer was given his own private prison, especially built on a hill overlooking his hometown. The compound was so opulent that the citizens of Colombia named it *La Catedral*.

"This bankruptcy," Quinn asserted, "is the Sacklers' cathedral."

Quinn was nervous about Drain's reaction. And rightfully so. At the next hearing, Drain treated Quinn like an errant boy caught smoking in the schoolyard. He referred to Quinn's clients as the "*so-called* Ad Hoc Committee."

After Quinn delivered his remarks, he switched to listening into the call on a headset. He went outside to work on the lawn of his family's Hudson Valley home, only to have Drain surprisingly pepper him with questions about arcane case law from the 1960s—while Quinn was spreading grass seed.

Those cases, "um, they don't come to mind," Quinn sputtered nervously. "But I have a lot on my mind."

At the end of the hearing, the Sacklers won the injunction they'd requested, and the litigation stay was extended once more. Though the date kept getting bumped back, negotiations were finally in the home stretch.

Quinn's next brief was an over-the-top critique of the "billion-dollar Chapter 11" culture. He compared Drain to a baseball umpire who unconsciously adjusts the strike zone to favor all-stars.

Quinn even included an illustration he'd made of a baseball player at bat on his computer, titling his head-to-toe strike zone the "Billionaire Bias."

Another argument in Quinn's brief featured a pencil drawing of Darwin's famed Galápagos Islands finches. Quinn compared the Bankruptcy Boys Club, full of repeat players, to finches who, through natural selection, manage to "take over their island and grow giant beaks to gobble up the system of justice."

A female lawyer would have never gotten away with that level of digression, humor, and insolence, noted Charlotte Bismuth, one of Goldin's advisers. "Mike's a powerhouse behind the scenes, connecting with politicians and the press," she told me. "But he's on the edge of being held in contempt."

At the following hearing, Drain made the threat real. There was surprisingly no transcript of that hearing; it had inadvertently (and astonishingly), a court official later explained, not been recorded.

"You're lucky that I'm a restrained judge," Drain scolded. "I could hold you in contempt for that pleading—including the *artwork.*

"Mr. Quinn," he intoned, finally, ending the admonishment with four emphatic words: "Clean. Up. Your. Act!"

Moving a bill to Biden's desk before the final bankruptcy order, scheduled for August 2021, was unlikely. Some insiders worried the SACKLER Act was simply a ploy by congressional leaders to score political points. Ryan Hampton, the co-chair of the bankruptcy's creditors committee, saw it as a Hail Mary that was too little, too late. Organizers were frantically trying to get a senator to co-champion the bill without turning it into a cumbersome total rewrite of the nation's bankruptcy laws. Alacrity was required. Bankruptcy guru Senator Elizabeth Warren was reportedly considering it; so was Senator Richard Blumenthal, who represented Purdue's home state.

According to billing records filed in the bankruptcy, Purdue spent over $1.2 million in lobbying fees throughout the case, which included "monitoring" of the SACKLER Act. Quinn sent me a video of corporate-turnaround specialist William A. Brandt Jr. speaking at a fall 2021 American Bankruptcy Institute conference. Brandt bragged that he'd personally "peeled off nine Democratic senators so far," coaxing them not to support the SACKLER Act.

In December 2021, the ABI hosted Judge Drain himself at a resort in Rancho Palos Verdes, California, to discuss, among other bankruptcy topics, the issue of nonconsensual releases. A corporate law firm–sponsored advocacy group that hosts a judge at a conference to talk about issues pending in an active case he oversees? To Quinn, it was the same kind of corporate cozying up that had launched the opioid epidemic—akin to Purdue paying 5,000 doctors, nurses, and pharmacists to give speeches to their peers about the miracle of OxyContin.

"We've all been played like a fucking chessboard," Hampton said. "The crushing thing is, there was an opportunity to fund all the things at a very robust level, but I'm worried that's being dwindled down to nothing," he added, referring to legal, consulting, and lobbying fees.

From her beautiful book-lined office, Kathe Sackler had insisted to Congress there was nothing she could have done differently. But just about everyone inside the Fairfax County Jail had a story that said otherwise. Even though they'd progressed to illicit heroin and fentanyl—data points the Sacklers touted as a way to distance themselves from subsequent waves of opioid deaths—everyone I met in the jail's bupe program had begun their journey into addiction with illicit pills, OxyContin foremost among them.

Economists have proven that their stories are not mere anecdotes. A 2019 study by economists at the Wharton School and elsewhere suggested that, in the few states with unusually stringent prescription monitoring practices—so-called triplicate programs—overdose deaths from both illicit and prescribed OxyContin remained significantly lower two decades after it was introduced. Purdue had avoided spending as much on marketing in Illinois, New York, California, Idaho, and Texas precisely because company executives understood that their hard-sell tactics wouldn't pay off where prescription oversight was highest.

Regulation, where it was employed, worked.

If she really wanted to understand what she might have done differently, Kathe Sackler could have consulted thirty-one-year-old Dema Hadieh, who became addicted to opioids following a broken-shoulder injury in 2009. The former softball player and community college student said she'd enjoyed alcohol and maybe a little weed. But not until a Virginia doctor, coached by Purdue's pro-opioid marketing machine, prescribed a three-month course of pills did she begin breaking laws to avoid the misery of being dopesick. For three years she bought OxyContin and Roxicodone pills off the streets and sold them so she could buy more. "I've been in and out of jail ever since," she told me, clad in a red jail jumpsuit.

When Purdue discontinued selling the abusable form of Oxy-Contin in 2012, Hadieh sought out heroin. She has two children she's never had regular custody of, including one who was still a newborn when Hadieh overdosed beside her bassinet. Her three-month stint at the Fairfax jail in early 2021 was the first time she'd ever been stabilized on buprenorphine. It was her longest period of sobriety in many years.

Hadieh was about to be transferred to an inpatient women's facility in nearby Vienna, where she hoped to reside for six months to a year, continue her bupe, and eventually get a job. "I never wanted to go to long-term treatment before because I just couldn't stand the withdrawals," she said.

In a nearby jail pod, thirty-eight-year-old Tiffany Riley was also on prescribed bupe for the first time. CAF peer Brittany Roberts was due to pick her up the day of her release. Roberts had already arranged a sober-living placement for her, including a grant for her first month's rent and connection to a government-subsidized buprenorphine provider. "Honestly, just having Brittany to talk to, I was so overwhelmed before with all the things I needed help with—rides to appointments, rides to court dates," Riley told me. "Even just getting a ride to detox. I didn't have the money to get an Uber—used to be they'd pick you up, but they had to stop because of COVID."

Her goal now was to find a job and regain custody of her son, who was living with her dad in West Virginia. Riley had begun using opioids with the explosion of OxyContin in her hometown of Hazard, Kentucky, two decades before. Around that time, the DEA swooped into her county in the nation's first federal OxyContin drug-ring bust, a press-hyped sting dubbed Operation OxyFest. That's when Purdue spokesman Dr. J. David Haddox first trotted out his standard talking points, explaining that overdose deaths typically involve multiple factors including alcohol and other prescriptions, and that people who misuse Purdue's drugs were the ones breaking the law, not Purdue. Haddox's was a version of the defense from Richard Sackler's mouth—"hammer the abusers!"—slightly sanitized for the media's notebooks.

Soon after, Riley delivered her son in custody while handcuffed to her hospital bed.

On the same Friday the SACKLER Act was introduced, Roberts picked Riley up from jail and drove her to transitional housing, setting her up with underwear, feminine hygiene products, an Uber card, and a Tracfone. By Monday, the pair were plotting how to get her an ID and craft a résumé. There was a shopping center nearby she could walk to for work.

But it had been so long since Riley had been in the workforce that Roberts had to teach her how to fill out a job application online. Both worried that Riley's felony drug and larceny record—using drugs and selling drugs; stealing to buy drugs—would keep her from being hired.

After three days at her sober-living facility, Riley disappeared. She started calling and texting Roberts from different phone numbers, saying she'd been robbed at a 7-Eleven. "Her story made NO SENSE," Roberts told me. "She never wanted to be picked up or taken home. Trust me, I tried!" In a week, Riley had blown off probation and drug-court appointments, and Roberts doubted she had even picked up her buprenorphine prescription.

Hadieh, the other CAF participant I followed, was managing better in the county-funded rehab. But there were no locks on the doors, and the possibility of relapse lingered. "You can give somebody all the tools and put them in the most supportive environment, but past trauma is so powerful," said Marissa Farina-Morse, the CSB administrator who oversees jail treatment. "So this might not be the time for her, but I hope it is."

Two weeks later, the women's fortunes flipped. Riley was back in another Oxford House and happy to see her relatives for a visit, but she was struggling with rules and accountability. ("No surprise—lots of us have problems with this in the beginning!" Roberts said.) Meanwhile, Hadieh had abruptly left rehab and was now on the run with her boyfriend, who was posting pictures of them on social media.

Weeks later, he beat her to the point of head injury and stabbed her, and she spent most of the summer in the hospital before returning to jail for a probation violation. She was back on bupe, reunited with her family, and hoped to be released to treatment again soon: "I'm not giving up on myself," she told me through a jail intermediary.

For people severely addicted to opioids, it takes two to three years *longer* to achieve wellness than it does those with alcoholism and other SUDs because they start out comparatively further behind in terms of their finances and health. "That's a huge disadvantage as they start their recovery journey," Harvard addiction researcher John F. Kelly told me. "This is why we need more resources for those with OUD, particularly housing, employment and training, and peer recovery supports." But such wraparound services were rare, another outgrowth of systemic stigma that viewed helping people with OUD as "coddling addicts" and "hug-a-thug."

With their army of lawyers and flacks, the Sacklers could still afford to buy their way out of trouble. So far in the bankruptcy, Purdue had spent $337 million on legal and professional fees—presumably not counting what was paid to surveil the activists and author Patrick Radden Keefe, who was threatened repeatedly by the same Richard Sackler lawyer who'd been writing letters to the Disney lawyers, questioning my journalism, and was also being trailed outside his Westchester County home. By May 2021, a Bloomberg reporter noted that the legal bill, tallied at almost $400 million, was more than half the amount that Americans harmed by OxyContin would be sharing under Purdue's proposed settlement.

The family's reputation was withering by the day. A few days after the SACKLER Act was introduced, the Serpentine Galleries in London, not far from the home of Sackler heiress Dame Theresa Sackler, the senior Mortimer's third wife, dropped the Sackler name. Goldin's team sent me a link to that story, adorning their text message with applause and tough-biceps emojis.

Quinn was busy trying to contact every senator he could think of. If you knew a senator, or if you even tangentially knew an actress who had ever once dated a senator—like, say, Senator Cory Booker's then-fiancée, Rosario Dawson, now portraying a DEA agent who tried and failed to take on Purdue in the Hulu version of *Dopesick*—Quinn beseeched you, please, call her up. And if you knew a Republican senator, Mike Quinn really, really wanted you.

"It feels good—we know we're fighting the good fight," he said, "but the reality of the bankruptcy is draining."

Some journalists working to hold power accountable had been at it for two decades—dogging Democratic and Republican administrations alike—and they were just as exhausted as the besieged peers, parents, and harm-reduction workers. It reminded me of an exchange I witnessed in 2016 between *Los Angeles Times* investigative reporter Harriet Ryan and Obama's first drug czar, Michael Botticelli, during a daylong seminar for journalists in Washington, DC.

Ryan asked him point-blank: Would the government ever hold Purdue accountable?

"The administration is continuing to take action and will continue to—" Botticelli began.

Ryan cut him off: "Senator Edward Markey called for an investigation of Purdue Pharma [earlier in the year]. That might be something you want to look into. He's from your home state."

Botticelli changed the subject and returned to the comfort of his talking points: veterinarians got more training around treating pain than physicians, words like *addicts* and *junkies* should be avoided in news stories, and more articles should be written about people in recovery. By and large, Botticelli pointed out, jails and prisons remained the nation's de facto treatment system for people with SUD. Great points, all.

But no mention was made of President Obama's demotion of the drug czar position from cabinet-level status with little explanation in 2009, when drug overdoses were doubling. Or that Obama had also failed to issue a "public health emergency" at several experts' request when fentanyl turned into the deadliest drug to hit American streets.

Ryan kept pressing the drug czar: But why did billionaires get away with breaking the law when those they addicted could not?

Botticelli refused to answer.

Five years later, Ryan's questions still hung in the air.

By the spring of 2021, President Biden was about to nominate former West Virginia health official Rahul Gupta to become the next drug czar. Public health leaders fumed. It was Gupta, after all, who as the state's health commissioner presided over West Virginia's overdose crisis in 2018 when NIMBY activists complaining about crime succeeded in shutting down Charleston's needle exchange. That closure had led to an emergency-level surge in HIV and hepatitis C cases in the city—sending the work of Prosperino, Solomon, and their peers underground.

While Gupta has said repeatedly that he supports harm reduction, his record is mixed. He remains under attack for providing cover for needle-exchange opponents in Charleston during the 2018 shutdown after criticizing the program for sloppy record-keeping and contributing to needle litter—even though, when operated correctly, such programs actually reduce needle litter. "There was an opportunity for Gupta to lead, but he took the opposite approach," said Robin Pollini, a West Virginia University epidemiologist and harm-reduction expert. "And I personally feel like we are still living with the wreckage of those decisions."

The volunteers at SOAR continued to run their needle exchange out of a church parking lot in Charleston every other Saturday, but SOAR's future was tenuous. The city council and the state legislature, with its Republican supermajority, were on the verge of officially outlawing their work, even though HIV had now spread to forty Charlestonians and residents of surrounding Kanawha County—putting the HIV infection rate higher than New York City's. Since HIV testing remained minimal in Charleston, the incidence was likely to be far higher than what was being reported, Pollini warned. The number of statewide cases related to intravenous drug use had increased seven-fold since 2014.

"We fear our crucible days are coming up," said Joe Solomon, SOAR's main needle-exchange organizer. He was frantically asking national opioid reporters to shame the naysayers with their coverage. "The only reason we're not on the front page of the *Washington Post* right now is because of COVID," Solomon said.

But Gupta had important ties to West Virginia senator Joe Manchin, the coal-state centrist who was now one of two key swing votes in the narrowly divided US Senate. In a move considered LBJ-esque, Biden's potential appointment of Gupta to the post could give the president leverage with Manchin in other important matters, like getting rid of the filibuster. Even though Biden was on record as supporting harm reduction, Gupta, a personal friend of Manchin's, got the job.

In a city of 48,000 residents, Charleston's needle exchange served nearly 25,000 people in three years. But the naysayers, led by a mayor who professed that people who use drugs "should be locked up until they're clean," were too angry to listen to stats. One opponent at a public meeting in Buckhannon got so upset that he had a stroke, and an ambulance was dispatched.

State reporters who quoted scientists like Pollini about the need for harm reduction were bullied, doxed, and harassed. Pollini herself was physically threatened. Federal money set aside for harm-reduction programs was initially blocked from receiving funds by the West Virginia State Health Department, though eventually it was released (but had to be spent quickly).

"I don't think most of you actually know what happens when you leave," a critic from the neighborhood told members of SOAR, which was still running biweekly health fairs that included not only needle exchange but also food and hygiene-kit distributions and HIV testing in the parking lot of the Unitarian Church. The critic argued that people who use drugs injected in broad daylight, defecated on church property, and left syringe trash strewn about. "Why should I lose my quality of life because you want to enhance theirs?"

The Unitarian Church happened to be in an African American neighborhood on Charleston's west side. A few ministers from Black churches had joined the chorus of critics, drawing comparisons to the lackadaisical response when Black communities were being ravaged by crack cocaine—and no one handed out crack pipes or held die-ins on their behalf. Solomon apologized profusely for not having met with Black leaders before setting up the biweekly fairs in the neighborhood.

Other opponents ridiculed the CDC data. "They were saying, 'Just thirty-six new cases of HIV. Is that really a lot?'" said Caity Coyne, a *Charleston Gazette-Mail* reporter who tracked the issue and who was also physically threatened. "When it was only two cases five years ago, that *is* concerning—especially when we're no longer doing anything to stop the spread."

The meeting grew so heated, the city council requested a vote delay. A day later, Senator Manchin submitted a congressional request that the CDC return to perform "a full inquiry," whatever that meant. (It had already released the official case count numbers. The data is the data—it doesn't require peer review.) "People don't trust the effing CDC!" Coyne told me, exasperated.

A few months later, Manchin waylaid Biden's "Build Back Better" social safety net and climate-change infrastructure bill, privately telling colleagues that parents would use their child tax credit payments to buy drugs and workers would fritter away their paid family leave to go on hunting trips. This, following a surge in corporate contributions made to Manchin's political action committee from corporations and billionaire business leaders, including lobbying by the Koch network against filibuster and voting rights reforms.

It was a microcosm of America's growing rural-urban divide:

a toxic brew of anti-government spew, fueled at its core by dark money, and amplified by passive-aggressive social media postings. The Facebook group called Charleston Has Had Enough! now had more than 4,000 supporters—nearly 10 percent of the city. Among the loudest naysayers was Jerry Waters, a Charleston fire-fighter-turned-radio-talk-show-host who'd gone on *Oprah* in 1987 to say that AIDS was God's way of punishing gay people. Though Waters came to regret his statements about AIDS, recently he'd begun flying his drone over homeless encampments to intimidate people who used drugs.

The more the syringe-services proponents cited scientific backup, the louder their critics deemed them suspect, along with the "fake news" journalists who reported facts and presented the harm-reductionists' side of the story. A troll sent Coyne a Facebook message: "I hope your dad dies from overdose so you can see how this feels. You don't know real pain." Coyne, twenty-six, was from San Diego, but she had been a Charlestonian for four years and loved her West Virginia friends and work. People in her immediate family had battled addiction, and Coyne lived in a low-income Charleston neighborhood. Her house had been pilfered by people who use drugs on the eve of her moving into it, so she knew firsthand that all was not rosy.

Almost every day that spring, a new complication emerged. The Kanawha County Health Department promised to go out and test more people. "If you're in the middle of an HIV outbreak, and you're simply testing to find cases but not doing anything to prevent them, that's public health malpractice," Pollini raged.

A Ryan White Program worker from the hospital had recently tested eight people who use drugs, and one was HIV positive. If you extrapolated that out to the projected number of users in the county—4,795, according to a recent estimate—the number of new HIV cases could potentially be as high as 600.

A city councilor in recovery publicly urged abstinence-based solutions, not syringe giveaways. Pollini called the councilman's story simply N of 1, an anecdote. "You want to be respectful of people's experiences, but I'm a scientist," she said. "Just because it worked for you doesn't mean it will work for everyone. Ideally, you have a whole buffet of options so people can pick the pathway that works for them."

As tempers flared and politicians fanned the fury, Pollini publicly warned officials that, unless immediate harm-reduction measures were enacted, the outbreak would prove to be worse than the 2014 outbreak in Scott County, Indiana. "People are going to want to know who's accountable," she told them. "If you shut down these programs, that's you!"

Like the Vancouver harm-reductionists before her, she vowed to make the politicians the grave diggers. "Make them wear the deaths!" as one VANDU member put it. But the state legislature, buoyed by the naysayers and their squeaky wheels, severely restricted needle exchange anyway, outlawing the work of SOAR and the "hill witch." The same week that the West Virginia legislature passed a law sending them further underground, Prosperino's social media accounts were subpoenaed. They were officially "under investigation." If the Kanawha County prosecuting attorney won the rights to their private messages, she would know not only more about their operations but also exactly who their clients were. That worried Prosperino.

But they had several sympathetic lawyers advising them and fighting on their behalf. Anticipating a raid on their home—the coalition's needles and safe-use kits were stored in a bedroom of their house—they got busy distro-ing supplies to secondary hubs operated by people they'd long served and trusted in the region. Instead of passing out 20 needles to each person, they were now giving out 1,000 so clients could share them with their friends. Secondary distribution is a best practice recommended by the CDC.

Karen Lowe (left) and the Rev. Michelle Mathis, co-founders of Olive Branch Ministry, run the nation's only biracial, queer, faith-based harm reduction group, offering low-barrier needle exchange and medication-assisted treatment.

As an Olive Branch volunteer, nurse practitioner Tim Nolan (right) signs up new patients in western North Carolina's most distressed areas. "I died two days ago" from overdose, said Zach, but he added that he was finally ready to seek treatment.

Photographer Nan Goldin used high-profile protests to heap shame upon the Sackler family and worked cannily to get hers and other victims' voices heard in the Purdue bankruptcy case.

Ed Bisch, an IT worker in New Jersey, works doggedly to hold the Sacklers accountable on behalf of the more than 1 million Americans dead of overdose since OxyContin launched in 1996. The first time he heard the word OxyContin, his 18-year-old son was dead from it.

Mike Quinn, the pro bono lawyer for the Ad Hoc Committee on Accountability, was the only attorney in the case who wasn't billing some $1,800 an hour. He saw himself as a kind of merry prankster, jabbing the Sacklers and the bankruptcy judge repeatedly.

Harm reductionist Alexis Pleus (with Nan Goldin in background) leads an annual Trail of Truth protest and die-in in her home city of Binghamton, N.Y.

Surry County, N.C., opioid response director Mark Willis, a former Marine and DEA agent, charts his progress on a wall-spanning whiteboard as he tries to shift his community's Overton Window of thinking about addiction treatment in his conservative, addiction-plagued region.

Sonya Cheek, one of Surry County's first peer-support counselors, was initially addicted to OxyContin. People in the local jail used to pass her phone number through the "chrome phone," for help with re-entry, housing, and finding work, and Cheek eventually became the county's Recovery to Work adviser.

As Mark Willis worked to get his transportation network and other recovery supports off the ground, James Stroud and Wendy Odum (below) traveled the county in their cars, passing out syringes and vital connections to care.

Harm reductionists
Joe Solomon and Lill
Prosperino (below)
delivered harm-reduction
supplies in Charleston,
W. Va., and elsewhere in
the overdose-plagued state
as legislators worked to
outlaw needle exchange
during an HIV outbreak.

Brooke Parker, an HIV outreach worker in Charleston, W. Va., traverses the city's homeless encampments to test, treat, and offers basic care to the addicted, in response to what the CDC called "the most concerning" outbreak of HIV in the nation.

Nurse practitioner Tim Nolan uses needle exchange as the "carrot" to entice people who use drugs into care. He meets patients literally where they are, from homeless encampments to truckstop parking lots to broken-down trailers in the North Carolina woods.

Nikki King developed an innovative, highly successful program to treat addicted probationers in Ripley County, Ind., but found herself ramming repeatedly against bureaucratic barriers and stigma.

Mike Moore was among the only lawyers in the sprawling opioid litigation to have first-hand experience with addiction in his family. He helped negotiate the first settlement with Purdue, pre-bankruptcy, as well as the 1998 Master Tobacco Settlement, still the largest corporate settlement in American history.

Jennifer Deneault works as a Certified Peer Recovery Specialist for the Fairfax County Community Service Board's Peer Overdose Response Team in Virginia.

Janet Wurie (center, front), a Doctor of Nursing Practice at the Fairfax County (Va.) Jail for twenty-two years, treats inmates William Wyatt (left), Anthony Batts (center, behind), and Cortez Settles (right) with medication-assisted treatment while they are incarcerated. The jail-based program is among the most innovative in the nation.

Laura Yager helped bust barriers to change thinking among jail staffers, some of whom were initially reluctant to see the addicted as people with a treatable medical condition. But her boss, Sheriff Stacey Ann Kincaid (below), studied successful jail treatment programs elsewhere and was committed to changing protocols. "We definitely heard our share of 'hug a thug,'" Kincaid said.

Shelly Young helps Northern Virginia families eschew "rock-bottom" thinking after nearly losing her son and then realizing that America's entrenched approach to addiction was all wrong. She works with the harm-reduction group, The Chris Atwood Foundation, run by Ginny Lovitt (below) who lost her little brother to overdose in 2013 and made it her life's mission to change laws and bust treatment barriers.

Daniel Adams is one of Lovitt's peer support specialists, joining the nonprofit after a thirty-year prison stint. He helps coordinate re-entry housing from jails to sober-living homes in a "warm handoff" for people like Tiffany Riley (below), who had never been on prescribed bupe until her 2021 stint at the Fairfax County Jail.

Kristy Howard (above) and Brittany Roberts worked as peer-support specialists for The CAF, helping inmates with re-entry issues and handing out harm-reduction supplies in the region, including at area methadone clinics.

Abbie Setzer hangs out regularly at Olive Branch Ministry in Hickory, N.C., where she volunteers and uses the harm-reduction facility's services, located behind a church. Mary Jo Silver (below) got treatment for Hepatitis and her addiction through Olive Branch and went on to become a leader in her community, hosting hepatitis testing gatherings in her home.

University of Buffalo historian David Herzberg's scholarship ended up in the crosshairs of the Purdue Pharma bankruptcy case. Herzberg unpacked the history of and fallout from the War on Drugs, including the brief period in the United States when the heroin addicted were offered treatment on demand, a system designed in the early 1970s by the nation's first drug czar, Jerome Jaffe (below).

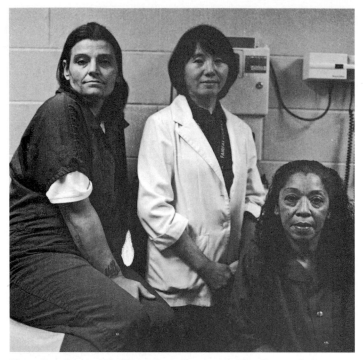

Nurse Practitioner Xin Wang (center) treats Fairfax County Jail inmates Diana Seaborn (left) and Missy Charpentier with bupe as part of their recovery program while incarcerated.

Robert Hutchins, an inmate at the Fairfax County (Va.) Jail, receives medication-assisted treatment for his addiction while incarcerated. Hutchins is also enrolled in a program in the jail to become a Certified Peer Recovery Specialist so that he could find employment helping others with substance use disorder upon their release.

Some participants burst into tears at the news. "Our friend was up on the porch a couple a days ago and he was crying, which was weird to see from a cisgender man," Prosperino told me. "We'd gotten him a grant to put a roof on his house. When I tell people about the search warrant and about the bill and all that, they have a really negative reaction. They're like, 'All y'all do is help people and, like, this is really fucked up.'"

Others responded by organizing, calling together allies, people in recovery, and people who presently use drugs. Solomon was planning another rally and a strategy Zoom session with Livingston in Vancouver to fire up SOAR's supporters. He had a text list of 300 people, but a few opponents had already infiltrated it—feeding stories to the local right-wing television station, which he blamed for amping up the animus that led to SOAR's Charleston operations getting shut down. Solomon was reluctant to invite them all to the first meeting, worried that the people who videotaped and harassed them would show up. As a nod to VANDU, he proposed calling the Charleston version *CANDU*. (Joe's cutesy that way.)

Prosperino hoped to cash in a chit they'd earned with the United Mine Workers of America. Two years earlier, Prosperino had stood in solidarity with the miners for two months—literally camped out near a railroad blockade built to stop the trains from moving the coal. The protest targeted owners of the Harlan, Kentucky–based Blackjewel Coal Company, after it closed without notifying its workers or paying them wages owed.

Paychecks bounced. People were on the verge of losing their homes. Prosperino and fellow activists supplemented the work of union officials and evangelical preachers alike, supplying the miners with food and organizing donation campaigns. Then-candidate Bernie Sanders sent pizzas. Eventually, after it seemed like the miners would really pull it off, even Mitch McConnell lent support. Local musicians set up and played songs, including the old labor tune written for another Harlan labor battle nearly a century before: *Until the battle's won, which side are you on?*

"I think it would be some work to convince the UMWA that harm reduction is a thing worth fighting for," Prosperino said. "Because it's not like anything they've ever engaged in." But at one blockade in an adjacent county, they noticed that many were on drugs, prescribed and otherwise. So, who knew?

When the miners' demands were finally met, including the restoration of their back pay, the UMWA donated the leftover funds to Prosperino's Southern West Virginia Harm Reduction Coalition. "Some of the wives were pissed," they said. "But the miners were like, 'Take that couple grand you raised for us and put it to good use because we really liked the work you did.'"

The treatment gap barely budged. West Virginia's overdose deaths had gone up 45 percent from 2019 to 2020, and statewide opposition to harm reduction was at a fever pitch. The only place with a higher death rate than West Virginia's was San Francisco, where fentanyl was finding fertile ground among that city's skyrocketing homeless population.

In most blue states and big cities, to have harm-reduction cred was not only scientifically proven; it was cool. Still, in rural places where the overdose crisis first broke out, Purdue's neediest victims continued suffering under bridges and inside tents. They were dying of untreated hepatitis C and, if past injection-related outbreaks were any indication, they could eventually be dying of AIDS.

Over an interview on Zoom, Joe Solomon showed me his copy of David France's *How to Survive a Plague*, and he pledged to organize in the spirit of ACT UP in the late 1980s. To draw attention to the HIV outbreak and the syringe-services restrictions, SOAR would spread their message through the media and engage in the kind of civil disobedience that captured politicians' attention about HIV/AIDS. At one point Anthony Fauci was burned in effigy in front of his office at the National Institutes of Health to draw attention to patients' poor access to medicines. SOAR would try to expose the fact that leadership on the overdose crisis remained a Wizard of Oz–type mirage, just as it was during the early years of HIV/AIDS. As activist Peter Staley put it in the 1980s, "There's no global strategy" to combat the AIDS crisis. "It's just this schmuck behind the curtain."

When better combination AIDS drugs finally came on the market in response to ACT UP, fifteen years after the virus was first named, an estimated 6 million lives were saved.

In 1995, during that same period, Purdue Pharma would take advantage of those same loosened drug-approval protocols to make false claims about the safety and efficacy of OxyContin. "Purdue literally had the FDA on speed dial!" Mike Moore told me.

Actually, it may have been worse than speed dial. Curtis Wright, the FDA medical review officer who approved OxyContin, reportedly had a web camera that directly connected him to Purdue's Stamford headquarters and pledged to "go to bat" for Purdue—two years before tripling his salary by going to work for the company.

Boston-based AIDS historian Dr. Joe Wright believed that the West Virginians' best bet was to draw upon parallel movements shepherded by coal miners' unions and Black Lives Matter organizers. But he worried that the recovery movement was too geographically and philosophically splintered, especially among twelve-steppers who remained opposed to bupe.

"It can't just be the moms of the dead leading the way—you also need the credibility of lived experience," said Wright, who directs addiction treatment for Boston Healthcare for the Homeless. "Focusing on the fact that's it's a *treatable* disease is savvy. You see that same thing happening with ACT UP in the US and later with the Treatment Action Campaign in South Africa. When people start believing it's a treatable disease, there's still stigma but the social death part of it begins to shift."

Unlike gay people who fled to San Francisco's Castro District from across the United States in the 1960s and '70s, the addicted don't geographically unite in a way that lends itself to advocating for better treatments and less policing of people who use drugs—the exceptions being Kensington in Philadelphia or the Tenderloin district of San Francisco.

Besides, Wright pointed out, people who use drugs and were living in disparate areas tended to remain in place throughout their addictions—unlike LGBTQ people who'd long sought more tolerant places to be. "So your thirty-year-old guy on Cape Cod won't connect to the fifty-five-year-old Black man in Roxbury, even though they're both shooting dope, and they may even get it from the same wholesale source."

Once again, the city on the North American hill remained Vancouver, where drug-user unions and activist allies showed up at public meetings carrying coffins and demanding access to treatment. As the author and AIDS historian Sarah Schulman has pointed out, "The more to the left your left is, the more credibility your center has."

In Boston, Wright and a fellow low-barrier buprenorphine doctor were treating people with SUD from a van, inside MASH-style tents erected during the pandemic, and via a jail program.

"Every day I feel like I climb down into the cracks of the broken world, work away, then climb back out and go back to my life," Wright said. "We're a Band-Aid."

I turned for advice to Dr. David E. Smith, an elder in the American harm-reduction movement. He was the San Francisco physician who battled NIMBYs to open the nation's first free clinic in Haight-Ashbury in 1967. The police didn't want him to do it—many practitioners ran the risk of being arrested for aiding and abetting a felony crime. A local drug dealer put out a contract on his life. "Our early days were dangerous, wild, and wooly, and we were getting grief from all sides," Smith said.

"But our goal was free, nonjudgmental health care, and we had overdose teams roaming the neighborhood resuscitating people." It was Smith who, drawing upon civil rights strategies, coined the phrase "Health care is a right, not a privilege."

A few years after the summer of love, when the first government grant hit his clinic's coffers, it was to fund the growing number of heroin-addicted veterans returning from the Vietnam War. Smith had already been treating the addicted; in the past authorities had tried to have him arrested for it, and now they were giving him money?

Casting addiction as a crime has long been a politically motivated way to stifle anti-government sentiment and dispossess already marginalized people, but that argument no longer held water when it came to returning veterans. The perception of who was worthy of care had shifted.

A decade later, when HIV started killing injection-drug users and gay men alike, a colleague of Smith's suggested that they start giving away sterile needles and safe-use supplies. Like the naysayers in Charleston, Smith initially thought it would encourage addiction. "But I'm also a scientist, and the evidence came out that it actually *decreased* overdoses, infections, and even drug use generally. I said, how the heck does that happen?"

Advocates for the homeless population call the work "therapeutic engagement." It's what Olive Branch calls "meeting people where they are." It basically means: When you treat marginalized groups like human beings instead of objects, they begin to trust you, eventually they get better and help others get better, too.

Smith hoped his story would inspire hope among the

Appalachian harm-reductionists I was following, but he was shocked and disturbed by the stories of setbacks I shared with him.

"If you don't believe in evidence and you don't believe in humanity, at least look at the costs," said Smith, eighty-three. "Every dollar spent on treatment saves nine dollars in public health and social costs."

But what about the dug-in politicians who refuse to be swayed by scientific studies and cost savings? "Well, that is a political problem...that I turn over to you."

History will vindicate treatment warriors like Tim Nolan, Nikki King, and the West Virginia "hill witch," he said. Whereas San Francisco's leaders once vilified Smith, they now gave him awards—so the moral arc still favored justice, in his view, however slowly it bent.

"I want you to celebrate them, and I will, too. As a nation, we have got to move beyond the idea that the person who gets celebrated is the one who makes the most money. It shouldn't ever be that one segment of the population gets care, and the other gets jail and the street."

PART THREE

Baby Steps

Nurse-practitioner Tim Nolan making a house call,
Nebo, North Carolina.

Chapter Ten

Encounters with the Unseen

Michelle Mathis delivering safe-use kits and encouragement,
Hickory, North Carolina.

The Olive Branch cofounders weren't sure what to make of the bearded, bespectacled nurse-practitioner, whose demeanor was as quiet as his idling Prius. Long before he took part in their mission to treat people where they were—including beside dumpsters in fast-food parking lots—Tim Nolan spent six months asking to volunteer before they accepted his offer to help with needle exchange.

Michelle Mathis and Karen Lowe had gotten used to being wary. When they began distributing needles out of the back of their pickup in 2012, it was illegal. Back then, they had a much smaller national network of harm-reductionists they could tap into for help. Friends in New York would order hepatitis C drugs from India, for instance, then ship them out to underground networks across the States. The effort was inspired by people with AIDS, who had joined together and formed buyer's clubs to import unapproved treatments before the activists finally shamed the federal government into approving better drugs. By the time North Carolina legalized syringe exchange in 2016, Mathis and Lowe knew how to run a lean and scrappy operation—and they were used to watching their backs.

"They were funny," Tim told me, as we wended our way to a trap house in rural Conover, North Carolina.

Protective, he meant. "I had to knock on their door for a long time before they invited me in."

It was Mathis who'd cringed hardest at the public meeting in Mount Airy, where the Kiwanis leader recommended people who overdosed be left to die—so that their organs could be harvested. For almost two years, I interviewed the couple over the phone before they permitted me to visit their Hickory and Gastonia needle exchanges. It was all managed inside a double-wide behind the church by a gravel-throated peer counselor whose T-shirt said, "I'm not Willie Wonka; I don't sugar-coat shit."

The shirt, a gift from Mathis, was an understatement. When participants lie to her, Karen Garcia playfully hands them a colorful unicorn-shaped eraser. "I'll say, 'The unicorn horn you're trying to shove up my ass isn't working, but here's your award for trying to feed me the biggest bunch of bullshit ever,'" Garcia said. ("She doesn't quite have the tolerance usually required of harm-reductionists," Mathis said, smiling. "But we're working on it.")

Garcia is Olive Branch's air traffic controller—handing out needles, arranging Tim's parking-lot appointments, holding weekly check-in sessions with patients. She also dispatches peer-support specialists to rural outposts when folks are too poor or too deep in their addiction to drive to them. Olive Branch hired one of its first peers, thirty-five-year-old Jessica Maloney, after meeting her in a jail-based education program—she was wearing shackles. Maloney had spent half her adulthood in prison and jail, with a drug-selling rap sheet so long that she once had to pay ten dollars to have the entire thing printed out. "I was as addicted to selling drugs as I was the drugs," she said. "To be honest, I was really, really good at selling drugs."

Now, Maloney gets paid to drive around the region's former mill towns, handing out needles, food, clothes, tarps, and even cat food to one participant who lives in a tent under a bridge with her boyfriend and her cat, Bella.

"I'm so proud of you!" Maloney tells a thirty-one-year-old named Brittany, who'd just started orientation for a job at a chair-making factory earlier that week. Brittany told us she was still injecting drugs—just enough not to be sick, she said—but she hoped to stop using soon.

"This job is your opportunity to shine, girl," Maloney told her, brightly. "Remember, baby steps!" She handed Brittany bags of donated food that also served as a cover for needle-exchange supplies. (Brittany's parents, with whom she and her boyfriend were temporarily staying, didn't approve.)

When someone expresses interest in bupe, Maloney makes referrals to Garcia, who sets them up with Tim for low-barrier buprenorphine and/or hepatitis C care, or gives them referrals for rehabs if that's their choice. "Most don't want to go into treatment; it's tricky," Maloney says. "You can't really push it on them. You kind of have to let them come to it on their own. I always tell them, 'I'm here for you, even after hours,' and 'There's a different route when you're tired and you're done.'"

But some people are so traumatized—including one of her participants who was repeatedly raped by his dad—that what they really need is full-on psychiatric care. Now thirty, this young man sleeps in a tent next to a big-box store clutching a flashlight and his knife. He tells her about his childhood abuse and how the needle (he injects meth) is the only relief he gets from his spiraling thoughts. "I can't blame him. You hear that, and you almost don't know where to start," Maloney says. Though she was trying to help him access psychiatric care, until that happened she would keep bringing him food and clean needles.

Garcia administers random drug screens for Olive Branch's low-barrier (or street outreach) bupe patients, the purpose of which isn't to prove abstinence but rather to confirm that the medicine Tim prescribes is really being taken and not sold for money to buy other drugs. Some clients sell their Suboxone on the black market, including twenty-seven-year-old Abbie, who's homeless off and on, and often games the system by waiting till the day before her appointment to take her medicine, so it will appear as if she's been taking it all along. "Some of them, they're goddamn chemists," Garcia said.

Abbie also volunteers at the center, checking people in and making Narcan kits, even when she's using. Wearing a T-shirt emblazoned with the word *SAVAGE*, she told me she'd gotten hooked on prescribed pain pills after a car wreck at the age of sixteen. She has a criminology degree from nearby Appalachian State and dreams of writing a memoir called *Degrees to Drugs*. Garcia deadpanned that she should reverse the title's order.

She's won her share of unicorn awards over the past two years, but welcoming Abbie's contributions is a form of harm reduction, too. Abbie was tweaking hard on methamphetamine the day we met—she kept jumping from one topic to the next before finishing her previous thought. She was processing having Narcanned a fellow user the day before, with the help of Garcia and Mathis, who coached her over the phone. But it took an hour before she could pull the story's thread to completion. It was like *Pulp*

Fiction meets the childhood ADHD classic, *If You Give a Mouse a Cookie*.

Estranged from her parents (who had the locks on their house changed to keep her out), Abbie had spent the night before at "that Asian guy's house," she told Garcia. There was boyfriend drama, something to do with a "side chick threatening to beat me down like a man," then another overdose inside a trap house that ended with friends shoving ice down the pants of the guy who overdosed. "Somebody else was conducting that one," she said, of the overdose reversal.

The day was so stressful, she told Mathis, "I was just like, 'I want to go somewhere and get high now.' I was going to kill somebody if I didn't."

"I'm glad you didn't!" Mathis said cheerfully.

Most Olive Branch staffers call Mathis "Mama Bear," and she pretends not to like it. "Whenever we're having a bad day or going through guy problems, she really guides us in the right direction," Maloney, the peer, explained as she drove me on her weekly route through Lincolnton. She pointed out places where she'd first recruited participants. "I would sit there by the courthouse and wait on people I thought looked like me."

Asked what she meant, she said she looked for people who "weren't real bougie-looking. Like when you see somebody with face tats or street clothes." Maloney has a broken-heart tattoo underneath one eye and a gang symbol from her former life under the other, but she usually covers them with makeup. "I just kinda talked to 'em," she added. "They didn't trust me at first, but then word spread."

Now, she visits about twenty people every week in various encampments, outside their homes, or in grocery store parking lots. She earns a fraction of what she made selling drugs, but she has her own place, she's regained custody of her teenage son, and she's attending Gaston College at night to become a substance-abuse counselor. Not long ago, she kicked out an abusive alcoholic boyfriend after Mathis taught her how to budget so she could live without his half of the rent. (Mathis's advice: cut out the junk food, and no more spending $1,000 on hair extensions you can't afford!)

"Now, my life's not chaotic no more. I make $600 a week, and that's plenty," Maloney said. "I don't have to go sell drugs or go prostitute just to afford what I like anymore," she said.

A year into the low-barrier program, Tim's roving Prius ran head-first into its first ethical snag. A Walgreens pharmacist texted over the weekend: One of Tim's patients was seen selling black-market Suboxone out of the pharmacy's restroom. The staff was uncomfortable. Customers complained.

Mathis wanted to kick him out of the program, but the man had been one of Tim's first low-barrier patients, and he had a soft spot for him, having already cured his hepatitis C. Before the Walgreens escapade, he seemed to be doing well on bupe. Mathis, an assiduous protector of boundaries, suggested some talking points but left the decision to Tim.

Her advice on the bathroom bupe situation: "I think we need to have a conversation around, 'Dude, this was reported to us. I understand the hustle, but at the same time you can't do that to the detriment of the program we created to try to help you. Otherwise, it'll put the entire program in jeopardy.'"

The following week, Tim gave the man a prescription for a two-week supply and told him he'd have to find another provider. "My guess is he'll return to buying it off the street, but it's tremendously expensive," he said.

That pained him. He worried about his patients, and he thought deeply about them. Their predicaments, he said, were best expressed by philosopher Simone Weil's description of *affliction*. They were afflicted more than they were addicted, experiencing suffering that Weil characterized as "physical pain, distress of soul, and social degradation all at once." Tim also took comfort in the words of Father Greg Boyle. Tim's brother had worked with the Jesuit priest at Homeboy Industries, the Los Angeles gang-intervention and reentry program. One of the things Boyle told struggling gang members was "I'll always help you, but I'll only help you." He wasn't really helping his patients if all they were doing was selling their bupe to buy heroin, was he?

Tim had been unbinding Lazarus, in one form or another, for decades, first delivering primary care to homeless men in Washington, DC, in the 1980s, during deinstitutionalization. In the '90s, he connected gay men and IV drug users in the South Bronx to HIV treatment through a Catholic ministry called Dominican Sisters of the Sick Poor. He'd had real successes throughout, hard-earned though they were. "They're inviting you into their space, and you see how really dark it is, and then some of them, eventually, they do get better," he said.

Some, but not all.

A week after their initial McDonald's meeting, Sam was still struggling. After he failed to make his next parking-lot appointment, Tim offered to drive to his home. But Sam lived with his father, who didn't approve of his taking Suboxone—the old "you're-trading-one-addiction-for-another" trope that continued to stymie so many. "So, we'll see where it goes."

The following week, they met for lunch with Sam's fianceé. The couple spent most of the meal blaming each other for their continued drug use; the fianceé dimed Sam for still visiting their dealer's house and offering to bring her drugs back.

"Sorry to disappoint you," Sam told Tim, as he left the table. Tim was puzzled. "I'm not sure how he thought he was disappointing me, but I'm less sure why he's still participating with us," he recounted.

The point was, though, Sam still had not fully disappeared.

Tim kept up their meetings and bupe refills. He would review his goals with him after two or three months, then ask if he felt his life was getting less chaotic. Sam missed some appointments but usually texted when he did.

The first time Sam came to the FQHC where Tim worked during the day, he broke the clinic's drug-screen records, testing positive for meth, benzos, cocaine, pot, fentanyl, tramadol, and bupe. Tim talked him into counseling, too, partly to address why he couldn't find the words to kick his girlfriend out of the house he owned. He'd started working again, which was good, and Tim hoped the counseling would help him delve into the roots of his addiction.

"I really need to stop 'cause if I don't, I'm gonna die," Sam said at every visit. Tim described his follow-ups with Sam and a handful of other patients I'd met over the phone or, more often, via lengthy e-mails he shared with me before his clinic shifts or between patients. He thanked me repeatedly for listening and being interested—for caring about his patients' lives.

En route to one visit, the gravel road was so rocky and crater-pocked that Tim's Prius had trouble making it to the patient's home. The house was so cluttered that Tim's patient told him she regularly chose to sleep inside her car. As Tim sat in the living room drawing her labs, sandwiched between fishing poles and other belongings, the woman's mother took notes. Her father offered Tim a piece of the toasted strudel they were having for dinner. Tim called it "an encounter with the unseen."

He wrote me about another of his patients, Natalie, who was HIV-positive and had overcome so much, despite having an abusive boyfriend who had shot and killed her cat—her one link to affection—and being an amputee with an ill-fitting leg prosthesis. After her cat's death, "she came to me pleading for 'something for my nerves. I'm about to lose my mind,'" Tim said. "I put her on a combination of Trintellix and Rexulti, which we're learning helps people use less meth."

The last time Tim saw Natalie, she told him she couldn't remember when she'd last done meth, and the bupe he'd prescribed her was also working—she'd not taken opioids for some time. "She had come so far and was doing so well," Tim said.

Tim said his favorite part of the job was when patients who got better helped others. The helpers became the leaders of their own small groups, in a grassroots structure that liberation theology refers to as base communities. "When they start helping each other, then it takes off like a wildfire—*that's* the gift. It is THEIR community that is doing the organizing, and we show up to learn from them," he wrote. Tim was hopeful that would be the case with Natalie, who had recently revived a friend with Narcan and told Tim, brightly, "I think this is the best I've ever been." She'd been injecting since she was sixteen. She was living with family members and "appeared as a different person!" Tim enthused.

But a week later, a relative found Natalie in an outbuilding on their property, dead from an accidental fentanyl overdose, and Tim was crushed.

Tim's newest pilot project began with Mathis picking up Papa John's pizzas and then accompanying him on a drive to a long-time patient's home in Nebo. The patient had invited friends to her house for pizza and also to get tested for hepatitis C. In Tim's experience, treating patients' hepatitis often paved his entrée into providing a broader range of care. Most weren't yet ready to stop using drugs, but all wanted treatment for their life-threatening, energy-sapping hepatitis C.

Duke University School of Medicine hepatologist Andrew Muir told me he had only witnessed such access to care twice in his career—in California's Bay Area and in Philadelphia. Muir and his colleagues had been brainstorming for years about ways to reach rural hep C–positive patients. "One of the most shocking things to me was that most patients don't even trust FQHCs, because they report being mistreated at them," said Muir. "If they don't feel comfortable going [to sliding-scale clinics], and the Ivory Tower is also beyond them, what are we going to do?"

Asked what advice he would give the Biden administration's future drug czar, Muir said, "What we don't have is a structure in place to reach people who are not in traditional health care. And that is because of where they live, how they live, and the fact that we don't have health care for all Americans."

Outside Mary Jo Silver's home, during my second visit to shadow Tim Nolan, he parked near a collapsing aboveground swimming pool and a smattering of broken-down vehicle parts. The thirty-two-year-old mother of two had grown up here, in a ranch house that had seen better days. She inherited the house after her mother's death at the age of sixty-three. Four years later, Mary Jo still mourned her mom, a much-beloved nurse who'd give people the shirt off her back while making them laugh so hard they'd literally "have tears running down [their] legs." Debbie Jack Silver had been the county's first woman to hold the position of assistant coroner, county firefighter, and EMT. In a small way, Mary Jo believed her hosting of the monthly gatherings for Tim was a way to carry her mother's legacy forward.

Her breakfast nook was now Tim's exam room. Prior to setting up there, he used to meet Mary Jo and her friends at a nearby truck stop for needle exchange. One night he noticed Mary Jo lingering after everyone else had gone home. She confided that she was pretty sure she had hepatitis C. Over the next couple months, using medicine donated by the manufacturer, Tim cured Mary Jo of the disease. After that, he started her on bupe.

Maybe her friends could similarly be helped?

It was Mary Jo's idea to invite Tim to test them at her house. Some nights, her friends' veins were so spent from injecting drugs that he couldn't draw enough blood for the test. Other nights, no one showed. Sometimes ten new people trickled into the nook. Most tested positive for the disease. Those who did were led into a back room in the house where Tim gently delivered the news.

Between patients, Mary Jo's kids chatted happily while watching TV and doing their homework, occasionally making appearances in the dining room to show off their pet ball python, King Noodle. "When my son was little, I was going through rough patches, and he lived with my parents," Mary Jo told me. "Now, sometimes he still stays with my dad."

In a year, Tim treated fifty-six people for hepatitis C this way. More than half were now cured or still in his care. Nine people had abandoned treatment, including one who'd overdosed and died; Tim learned of the death on Mother's Day, when the man's mother phoned to explain.

Overall, especially when compared to nationwide treatment-gap data, the project was a roaring success. A few patients, including Mary Jo, were no longer injecting drugs.

So it happened that Mary Jo Silver's breakfast nook became a de facto addiction triage center in a small corner of Appalachia, something a local health department could have been running—if funding for local health departments hadn't been decimated by budget cuts over the past fifteen years. If only local health officials welcomed people who use drugs instead of treating them like criminals or overwhelming them with bureaucratic hurdles they were incapable of clearing.

As Tim built up trust, word spread, and even strangers began phoning Mary Jo about that doctor who might be able to "fix my hep or get me off the needle for once and for all."

"I hear you can treat me" came another text on Tim's phone.

On a chilly March 2021 night, only four people showed up at Mary Jo's house. Among them was a middle-aged woman named Brenda, a supervisor in a steel factory. She had recently dedicated a two-week vacation toward weaning herself from opioids, which she'd been injecting for three years. But her DIY detox didn't take. (It rarely does, despite all the television-show portrayals).

"I was so sick, I just couldn't do it," she said. It was getting harder to be a functioning user; she feared she'd soon be fired from her job. "I want to get off this shit so bad, I just want out," she said.

Because Brenda was more self-sufficient than most, Tim asked her to come by his office later in the week; the plan was to treat both her SUD and her hepatitis C. He had a hunch she would show up, and she did, though they quickly shifted to evening meetings in a parking lot near her home because it was hard for her to get off work early.

When patients continued using illicit drugs while on bupe, Tim usually increased their care rather than kicking them out—sometimes upping their dosage or adding a counseling component. Sometimes he just let them be. As patients were cared for, gradually they got better, and eventually, some had the wherewithal to drive themselves to care.

That was the theory. In reality, relapses occurred, people lost jobs, cars broke down. "It's amazing how many deaths we hear about from others on a weekly basis. Fentanyl," he wrote in early June.

Just as Tim was getting Brenda into care, Mary Jo disappeared for the first time in two years. When he tried to call, her phone had been cut off. Child Protective Services had taken custody of her kids, he later learned.

"This morning I'm reflecting that for me there is no 'formula' in how to respond to these broken lives," Tim e-mailed. "Many in the treatment community seem to want to treat these folks in such a formulaic manner, and if they can't fit into that formula for whatever reason—they live in a tent, they don't have a car, they have trauma beyond our imagination—then they don't fit into the treatment plan."

A week later, Tim was still very concerned about Mary Jo. "She usually touches base when she's due for a refill, but I may go by her home tomorrow and see if I can find her," he wrote. He worried she'd be too depressed and ashamed to answer the door. He worked his contacts until he located a cousin of hers, and he kept reaching out. Within a month, she had reengaged in care and was hosting testing parties again.

The secret sauce to street medicine, Tim now understood, was to envelop the unseen. Pizza parties and old-fashioned house calls were the carrots. Continued medicine was the carrot. So were clean needles for the 40 percent of people who use drugs who weren't yet ready to stop using.

The sticks were—as long as you didn't turn the local Walgreens into a trap house—well, there shouldn't be any sticks.

Still, among some of his clinic colleagues, Tim was perceived as being too soft. He joked to one that "I'm becoming known as the Suboxone guy, and she said, 'The horse is out of the barn on that one, Tim,' with a scowl on her face!"

But the proof of his approach was, literally, in the clinic waiting room. On her break from work as a home health aide, Alisha Martin told me how Tim's low-barrier approach had saved her life—mainly because, for the first month, he was willing to overlook the fact that she was still using marijuana, Xanax, and opioids while taking her prescribed Suboxone.

Before that, she'd been homeless, staying in motels and selling drugs, recalled Martin, thirty-seven, of Morganton, North Carolina. She was twenty-one when she got hooked on prescribed OxyContin in the wake of gallbladder surgery. In a small town where pill mills had replaced the shuttered furniture factories, black-market follow-ups were easy to find. Martin just drove around looking for groupings of cars.

"You'd see people's driveways filling up on pill day," she recalled. "Drug dealers never have company unless they have something somebody wants."

Martin's drug use spiraled in waves befitting a Johnny Cash song. She lost her thirteen-year-old in a four-wheeler accident. Before long she'd lost custody of her other kids. She swore to Tim and me that an in-law had recently tried to kill her at a family gathering by poisoning her cheesecake with brake fluid ("she'd made it special for me, knowing that everyone else in the family likes chocolate").

For Martin, the front desk of the FQHC where Tim worked was where her recovery took its first baby step. Front-desk clerk Nicole Montelongo first spotted Martin running back and forth to the clinic bathroom—dopesick and diarrhea-plagued.

In recovery herself for seven years, Nicole has a sixth sense for what to say to broken-down people approaching her front-desk counter for the very first time. ("When I say Nicole runs the clinic, I mean she *runs* it," Tim had said.) Nicole gives new patients her direct phone number. She pulls the tearful ones aside and convinces them to be honest with their providers.

Then she decides which practitioner they'll see, based on whether she thinks they'd thrive better under Tim's harm-reduction approach, or the other nurse-practitioner's, whose style is stricter and more tough-love.

When thirty-six-year-old Julie Steen first approached the clinic counter wearing an oversized pink T-shirt, Nicole noticed her hangdog look and gently asked, "What are you here for today, honey?"

And Steen could only whisper, "It's awful."

"I'm in recovery," Nicole offered, cheerfully.

"But I don't work. And I'm an IV drug user."

"So was I," Nicole said, loud and proud. "And we can put you on a sliding-scale fee."

"Yeah, I'm homeless," Steen said, still whispering. "My children are in another home."

"I'm so happy to see you," Nicole said.

In the four hours I watched her man the front desk, Nicole calmed a psychotic patient who couldn't stop pacing, and counseled an elderly man with dementia who'd just been discharged from the hospital and had no memory of how he'd arrived there. Between patients, she opened a new box of COVID vaccines.

After a pharma sales rep dropped off lunch from Olive Garden for the staff, Nicole distributed the leftovers to patients in the waiting room. (On principle, Tim refuses to eat the pharma-funded freebies, a fact that other staffers find weirdly hippie-ish.)

Tim and Nicole knew that Steen could turn her life around, just as Martin had done. Once the buprenorphine stemmed her cravings, Martin stopped taking illicit drugs. Calculating precisely how long that would take was something experts were only just beginning to understand. Most patients still don't stay on buprenorphine long enough for the treatment to be effective, according to research published by University of Washington researchers in 2021. (Research still hasn't pinpointed a time frame for staying on addiction medicines, though most experts believe the duration should be years, perhaps even indefinitely, and there should not be arbitrary limits placed on treatment length.) Older females were better at staying on the medicine longer, which increased their chances of success; the more times people tried, the more inclined they were to eventually stop using.

Martin has since reunited with her kids and bought a brand-new-to-her car, a 2014 Chevy Equinox, which she drives to her full-time job as a home health aide. It had been a year since she'd last used Xanax or marijuana, she told me.

"It's the first time I've been clean since I was a teenager," she said proudly. "I feel good. I don't hurt no more. The diarrhea is all gone.

"Those pain pills come with pain, boy. They inflict pain if you don't need 'em."

I posed what I began to think of as my "magic-wand question" to the clinic's mental health counselor, Crystal Watson. By the end of my reporting for this book, I had asked scores of people this question. Watson had grown up in Morganton, where her dad worked in the furniture factories that once made the town hum. When I asked her what it would take to turn the overdose crisis around, she didn't have a nifty recipe—no one did—but she was positive that the lack of meaningful work and limits on higher education, vocational, and retraining opportunities bedeviled her patients.

In 2008, when Google announced it would open a $600 million data center in nearby Lenoir, Watson hoped the technology giant would help the state recover from the 250,000 factory jobs it had lost. But Google initially hired just 210 people, many of them relocated from elsewhere. A glowing 2018 economic report gave the company credit for creating 1,024 jobs, a figure that counted supply-chain affiliates and the "multiplier effect" of enhanced spending in the community.

But it rankled Watson that the government gave Google millions in tax incentives when it did so little for the actual people who'd lost their jobs. Procedures for taking federally funded Trade Adjustment Assistance courses were so onerous that fewer than a third of the displaced could afford to take advantage of them. At the same time that work evaporated, no one in power batted an eye as Burke County morphed into a pain-pill epicenter. Between 2006 and 2014, its pharmacies distributed 58 million prescription pain pills, enough for every resident to have 71 pills per year. In 2010 alone, area doctors prescribed opioids at a rate of 146.5 prescriptions per 100 people—far more prescriptions than people.

In regions with higher rates of OxyContin misuse, disability rates had gone up 7 percent more than the average, and Lenoir—home to once-mighty manufacturers like Broyhill, Bernhardt, and Kincaid Furniture—now had the highest disability rate in the state. (Surry was a not-too-distant fourth.)

Maybe the opioid-selling and -distributing tycoons testifying in courtrooms from California to New York should be forced to trade places with the "abusers" seated in America's jails, tent camps, and free clinics. Maybe every doctor who profited from opioid prescribing should be required to prescribe bupe or methadone free of charge.

Maybe some of the $262 million the state offered to land the Google server farm would have been better spent preparing the laid-off factory workers and their children for a knowledge-based economy. From economist Tim Bartik's point of view, the problem was power, or the lack of it: the victims of the corporations' rent-seeking practices possessed zero political clout.

"Going after data centers is not a solution," said Bartik, of the Upjohn Institute. He hoped COVID-driven telecommuting might entice more people to relocate from cities to rural areas. But would many outsiders move to distressed places where schools were notoriously subpar? "If you want to revitalize a local labor market, you should work on both the demand and supply sides," Bartik said. "Economic developers tend to only rely heavily on business tax incentives"—the demand side.

But on the supply side—that is, the *human being* side—funding for workforce training programs and substance-use treatment remains woefully scant, and, he added, the people operating them tend not to talk to each other. Bartik suggested giving tax credits to employers willing to hire people with substance-use histories—and nurture those workers like both their very businesses and the health of their communities depended on it, which they do.

Was it possible to scale up the work of the nation's Jessica Maloneys, Tim Nolans, and Nikki Kings? Most experts I talked to were skeptical, given the political climate. "It's possible you could create an environment that has fewer barriers to what they're doing and inspires other people to do similar work," offered China Schertz, a medical anthropologist at the University of Virginia who studies addiction across the globe.

She cited Partners in Health, founded by Harvard professor Dr. Paul Farmer, who demonstrated that it was possible to deliver novel, community-based treatment to HIV-positive people in Haiti and other resource-poor places in the late 1980s—even if his team initially had to literally transport the antiretroviral medications in their personal suitcases. Farmer didn't let the enormity of the problems overwhelm him; he refused to be swayed by bureaucracy, the skepticism of colleagues, or political apathy.

"What they pulled off was a kind of spectacle," Schertz said. "They used a spectacular form of giving to humiliate the international community," which eventually spurred new World Health Organization guidelines and helped lower the price of drugs.

I noted that Farmer, who died in February 2022 at the age of sixty-two was a proponent of applying liberation theology to medicine, as was Martin Luther King Jr. Its tenets:

- Poor people should get preferential care because they're the most likely to get sick. "Imagine how much unnecessary suffering we might collectively avert if our health care and educational systems, foundations, and nongovernmental organizations genuinely made a preferential option for the poor?" Farmer wrote.
- Denying poor people the benefits of science is a form of structural violence that's embedded into our cultural, political, and economic systems. As King put it, "Of all the forms of inequality, injustice in health is the most shocking and the most inhuman because it often results in physical death."

- Forget casting aside patients who missed appointments and don't adhere to the advice of medical experts as "noncompliant." Rather, community health workers should go to the afflicted where they live, Farmer urged, and ask, "How can we accompany you on your path to wellness, or a life with less suffering due to a disease?"

In reality, such largesse was reserved for tech giants, not people like Sam and Natalie. When North Carolina was trying to lure Google, county commissioners rolled out the welcome mat, noting that the company's Stanford University–grown employees would have to hire locals to clean their houses, mow their lawns, and perform other service tasks.

That bothered Watson, who said: "You see the people who work there coming out of the center driving Teslas, and that's just not our community." A former teen mom with generations of addiction in her family, Watson credited her own white-collar position to having had "a counselor who acted like she gave a shit about me," she said. "I want to be that for other people now."

Asked how she approached teary patients like Julie Steen, Watson used a psychological term. She tries to meet them all with *unconditional positive regard.* "I always start with, 'We're so glad to see you. We're so glad you're here.'

"We always seem to go back to stigma, but I'm telling you, it still plays the biggest part," Watson said. "I mean, just look around in our lobby. There's clients sitting there right now with their heads hung in shame." And no wonder: three-quarters of America's primary-care doctors say they are unwilling to have a person with SUD marry into their family, and two-thirds believe addicted people are "dangerous."

An addiction specialist in Baltimore told me her patients just assumed that when the dingy methadone clinic building where she practiced was renovated that the center must be planning to move. The building's upgrade had to be for other people; they couldn't imagine the operators investing money to beautify a structure dedicated to treating people with SUD.

Researchers were only now beginning to crack the multifaceted code of keeping people from disappearing. An author of a study based in Fresno, California, looked at the behaviors of 500 people with SUD who had managed to stay in treatment.

As an aside, Watson told me that the professional most critical to a person's initiation into recovery wasn't their doctor or even their nurse. It was the attitude of the person running the front desk.

For months, Tim's patients took turns disappearing. Once when Sam did show up, he falsified his urine drug screen, incurring the wrath not only of Tim but also, and maybe more important, of Nicole. ("Nicole doesn't mess around," Tim said).

Still, Tim took victories where he could, and he was thrilled about the progress of Brenda, the steel-mill supervisor. Though he initially worried when her boyfriend said he wasn't ready to stop using heroin—a problem Tim picked up on quickly at Mary Jo's house—he was buoyed to see an independent streak evolving in her.

The minute they sat down, she confided, "I want to talk about treatment."

"She was looking for a lifeline," Tim recounted. Within a week, he'd started her on hepatitis C meds and low-cost buprenorphine.

Weeks later when he stopped by her house, the boyfriend was gone. Brenda greeted Tim proudly with "I'm twenty-nine days clean!"

She had replaced the problematic boyfriend with a cat.

Chapter Eleven

Backburn

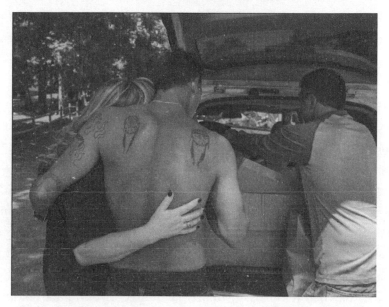

Birches needle-exchange workers delivering supplies, Surry County, North Carolina.

B ack in Mayberry, the unseen were still talking to each other through the chrome phones of the Surry County Jail. They were still living beneath the Chang and Eng Bunker Memorial Bridge, named in honor of the famous conjoined twins who settled in the town.

And on one sweltering afternoon in April 2021, they were holed up in a tiny Mount Airy trap house, monitoring the cameras on the other side of the door, shooting dope, and waiting for James Stroud to come to them.

For the next hour, a steady stream of people made their way

to Billie Campbell's stuffy, rent-by-the-week room. They came to get Narcan, fentanyl test strips, and needles—which they called points, rigs, hippie pistols—from Surry County's new needle exchange. They came to sign their names to a card stamped with the North Carolina statute that protected them from drug paraphernalia charges the next time they got caught by police with needles and trace amounts of drugs. The program, called Birches, was neither county-approved nor health department–supervised—a fact that appealed to the participants James was serving from the trunk of his cluttered car.

"Used to be, they'd take you to jail quick as hell for a dirty rig," said Billie, forty-seven, who'd once used drugs with James. She'd spent years inside the Surry County Jail, including nine months for possession of heroin and for operating what police called "a drug dwelling." She'd done time not long ago in a Raleigh prison, too, where she paid a guard to smuggle in Suboxone strips she could sell. Her drug of choice was meth; she'd only started snorting heroin three months before. Selling was more Billie's thing.

The day before our visit, Billie Narcanned a young man named Jacob with supplies she'd gotten from James on his last visit. "I told her, 'Billie, I don't feel good; something ain't right.' And I started crying," Jacob recalled. "She knows when I cry, I'm about to overdose." It was his sixth overdose, and the tears were always his tell.

While Billie's trap house morphed into a needle-distribution hub, something even more surprising happened. A slow and fragile turn began in Mount Airy's diners, in the back seats of its police cruisers, and, eventually, even in the Surry County Jail as a few detectives quietly and tentatively dipped their toes into the world of helping people with SUD.

James was excited to see it unfold, finally, but he was operating at the ragged edge of capacity, as was everyone I knew doing this work. One told me that her dream was to take a two-week vacation for the first time in her life. (She settled for a weekend away at one of those resorts where they constantly pitch you to buy a condo.) Another spent most nights laid out on her floor clutching her cat. As recovery activist Tracey Helton Mitchell put it: "If you work in any way adjacent or directly with overdoses, I strongly recommend having nonverbal hobbies, disconnecting from social media, having a playlist of funny movies, and making time for walks and/or physical exercise. Burnout and grief are killing the helpers."

Night and day, James got about a dozen texts an hour. When I asked whether being in Billie's trap house triggered him or made him nervous, he said it only made him more determined to make sure that people who wanted help got it.

After we left Billie's house, he asked, "Did you notice how miserable they were?"

The first time I met the Birches team, they were packing up Narcan kits in the back room of a Mount Airy Pizza Hut, preparing for a quiet launch of the region's first needle exchange. It was late 2020, and founder Wendy Odum had already filed the state-required safety plan with the county. Hearing nothing back, she plunged ahead.

That it didn't immediately backfire had a lot to do with her No. 1 volunteer and right hand, James Stroud, the former banker who knew people in all corners of the county, from board rooms to under the bridge. Before his fall into meth addiction, James had been a top salesman at the Royal Bank of Scotland, the third-largest bank in the world. "I'm used to networking," he said.

Rather than kowtow to the region's power structure, James strategically greased its wheels—calling people, setting up lunches. "My thinking is, if I can get a handful of deputies on board with what we're doing, they can refer people to us instead of just arresting everybody," he told me.

Three years earlier, the last time he'd seen narcotics detective Sergeant Brandon Johnson, the sergeant had James pinned face-down on the pavement, in handcuffs. Later at the station, James remembered, Johnson told him, "If you ever want to get out of this lifestyle, call me." Now, almost three years into his sobriety, James took the detective out to lunch. He wanted him to understand that people who participated in needle exchange were five times more likely to enter treatment, and that, absent intervention, these were the people most likely to end up in Johnson's handcuffs again.

Previous efforts to offer harm-reduction services in Surry County had backfired spectacularly. When a public health department worker suggested in 2017 that Mount Airy open a needle exchange, the outcry was so loud and immediate that she was fired.

"One good cop can make all the difference," said Fred Brason, a nationally known treatment innovator in nearby Wilkes County. Birches leaned on Brason for syringes when supplies were low, as well as for advice. "If you really want to make change, you don't go to the politicians who have no clue; you go to the people who are working the streets," Brason said.

Wendy and James started delivering needles and Narcan from their cars just before the pandemic hit, and they had not wavered, not even when participants showed up maskless because they had more pressing things on their minds—like not being dopesick. When supplies ran low, the pair used their own money to mail-order more. In the first six months, they signed up 300 users and ferried more than a dozen to treatment. Some went to abstinence-based residential rehabs, which had been James's route, and some went to outpatient bupe or methadone (Wendy had taken daily methadone for ten years).

"It's to the point now that people I don't even know message me," James said. "After about three visits to deliver them needles, they'll ask, 'Hey, can you help me get clean?'" Getting people admitted to quality residential treatment remained his biggest hurdle. Half the people with OUD in Surry County couldn't access treatments because they didn't have Medicaid or private insurance; it was that way in the dozen states that still hadn't expanded Medicaid under Obamacare. And most church-affiliated centers still refuse to allow treatment with medications; some say they don't have the medical staff to supervise it, but many cling to abstinence-only models and are philosophically opposed: *Jesus loves the "addicts" but he doesn't want them taking bupe.*

It is perhaps the sorest point of the ongoing overdose crisis that the very sickest people—many of them unhoused and devoid of support from friends or family—are the ones left to navigate this thorny divide.

Unlike the counties where Michelle Mathis and Tim Nolan worked, Surry County has not one sliding-scale FQHC for adults. The largest Medicaid-funded option for addiction medicines remained Daymark Recovery Services, but most drug users I met found its mandatory counseling requirements exceedingly onerous, and roughly half of the addicted working poor in the community don't qualify for Medicaid because state politicians had shunned Obamacare as socialism. An estimated half-million North Carolinians would benefit from closing the Medicaid coverage gap. (It would most help those who earn too much to qualify for Medicaid but still can't afford insurance and too often end up using costlier emergency rooms rather than primary care.) Even those who did qualify for Medicaid had trouble getting to appointments.

Daymark patients starting bupe are required to attend nine hours of counseling, or intensive outpatient (IOP) therapy, a week—but its center only operates during the day, when most people work. While Daymark provided free smartphones during COVID so patients could connect via Zoom, only 30 of its 100 publicly funded slots were filled.

"There's just not evidence for mandating counseling in my view," the Columbia psychiatrist Carl Erik Fisher told me. The scientific consensus is crystal clear that bupe or methadone should be the first-line treatment for OUD, and that it should be offered without the requirement of counseling. But across the country, local treatment providers stuck in outdated twelve-step-only ideologies designed for alcohol, not opioids, often ignored that consensus—especially when they get paid for counseling services, not patient outcomes.

"There's got to be something [publicly funded] that's between Daymark's nine hours a week and nothing," said Brason, the Wilkes County treatment innovator. The best evidence points to a stepped-care model in which patients who struggle get increased treatment, including alternative treatments to bupe like methadone.

An hour west, Brason's nonprofit, Project Lazarus, had been triaging the addicted for going on fifteen years, and Brason had consulted in more than 100 communities across the country. At the start, he'd scared local leaders in his rural North Carolina community, too—by pushing too fast for change. "Baby steps, I tell people," he said.

But even baby steps were a tough sell in sprawling Surry County. Traversing its 536 square miles requires precise organization, a better schedule, more hands on deck. Also: boundaries. Wendy had yet to complete the paperwork to become a tax-exempt nonprofit—in her mind, she was too busy saving lives to tend to record-keeping. Technically, Birches worked under the umbrella of Winston-Salem's Twin Cities Harm Reduction Coalition, whose director had just relapsed. That was happening at harm-reduction organizations across the country, with beloved leaders dying from overdose and drug-related infections in several cities. "The past few years have been really traumatic," the Twin Cities director, Colin Miller, e-mailed me from rehab. "Lost a lot of friends to overdose and such and ended up going back to familiar self-medicating with dope and benzos."

Wendy answered every person who reached out with a message, day or night. James spent $11,000 of his own money bailing a friend out of jail.

Brason worried about the pair. "They're doing great work, but the way they're doing it won't be sustainable. I haven't told them that quite yet," he said.

It was hard to set boundaries when old friends were overdosing all around you. It was hard when the homeless young women who were couch-surfing in trap houses reminded you of your dead daughter. After a stop in a trailer park to deliver needles to a frenetic young meth user whose teeth were missing, Wendy sighed. "My daughter, she wandered like that, too. She'd just carry a bag."

By the end of May 2021, Surry County's official count for the year was 200 overdoses and 22 overdose deaths—but those numbers were likely an undercount. Billie alone had lost fourteen people in her circle to overdose death, and among Birches' clientele, those who revived their friends with naloxone usually refused to call EMS in order to avoid possible arrest.

During my first ride-along with Wendy and James, they spent most of the day trying to help Eric Snow, a forty-three-year-old welder, get into a faith-based rehab called Hope Valley. They'd met a week before at a well-known meth house, where James passed out needles, naloxone, and fentanyl test strips he'd personally bought online. A few days later, a friend from that house called him frantic—Eric was overdosing, and she needed James to talk her through using the reversal drug. James sped to the house with extra naloxone—with fentanyl-packed drugs, sometimes it takes several doses of Narcan to bring someone back to consciousness—while giving instructions for rescue breathing over the phone.

"The heroin that's around now, it's stout," Eric said.

James drove him to a medically supervised detox in Statesville an hour away. But when he picked him up five days later, there was no plan for follow-up care, no way for him to continue his Suboxone. The rehab that James arranged wouldn't admit him until he showed proof of a negative COVID test. And finding a test at the pandemic's height in Mount Airy took us three stops and, between other needle-exchange stops, four hours. By the time Eric got his test, his rehab was closed to intake for the day, forcing him into active withdrawal—diarrhea, nausea, and crushing anxiety—for a minimum of twelve hours.

"This right here is the bullshit of everything," Wendy fumed. "People say, 'Well, they can just stop.' But I want them to know the truth about the utter lack of choice to do anything different."

She compared their work to firefighters creating a backburn, an outside ring of fire that paradoxically creates a boundary, sucking oxygen away from the wildfire. "What I'm talking about is, if we can contain it and then slowly smother out the damage, then fire always brings new growth," Wendy said.

It wasn't standard protocol—and it was definitely a boundary-buster—but that night James took Eric into his home. They ate takeout and watched *Cobra Kai*, the follow-up to *Karate Kid*, and fell asleep on the two couches in his living room. Without calling attention to it, James made sure Eric's belongings stayed locked in his car so he could sleep without worrying that he might bolt.

The next morning, James took him to rehab and breathed a sigh of relief.

The Birches team thought that Mark Willis, Surry County's opioid-response director, with his emphasis on charts and data, was too encumbered by the bureaucracy that employed him. "There's like a whole underground world operating underneath the official world, and it's booming, and it's not going to suddenly get better by [officials] meeting on Zoom and playing nice," Wendy said. "You gotta be willing to get out here and build up little threads of trust."

The skepticism was mutual. Willis didn't trust Wendy because her husband, Steven Odum, had become a political lightning rod. He frequently took to Facebook Live to criticize county officials and accuse them of corruption. (A family member had run against the sheriff, unsuccessfully, the year before.) Willis feared that associating with the Odums would backfire and hurt his program, and he wasn't wrong. He didn't trust James entirely, either, recalling a nasty run-in they'd had in a martial-arts class years earlier, before James stopped using meth.

A native Californian, Willis was still considered an outsider in the small town, even though for decades he'd owned Surry County land. Still, by mid-2021, he had managed to turn about half his items on the Operation Vital Links board from red to green, though with several footnotes and caveats. A year after the 2018 "let 'em die and take their organs!" meeting to organize a volunteer transportation network, Willis nabbed a Department of Justice grant to pay for an official one. The grant funded a coordinator and four drivers and paid for the cars, but because of COVID-related funding delays it took another year before he could get it launched. "It's a software thing; they 'apologize,'" Willis said, making air quotes.

When his Ride the Road to Recovery began in June 2021, drivers were not allowed to carry more than one person at a time, per COVID restrictions, and everyone had to be masked. Willis worried that some residents would take advantage of the program and treat it as a free concierge service, but he was surprisingly buoyed by the initial results: In the first two weeks they'd driven twenty-seven people to treatment, with occasional stops to pick up prescriptions and diapers, or drop someone off for his late-shift job at the chicken plant, which was still facing a severe labor shortage. All were polite and appreciative. No one overdosed or nodded out.

"Right now, anybody who asks, and as long as it improves the health of this community, we'll transport them," Willis said.

After two years of bureaucratic box-checking, Lazarus could finally get a ride to treatment in a county-owned vehicle.

The month of June 2021 heralded the fiftieth anniversary of the War on Drugs, the moment Richard Nixon began his police offensive against "public enemy number one"—drugs and the largely poor and minority people who used them. If communities ever managed to unwind the drug war, Willis now understood, the shift would not be determined by logistics, funding, or even national policies.

The biggest factor remained politics, exactly as Jerome Jaffe, the nation's first drug czar, had predicted: What were voters willing to accept?

"I think we're pushing the limits of it right now," said Willis. He'd spent months trying to calculate the answer to Jaffe's question down to the percentage point. He'd created an online survey asking citizens whether they believed that the county's law enforcement officers and the courts had adequately responded to the overdose crisis. By a margin of 75–25, respondents said no and no. Almost everyone personally had a friend or family member with SUD.

To chip away at stigma, Willis got a grant to create a series of high-production-value videos. The mini-documentaries combined data with heart-tugging stories of recovery, not only from local people in recovery but also from innovators like Michelle Mathis at Olive Branch. One video featured the story of East Tennessee drug-prosecutor-turned-judge Duane Slone, who'd been adamantly opposed to allowing his probationers to take buprenorphine—until he and his wife adopted a child born with neonatal abstinence syndrome in 2011. Soon after, Slone "took a deep dive into the science of addiction," a self-directed study that led him to finally *understand* how nearly impossible it is to battle opioid addiction without bupe. Slone's recovery court now allowed all forms of addiction medicines, under the direction of a clinician, plus recovery housing that Slone spear-headed in a three-story log cabin surrounded by eighteen acres of Appalachian woods.

Overdose deaths went down 50 percent in the region as Slone picked off the naysayers one at a time, gradually winning over resistant officials in several surrounding counties. He piloted court projects that ultimately led to reduced jail occupancy and property crime and increased healthy births, after which 90 percent of mothers retained custody of their kids. "Call it a *pilot* instead," Slone told me, echoing Brason's baby-steps advice. "When people are scared of new things, call it a pilot—that's the key."

While Slone remained an outlier in rural law enforcement, he was also a powerful reminder of what enlightened elected officials could do when they worried more about doing the right thing than about winning their next reelection campaign.

"The overarching thing is that we go as upstream as we can, we meet people where they are, and we let the clinical professionals guide us," Slone told me.

Willis worried that the Slone videos would ruffle the feathers of local judges, and when I asked him about them later, he shook his head. His boss, the county manager, was afraid the videos would offend the judges and wouldn't let Willis release them.

In 2019, United States Supreme Court chief justice John Roberts gave Slone the court's highest judicial honor for his work on the opioid crisis. Slone was masterful at turning skeptics into collaborators, figuring out how to schmooze a pilot project into being and, once the benefits were too obvious to be ignored, get it officially stamped. North Carolina policing consultant Donnie Varnell boiled this change-making formula down to a technique he dubbed Barbecue and Sweet Tea. Varnell had talked many a reluctant sheriff into adopting pre-arrest protocols to divert the addicted to treatment across the country, including eight sheriffs in North Carolina. He'd touted drug courts because they saved taxpayers' money, and needle exchanges because police officers were less likely to get stuck with infection-harboring needles. In Indiana, where the sheriffs once slow-clapped my message about offering bupe in their jails, a few eventually changed their tune after the governor's office attached more than $4 million of state and federal funding to the initiative.

Like Slone and Mathis, Varnell believes the personal approach is paramount, and so is culture. In rural areas like Mount Airy, it was wise to physically enter the sheriff's lair: "You don't simply call or e-mail him with an invitation to come to you. And you take decent food when you go—never, ever doughnuts. As a police officer, I love a doughnut. But you will never see me eating one in public. Instead, you take real food," he said. "You take actual lunch."

On the theory that no elected sheriff wants to be the first to do anything—it's too politically dangerous—Varnell passes out testimonial "quote sheets" from other sheriffs who have seen criminal recidivism and property crimes plummet after implementing pre-arrest diversion. He hands them copies of glowing newspaper stories, not mentioning that he has personally spoon-fed the articles to overworked, content-starved news reporters along the way.

I shared these strategies with Mark Willis as I learned them, personally introducing him to Varnell and Judge Slone, among others. I told him about a Martinsburg, West Virginia, health department nurse who'd coaxed local police officers into permitting needle exchange through the simple act of buying the Narcan for them to carry. That small act of generosity showed them that she cared about them as people, with real-life budget restraints: "It was really our relationships that saved everything," Angie Gray said.

I told him about the emergency-department administrator in my hometown of Roanoke, Virginia, who'd changed his mind about addiction medications and now had buprenorphine pre-scribers and peer specialists stationed in emergency rooms across the western half of Virginia, with connections to outpatient clinics and peer-support specialists. "For twenty years we just didn't be-lieve it was within our purview," said Dr. John Burton of Carilion Clinic. "But once we finally dove into the science and the medical literature, we said, how can we *not* be doing this?"

More than almost anything else I'd witnessed, that simple act of an empowered physician changing his mind—then admitting publicly that he'd changed his mind!—brought the city of Roa-noke closer to the "urgent care for the addicted" that Tess Henry envisioned before her death. And Burton wasn't just pleased with the results, he was reinvigorated about his work because he was no longer seeing the same people cycling in and out of his ERs. "I feel like turning mental cartwheels every day," he told me.

Within a year, Surry County's private hospital, Hugh Chatham Medical Center, was prescribing bupe out of its emergency depart-ment, and Willis's intervention team had an office in the hospital, thanks to a young female physician who'd been eager to launch the initiative. "Any time I tried to go, 'Let's build this together,' it didn't work. But any time I found one individual willing to pick up the torch, it worked," Willis said. He was going to go back to the county's other hospital and very casually brag about the first hospital's fine work. "Rather than direct confrontation, this is *hapkido*," he said, referring to a martial-arts style employing a redirection of force.

I also introduced Willis to the Indiana small-town phenom,

Nikki King, who'd managed to co-locate her hospital's drug-treatment team inside a courthouse by sheer pluck and force of will. Over the course of three years, Willis and I spoke most months, and every time, I shared strategies I'd seen working in other locales—initiatives I came to think of as my Harm-Reduction Greatest Hits. While he appreciated the connections and followed up with most, for a long time they also made him want to smack his head against his color-coded whiteboard—and mine, too. (Our interviews, he told me repeatedly, half joking, reminded him of interrogations he'd once conducted for the DEA. "The hot lamp on my forehead is the only thing missing.")

"This is the frustration I have when you send me these things. They're fantastic, but they're not asking what other options are out there. They're just saying no!"

For now, he would back-burner the drug-court plan and concentrate on initiatives where he'd already formed allies. Two counties over, a grant designed to divert addicted and mentally ill people to treatment instead of jail had fallen into his lap by way of a SAMHSA grant that hadn't worked out for the usual reasons—stigma and bureaucracy. Willis and the grant team removed the word *diversion* and renamed the project the Mental Health Assistance Program, so it wouldn't sound like he was telling the sheriff or the district attorney what to do. *Hapkido*.

The county donated an old building to house the program, but when a black-mold problem was discovered in the basement, progress ground to a halt—an irony, considering the county had never had trouble housing inmates in its overcrowded, mold-riddled jail.

Overdoses were at an all-time high when Willis got more bad news. The head of Surry County's EMS, Johnny Shelton, who'd been an ally to Willis at every turn, died of a self-inflicted gun-shot wound. He was sixty-seven. The suicide weighed on Willis, who considered Shelton a close friend. "During the last three days of his life, he'd tended to five deaths. So, sixty-seven years old and all of that weight on his shoulders—was that part of it?" he wondered.

Willis had met a woman at a community-wide addictions summit. Sonya Cheek was thirty-nine, with a lot of "lived experience," as the saying goes. And he could tell from the way she spoke that she could hold her own with county leaders and law enforcement. An outspoken lesbian, Sonya had a brother who worked for the county, and her family had stature in the community.

Sonya had been sober for two years, following several years of heroin and meth use that culminated in her losing custody of her daughter and living out of her car. It had all started with a 2013 OxyContin prescription for her psoriatic arthritis, she told me. Her doctor told her that Purdue had reformulated the drug to be abuse-resistant in 2010 "so it's not addictive anymore," he said—but there was nothing to keep her from simply swallowing the pills, which she did, first as directed and then taking more until she eventually progressed to heroin after two people close to her killed themselves, and the pills no longer kept her pain at bay.

Sonya became intimately familiar with the vomit buckets inside the moldy jail. If she could survive that, Willis thought, surely she could handle Mayberry's CAVEs.

At their initial meeting, Sonya was still on probation and working at her uncle's road-paving business—the only place she'd been able to secure work because of her felony record. She owned her own car now and had a home, and her daughter lived with her most of the time. When her probation ended, Willis made her the second member of his intervention team. Sonya's job was to contact people within a day or two of an overdose, and, if they were willing, help them get into whatever form of treatment they chose. Sonya herself had gone to a Christian-based rehab. It was abstinence-only, but Willis made sure she also understood the science and wasn't opposed to addiction medications.

Within six months, Sonya had become the heretofore missing link between the official Surry County and the one existing—barely—just below ground.

In the beginning, Sonya's main source of referrals came from EMS workers, who asked people, just after reviving them from an overdose, to sign a simple form saying they agreed for the intervention team to reach out to them. But when Sonya followed up by phone, she learned that many had written down bogus numbers, or didn't have cell phones, or simply refused to answer when she called.

Though funding for her job came through Willis's office, Sonya and the other peers were supervised by mental health administrators at Daymark who didn't permit them to leave their home offices during COVID. Because Willis subcontracted with Daymark to oversee the peers—a decision he now questioned—the program was stuck in a bureaucratic quagmire just as Sonya was gassed up and ready to go.

From San Francisco to rural Appalachia, I heard that refrain everywhere I reported: To reach people who use drugs who were most at risk of dying, outreach workers had to physically enter the spaces where they were living, from truck-stop parking lots and riverside encampments, to "bandos," or abandoned homes—exactly what Tim Nolan had been doing for two years.

Though they were trained to work in the hospitals and on the streets, Sonya and her fellow peers were literally grounded, at home, their phones their only tool. Because of COVID, Sonya wasn't permitted to attend twelve-step meetings in person; she wasn't supposed to work weekends or nights. The texting app she was required to use was the same one she'd used to buy drugs—a potential trigger.

"I'm looking for loopholes so I can get out and meet people and be in the community," she told me, a month into her job. "My passion is to help people, and me and my personal life would love something 8:00 to 5:00. But when I was getting high, I didn't just get high Monday to Friday 8:00 to 5:00."

She called one woman's cell phone every day for two months—until finally the woman picked up and said, "Okay! I guess you guys really *do* care."

Wendy and James were not so encumbered, a status that sometimes helped and sometimes hurt. Whereas Sonya had a list of things Daymark forbade her from doing, Wendy and James were grant-funded volunteers who went wherever they were called. I told Sonya about James and gave her his number. When James suggested the three of them meet for lunch, thus commenced the first baby step of a Surry County portal to treatment instead of jail. It wasn't official, but the hope was that, in time, it would be.

The trio talked constantly about the status of people who use drugs in the community: who needed clean needles, who was ready to go to treatment or needed a ride to detox, which rehab had a bed. "I've talked to Sonya five times already this morning," James told me one day at 10:00 a.m. Sonya told me James was her best friend.

By midsummer 2021, Birches had more than 600 participants, COVID restrictions were beginning to lift, and Sonya was now literally getting regular referrals through the chrome phone—the toilet intercom—of the Surry County Jail. "Some of us, we talk for twelve, sixteen hours a day," one told me.

Thirty-four-year-old Dylan Goughary had just spent four years in prison for meth possession and illegal possession of a firearm. He was awaiting reentry at the Surry County Jail when a woman in the next cell block stuck her head into the toilet and recited Sonya's phone number from memory (the woman and Sonya had been friends since childhood). Estranged from his relatives and due to get out in a few days, Dylan had only the clothes on his back and that was it, he told Sonya over the telephone. She arranged for him to move to a halfway house. A few days later, when she met him there with his parole officer and handed him clothes, he broke down crying in the parking lot.

"Listen, I know you're nervous," she told him. "I know there's a lot going through your mind. Just breathe, and if you need anything, call me."

Sonya was the first person who'd ever gotten him into treatment, Dylan told me. And she kept helping him—with housing, with medical care, and when he was between places and needed a couch to crash on, she took him into her family's home for the night.

Within four months, Dylan was working full-time, sharing both a car and a rental house with a friend from the halfway house. "There have definitely been a few times I've thought about using again," he said. "But whenever I think I'm having a really bad day, the first thing I do is I think of Sonya, and I call and talk to her.

"Words don't even cover what all she's done."

When James introduced Sonya to the thirty-one-year-old narcotics detective, Sgt. Brandon Johnson, it turned out that Johnson had once arrested Sonya, too. Rather than ask immediately for Johnson's help, Sonya and James asked if there was anything they could do for the sergeant.

What Johnson needed, he told the pair, was for former drug users to tell their recovery stories at the drug-awareness events he was putting on in area schools. And another form of back-scratching commenced.

So James and Sonya shared their stories at Johnson's school events, after which Sonya handed the sergeant a stack of her business cards. Going forward, the detective told them, whenever he or his colleagues arrested someone for possession, he would give out one of her cards.

"It can be 9:00 at night, and I'll call Sonya with that [arrested] person sitting in my police cruiser," Johnson told me, six months into the pilot. "If I have a person, and they're breaking down, telling me they got kids and they want to get their life on track, I'll cut them loose and give them a chance to get up with Sonya."

When Sonya's busy, he calls James, even though he initially opposed the idea of Birches' giving out needles to people who use drugs. "At first—I ain't gonna lie—I was against the needle exchange," Johnson told me. "I thought, 'What in the world? You're *giving* drug users needles?'

"But after looking at the bigger picture and talking to James, I see it gives him a chance to get inside their houses, get into their personal lives, and he's sharing his positive story about getting clean and coming where he came from. So I can see both sides now," Johnson said. "Drug users are gonna get their needle to shoot up—whether it's dirty or clean."

And though they didn't exactly take the sheriff barbecue and sweet tea, Sonya, James, and Wendy did meet with him after Johnson was fully on board. By mid-2021, and with the sheriff's approval, Johnson and his colleagues were offering treatment rather than arrest to five or six people per week. By fall, Sonya told me, "I think I'm changing the minds of politicians and bureaucrats. My goal is, now, I want to meet the judge that sentenced me and the judge that set my bond—not as 'work with me' but as 'I want you to meet the person I am today.'"

Ultimately, it would be stories like Sonya's that pried open the clenched hearts and minds. It was not something you could calculate on a whiteboard, as much as Mark Willis wished it was. But, culturally, it fit Mount Airy to a T.

In mid-May, two weeks after I met Billie Campbell inside her tiny trap house, Brandon Johnson's police partner pulled Billie over. She was driving back to Mount Airy from Winston-Salem, where she'd gone to buy heroin. She had four grams on her at the time.

With six other drug charges pending, that was enough to provoke federal charges and a potential incarceration of fifteen years. An officer at the scene who recognized her asked her plaintively, "Billie, what the hell are we gonna do?"

The next day, Billie sat in a tiny isolation cell on a thin, urine-soaked mattress, detoxing and getting sick. For the first time in her six years of dealing drugs, an officer visiting her in jail did not try to turn her into a confidential informant. This time he told her she needed to get help, or she would die.

"Get me some help, then," Billie told him. "I can't do it alone."

The officer handed her a card with Sonya Cheek's name and phone number. A few days later, Billie left the urine-stained mattress for a yearlong treatment facility called Tabitha's House near Greensboro. An hour away from the people, places, and things that had long been rocket fuel for Billie's addiction, Tabitha's was the same facility where Sonya had gone for treatment four years before.

"I was so dopesick when Sonya come and got me," Billie recalled. "I was crying, and I was so grateful to get some help."

At first, Billie struggled with the religious aspect of the program. She'd gone to another residential rehab a few years before, a religious-based facility in West Virginia that made patients fundraise in front of Walmart stores, selling Jesus-themed T-shirts and bumper stickers. "That last place, they Jesused me out," she said. "I told Steve [her stepdad], 'Get me the hell out; this is a cult.'"

But she ended up loving Tabitha's House. Billie still suffered from restless leg syndrome—exacerbated by her opioid withdrawal—but a counselor at the facility connected her to medical care and advocated for her with the prosecutor and the judge. As long as she showed progress, the judge and district attorney agreed to let her remain in treatment, placing her charges on hold. She was making sober friends for the first time in many years and working in a rehab-run thrift store called Tabitha's Closet. I bought a desk lamp during my first visit to see her there, and after that Billie phoned me excitedly whenever she got a new shipment of overstock lamps that she thought I'd like. From heroin to home furnishings, she was a born saleswoman, it was clear.

She was sleeping through the night for the first time in months. "I'm used to sleeping in thirty-minute increments because I was always being robbed of my dope and my money," Billie said, early on. After her arrest, her trap-house friends tore the place apart, stealing everything and pulling the ceiling tiles down looking for money and drugs.

She said she'd never forget walking into Tabitha's House and, for the first time in her life, "I felt so safe and so much love."

It wasn't the help that science said worked best—Tabitha's House, like many such facilities, does not allow addiction medicines. But, according to the lingo of harm-reductionists, if Billie saw it as a positive step—and she did—then it was. She lived in an actual house. Through intensive counseling, she was dealing with her childhood sexual abuse and other trauma. Without question, she was in a much better place than she had been in the stifling, one-room trap house with security cameras, the shades pulled, and people disappearing into her shared bathroom to shoot dope.

I asked Tracey Helton Mitchell, the recovery activist, what she thought of Billie's story—the fact that it didn't fit the bupe-first narrative championed by harm-reductionists; that it relied on twelve-step and Christian principles that many addiction experts deem dangerous and insufficient for people with OUD.

"You can't tell the story of addiction in rural America without Jesus, or without talking about the value of self-sufficiency," she said. "In some ways that's the rub with harm reduction versus abstinence. With abstinence, you're supposed to be pulling yourself up by your bootstraps, but actually it's all based around mutual support—which is why telling the story of addiction is so complicated."

Abstinence-based treatment worked for some because it gave people like Billie a peaceful place to go where she could get herself together emotionally and physically. For the first time in her life, she had advocates offering not just to pray with her but also to help her access mental health care and get her teeth fixed. The role that religion and spirituality played in many people's recoveries shouldn't be dismissed, Helton Mitchell said, which is why multiple recovery options should always be offered. It isn't about one being better but rather about each individual being a unique person with unique needs. She credits a secular, peer-run program called LifeRing for her own recovery from heroin addiction, which she recounted in her 2016 memoir, *The Big Fix: Hope After Heroin*.

"Bupe is great. If I got on Suboxone today, it reduces my risk of overdosing, of getting life-threatening infections," Helton Mitchell added. "But there is not going to be buy-in from everyone, no matter what the research may show about bupe. And if I'm still homeless, I'm still homeless. So I think there's something to be said for the abstinence-based service model. But it has to be good rehab; it can't just be whatever I slap together for twenty-eight days."

Stanford University addiction psychiatrist Anna Lembke's skepticism about the widespread use of bupe ran deeper than Helton Mitchell's, even though she prescribes it every day. Lembke worried that all psychotropic drugs—and bupe in particular—had worrisomely become viewed as the savior to the overdose crisis when what was needed was a wholesale reinvestment in communities, starting with universal health care. If doctors keep simply medicating people who are anxious and depressed, she argues in her new book, *Dopamine Nation*, society will be robbed of the energy that incites the political will to create change.

"I would never not want to have the tool of buprenorphine," Lembke said. "But frankly, it doesn't work for everybody...I have qualms about the fact that we are broadly using these drugs to fix what are essentially social problems."

I understood what Lembke was saying, but in an era of super-potent fentanyl, the fact that patients with SUD were left navigating the uncomfortable space between abstinence and medical treatment seemed like the harshest abandonment of all.

"When a disease is seen as treatable, you significantly knock back the stigma, and bupe and methadone are the treatments," said Dr. Josh Sharfstein, the Johns Hopkins public health associate dean. "Think about HIV: When HIV became an illness managed with medications, much of the taboo fell away. The same concept could work for addiction. The critical first step is for the medical community to fully embrace effective treatment with buprenorphine and methadone.

"There isn't a zero-sum game between treatment and prevention," Sharfstein added. "Saving lives through treatment can create momentum that gets people to say, 'Let's take on a bigger chunk of the problem.'"

A month into her stay at Tabitha's House, Billie brought home a pajama set from the thrift store. Growing up, she'd never owned matching pajamas. But that night Billie put on her new-to-her PJs, and, sitting there on her twin bed in the room she shared with another former drug user, she beamed.

"You look like a sweet little girl sitting there," her roommate told her.

Billie felt like a sweet little girl. "That's all we are, a bunch of little girls, living our childhoods again, only now we're in a safe place," she told me.

I don't want to overstate Billie's newfound sobriety. It was early days, and she was still feeling raw, reliant on phone calls with Sonya and sometimes bored with her new life. She called me in tears once, angry because she wasn't allowed to vape.

It was entirely possible, statistically speaking, that Billie would check herself out and go back to her trap-house life. Eric did, after just three days at the rehab James had worked so hard to arrange. "We're still in touch, though," said James, optimistically. "So that's good."

It was also possible, statistically speaking, that Billie's abstinence-only treatment might one day increase her risk of overdose and death, extrapolating from studies suggesting higher risk of death after detox.

But four months into her stay at Tabitha's, she was doing great. Asked how the not-vaping was going, she chuckled and said, "No comment." She was still in touch with Sonya several times a week.

Sonya told me she was 100 percent determined that by showing the commissioners and the other higher-ups how well she was doing in her job as a certified peer, eventually she would change their minds and soften their hearts. "I feel like people are starting to have respect for me now," Sonya said. "I have purpose. I may not make a ton of money, but I'm touching people that may not have ever heard of somebody getting clean before. To be honest, I'm grateful now for my addiction; I wouldn't change it for nothing."

Very slowly, some fragile threads of trust were braiding together. In my most hopeful moments, I found myself thinking that even Sheriff Andy Taylor—who was never above bending a rule if he thought it would benefit the people he'd promised to protect—would approve.

It remained a conundrum, though, that people in recovery were both the best people and the most vulnerable people to do the work of helping people get sober. Though she'd been sober for three years, Sonya told me, she had only recently stopped experiencing the tastes and smells of heroin. Every time she had a craving, she told her mom or girlfriend about it, and "the moment it came outta my mouth, it left."

The job was also starting to weigh on Willis, the buttoned-up bureaucrat. Three years into the post, both hospitals were fully on board with his program, but he worried about the stress on peers like Sonya.

When his wife jokingly said, "'Bye, stupid," as he left for work, he responded with his usual deadpan "I'm off to save the world."

To which Theresa Willis replied, "Okay, but if you can't save the world, at least save yourself."

Willis took his supervision of the peers as seriously as he had when he was sending fellow Marines or Special Agents into danger. He increased his check-ins on Sonya and the other peers and had a counselor on standby for them. A Marine who was the son of a Marine, Willis wasn't a talk-about-your-feelings kind of guy, but he made a genuine effort to lighten the mood for his staff, from bringing in baked goods from home to putting a nine-foot-tall inflatable Frankenstein behind the county manager's desk when he was out of town. (The assistant county manager made him take it down.)

"I thought I could just wind the peers up and let them go, but they're literally going into harm's way. You order someone into a house or to take a hill, you're *responsible*." When he needed advice, he called his favorite purple-haired harm-reductionist. By August of 2021, the annual stats weren't looking good: There'd been twenty-eight overdose deaths so far, up a third from the same period the year before.

At the end of my last visit to Surry County, as we walked from a restaurant to my car, Willis took a call from one of the local hospitals. A block away, bulldozers worked to clear land for the new $45 million jail. It would open in fourteen months, and Willis had personally gotten his boss to alter the architectural plans so it would include rooms for SUD treatment and offices for his peers to work with inmates on reentry issues. When the opioid-litigation money landed, he would hire more peers and three clinicians to staff the jail. Plans were also in progress to move the entire recovery office staff, now eleven and counting, to the basement of the county building—his wife, Theresa, was already working on decorating it.

On the phone, the hospital's CEO was calling with a first-time request. An eighteen-year-old had overdosed a few days before, and the staff was keeping her on life support. The CEO invited Willis to join the family as staffers pushed her body down the corridor from the ICU to the operating room. They would harvest her organs, but first they would honor her journey in a ceremony the staff called the Walk of Life.

I said I was sorry. Parks and rec directors got to organize the Special Olympics and the county fair and make sure the county lawns get mowed, but Willis spends eight to ten hours a day talking about mental illness and drug use and, now, organ transplants.

"I don't get many calls with good news," he said.

I thanked him for his openness and insights—they're hard to come by from a bureaucrat—and we bumped elbows again.

"'Bye, stupid," I said, but the joke fell flat.

PART FOUR
Judge for Yourselves

Mark Willis updating business leaders on overdose data, Surry County, North Carolina.

Chapter Twelve

"You Literally Cannot Give a Shit"

Tim Nolan (right) delivering supplies to Brittany in Connelly Springs, North Carolina.

Their was supposed to be a hopeful book. It says so right there in the subtitle.

Then came the Friday when every story I was tracking blew up at the same time. It was late summer 2021, and the stone-rollers were fraying and freaking out, some to the point of relapse. People who thought they were making strides—because they were—suddenly lost their stride-making jobs or were on the verge of quitting because, in a word, politics.

Cops were complaining about the trap-house visits of Tim Nolan, the nurse-practitioner who'd recently added refrigerated vaccines for hepatitis A to the things he carried in his Prius.

Mike Moore's nephew, Damian, was MIA from Home of Grace, the rehab where he was supposed to be working as a peer coach—Moore had secretly donated to the rehab to speed Damian's job offer along.

James Stroud was so burned out that he began shooting up methamphetamine again (he blamed it on job stress and "a girl"), and, in typical Mayberry fashion, everyone in town knew about it. Sonya and Wendy were very, very worried about him. The last time they'd seen him, he looked as if he'd dropped forty pounds. "I told him, 'You ain't gotta be ashamed. It happens. You have no idea how many times I relapsed. You can come back from this,'" Sonya said.

Nine months into their collaboration, Sonya and James were no longer speaking, and Wendy now relied on other volunteers. Billie asked everyone at Tabitha's House to pray for James.

At a public meeting in Mount Airy, Steven Odum, Wendy's outspoken husband, lashed out at Mark Willis, jeopardizing the future of the needle exchange she'd created. That night, Willis walked into his house in Lowgap to the jarring sight of "my wife standing in front of the TV with the commissioners meeting on the screen, and she's jumping up and down like she's stomping on a snake!"

When Michelle Mathis watched the meeting later on YouTube, she cried. "You remember, I didn't think the community was ready yet [for syringe exchange]. And so, if you are gonna do something like that, you keep your head down and your mouth shut to protect your programming so you can do the work while educating the community and changing hearts and minds. You don't attack your biggest supporter in county government!"

To watch people trying so hard get kicked so hard in the gut—I was somewhat removed from the drama, and even I was devastated.

"These are potholes," Fred Brason reminded me. "And potholes do eventually get filled in."

Do they?

In Charleston, a woman was shot to death as retribution after allegedly giving her killer HIV through a shared needle. A severe national naloxone shortage struck hardest in communities where harm-reduction services were least supported, not coincidentally in the same places where bystanders were the least likely to call 911 for an overdose because they feared criminal repercussions.

My friend and BuzzFeed News science reporter Dan Vergano summed it up best: "We're right in the middle of this moment when we're moving away from the War on Drugs and from putting people in prison for having the disease of addiction. We're watching the wall come down. But sometimes the bricks are falling on people's heads!"

The teenage daughter of a woman Vergano had gone to high school with had reportedly been executed by her drug dealer in rural Pennsylvania. "A nineteen-year-old. The daughter of some girl I held hands with once at a dance," he said.

Police initially said the dealer injected heroin into the young woman, then moved her body to her car to make it look like she'd overdosed. But Vergano later learned that it was "just another goddamned dumping of someone overdosing by a scared user" who feared being arrested.

While the nation's judicial apparatuses did little to hold Big Pharma's feet to the fire, parts of the planet succumbed to fires and floods. COVID roared back with deadly new variants. The climate crisis mirrored the overdose crisis in that each had been triggered by greed, deepened by political inaction, and defined by those intent on subverting science and manufacturing doubt so Americans wouldn't understand the risks to their health and safety.

But the immediacy of COVID sucked up most of the

public's bandwidth from those crises because it felt more immediate—unless, that is, you were one of the Americans who didn't believe a word of any of it.

Also, a billionaire rocketed into space.

Then, another.

The real crisis wasn't the overdose crisis but the one underlying it and all the other crises in the developed world: It was greed, on an order of magnitude that allows corporations and bought-off politicians and families like the Sacklers to turn Americans against ourselves. To persuade us that the "junkies" and Black people and hillbillies and immigrants are why we can't have nice things.

In White Plains, Purdue's bankruptcy lumbered toward closure while explosive and exhaustive new journalism about Purdue, including an HBO documentary called *Crime of the Century*, did little to penetrate the Sacklers' protective coating. For the third time in as many years, comedian John Oliver delivered a scorcher of a show on the Sacklers, this one focused on how the family was using judge shopping and a bankruptcy loophole to nab another get-out-of-jail-free card.

"When your family's company recklessly sold a product as damaging as OxyContin, the question might not be 'How many billions is it right for you to pay?' It's 'How many billions is it right for you to keep?'" Oliver punched. "And I would argue: no billions."

Between the Delta variant and the wildfires, so many bad things clamored for the public's attention that the Sackler saga barely registered a blip. NPR's Brian Mann noted the near-silence on the radio, even as he reported from a conference room where he and other journalists worked to follow developments in suburban White Plains—after Judge Drain declined to permit a public webcast of the proceedings.

Journalists and victims would have to follow along via

conference call. Mann noted that the sound quality was often unlistenable. "One of the major public health legal proceedings of the last half century, and it's often impossible to hear what's going on," he wrote.

The Sacklers' guards—their lawyers and public relations consultants, not to mention their accountants—were masters of the long game. All along they had predicted that the story's wonkiness as well as other tragedies taking place in the world would narcotize the country from caring, not unlike the Purdue sales official who gave his staff the day off after 9/11—saying that at least now OxyContin would be off the front pages for a time.

The company had now pleaded guilty to federal felonies and fraud—*twice*. And yet things were still looking good for the Sackler family, whose hand-picked judge, Robert Drain, bristled whenever anyone questioned his handling of the case.

Drain seemed poised to allow the Sacklers and thousands of their associates to receive a controversial third-party release, a loophole that meant the family could keep most of its $10 billion in OxyContin profits. (In court papers, some Sacklers claimed that the family retained less than half that, with almost half going to taxes.) Broadly, the law was unsettled—some federal circuits allowed the releases; others didn't.

In June, on behalf of a father who'd lost his daughter to an OxyContin overdose, bankruptcy law professor Jonathan Lipson asked Drain to appoint an examiner, an independent investigator to analyze and report on the Sacklers' involvement with Purdue's board after the company had decided to settle with creditors in 2018. Pete Jackson's eighteen-year-old daughter, Emily, died in 2006 after a single dose of OxyContin, and Lipson, who'd lost a relative himself to an addiction that began with a single OxyContin, believed the court owed Jackson that much.

It was clear the Sacklers stood to benefit from the bankruptcy settlement—they'd get to protect themselves, their children, and their wealth from any future civil lawsuits. But the decision to file for bankruptcy was seemingly made after members of the Sackler family resigned from the company's board. Lipson wanted the examiner to investigate whether they'd continued to pull strings after the initial 2019 settlement proposal, the one negotiated by Mike Moore. Had the Sacklers exercised undue influence on the Purdue board after the initial deal? If so, Lipson argued, they would have orchestrated their own liability releases.

The Sacklers had recently upped their cash contribution from $3 billion (the deal orchestrated by Mike Moore) to $4.275 billion, but Lipson believed the public still deserved to know: Who at Purdue made the decision to settle rather than sue, and why? And were the Sacklers still pressuring the board of the company they had long owned? These were pertinent questions, given that Richard Sackler was known to be a micromanager.

But Drain was outraged at even the possibility of impropriety. His voice raising repeatedly, he berated Lipson, calling his filing "slanderous" and full of "unsupported, inflammatory allegations," and at several points questioning whether Lipson should even *be* a law professor.

And then, after four hours of belittling and interrupting, Drain granted part of Lipson's request. Saying he believed the examiner would find no irregularities, Drain limited the investigation of influence to a "special committee" of the Purdue board formed shortly before bankruptcy, with an examiner budget capped at $200,000—a pittance, compared to the *$600 million* already spent on legal fees in the case. "I am concerned that if I don't appoint an examiner, the next press release will be 'Court refuses to appoint examiner to show process was fair' but not add 'because there was no evidence,'" Drain fumed.

No matter that judges, according to their own code of ethics, aren't supposed to make decisions based on public clamor or fear of criticism. The code also states that judges should be "patient, dignified, respectful, and courteous."

Lipson was left bereft by the judge's dressing-down. While he appreciated the partial approval of his motion, four hours is a long time to get yelled at in front of your peers by a federal judge you've long respected. "I feel like I'm still coming out of some post-traumatic-stress state of mind," he said, a few days later.

Early in his career, Lipson had worked together with Drain at the same law firm. Lipson remembered Drain enjoying his impression of the character Worf from *Star Trek: The Next Generation.* "He's a quirky, interesting guy; he was my favorite person to work with there," Lipson said of the judge. In 2013, Drain self-published a novel featuring a woman addicted to opium; an early version of the book drew praise from John Hersey, a Yalie like Drain.

Halfway through the hearing, around the time Drain called Lipson's examiner request "a load of hooey," Lipson found himself contemplating whether his family's umbrella insurance would cover a legal sanction from Drain. "At this point, I'm the only person Judge Drain hates more than Mike Quinn," he said.

As Drain predicted, two months later the limited examiner reported no smoking guns. But Drain's attitude toward Lipson in open court served as a warning to everyone involved in the case, from the Sacklers' lickspittle lawyers to the victims: Judge Drain was mercurial, and he took this case personally.

Quinn was relieved not to be the bad boy, for once. In more than a dozen objections he filed on behalf of the Ad Hoc Committee on Accountability, Quinn argued that a forced bankruptcy settlement designed to protect the not-so-very-bankrupt Sacklers was the "poster child of what wealthy people gain by spending their money on lawyers." If Drain's refusal to confirm the plan or his confirmation of it ended up in appeals, the Sacklers would still be so rich that they could spend the rest of their lives fending off lawsuits from the very long list of personal-injury victims who didn't qualify for any settlement money because they were unable to produce an OxyContin prescription from two decades before. "Bright students who are still in high school today could go to college and law school, join a firm, and become millionaires defending the Sacklers before the money is all gone," Quinn wrote. You could almost smell the burn of his keyboard.

It would be better, Quinn argued, to resolve the case with a trial on the allegations against the Sacklers, which wouldn't violate victims' rights to due process. After all, other opioid manufacturers were being sent out for "bellwether" cases by the same Multidistrict Litigation judge in Cleveland that Purdue Pharma and the Sacklers had managed to escape. During the late spring of 2021, reports were coming from Orange County, California, about opening statements, expert testimony, and closing arguments in a state case—not part of the Multidistrict Litigation—that had been intended to include Purdue Pharma. And yet here they were, stuck in a bankruptcy court designed to divvy up assets, not deliver justice.

So Quinn kept poking the judge. "We're like ninjas running up in the dark and taking swipes," he told me. Working hard to get more co-sponsors for Congresswoman Maloney's SACKLER Act, he had feelers out with several senators, including Elizabeth Warren, the Massachusetts bankruptcy professor who had long argued for an overhaul of the bankruptcy system.

Asked if he had anything to do with getting a second Congressional Oversight Committee hearing scheduled for the SACKLER Act, Quinn chortled and said, "I'm just a simple guy from upstate New York." He was a simple guy from upstate New York with an Ivy League education and generations of lawyers, judges, and politicians in his family tree. Quinn had a whiff of hipster combined with the kind of confidence born of East Coast old money. And he had friends literally everywhere, it seemed. At a funeral for a friend's father in Florida in early 2022, Quinn found himself chatting with Purdue's longtime lawyer and Sackler-family protector and secret-keeper, Stuart Baker.

Quinn considered confronting Baker, but it was a funeral. Besides, he reasoned, Baker didn't deserve to put a face to the young lawyer who'd spent two years fighting to expose how the Sacklers were gaming a flawed legal system. He didn't need to know that Quinn was the one who'd quietly pushed for the SACKLER Act; or that he was the author of the wild, illustrated briefs filed in Drain's court.

And Baker had no idea that Quinn had just planned a meeting between his Ad Hoc Committee and the newly sworn-in New Jersey US attorney to press for holding individuals at Purdue and in the Sackler family accountable for criminal activity.

Though some of Quinn's jabs misfired, who else but a fourth-generation lawyer would even entertain the idea of locating every other attorney named Michael Quinn in the country, then calling them to ask if they'd be willing to create their own Ad Hoc committees for the case—*the Ad Hoc Committee on Justice, the Ad Hoc Committee on Transparency*—just to irritate a federal judge who had already threatened to hold him in contempt?

Quinn found three other Michael Quinns but dropped the idea after the poor response of the first one, a real estate attorney in Florida who thought the original Michael Quinn was loony tunes. "The call got awkward very quickly," he said.

Quinn reveled in poring over the case minutiae—looking for scoops that reporters and others had missed—like the fact that Richard Sackler had renewed his controlled-substance prescribing license during the final throes of the case.

Or the fact that Purdue spent at least $1.2 million on lobbyists to "monitor" the SACKLER Act and other proposed legislation during the year and a half of bankruptcy negotiations. Quinn found that one by trawling public congressional records, then funneling the scoop to a reporter at *The Intercept*. That same reporter had already written a story a year earlier when Purdue was caught donating money to both the Democratic and Republican Attorneys General Associations after declaring bankruptcy—forcing both groups to return the money.

Quinn loved nothing more than studying the seven-figure bills submitted by Purdue's lawyers, PR professionals, and consultants. That legwork had led to his February 2021 conflict-of-interest objection, the one about the supposedly independent law firms that were working for both Purdue and the Sacklers. "It's the whole case, the whole corruption!" he'd railed at the time.

Everyone else yawned at the story when it finally landed in the *Wall Street Journal*—it was too wonky, too loaded with legalese. "I filed that objection and—crickets," Quinn said. But three months later, the story rebounded when the US Trustee Program echoed Quinn's assessment and settled with the three firms for $1 million for their failure to fully disclose the joint defense agreement to the court.

Someone was paying attention to Mike Quinn's arguments on behalf of the *so-called* Ad Hoc Committee of five, after all. "That's another million bucks for creditors—for actual people! Imagine!" Quinn enthused. Lipson called it one of the most significant victories anybody had won against the Sacklers and Purdue to that point in the bankruptcy.

By May, more than thirty members of Congress had signed on to support the SACKLER Act (all Democrats), and Quinn was toggling between his real job and his Ad Hoc Committee sleuthing. He was trying to hustle up more sponsors for the bill and advocating for a public document repository that would reveal the entire sordid tale—footnotes and depositions and e-mails that didn't self-destruct—all of it.

He felt for Lipson after Drain's four-hour tirade. "I don't know how he feels, but I live in fear most of the time," he told me. "It's the side effect of having courage—you're scared a lot."

In July 2021, in the final Zoom before the bankruptcy confirmation began, the OxyJustice warriors were morose. The attorneys general of Massachusetts and New York, who had long been the most vocally opposed to settling, had caved the day before. After insisting for two years that they would never settle, AGs Maura Healey and Letitia James and thirteen other nonconsenting states announced they would.

It was spun, of course, as a major win: The Sacklers had upped their cash contribution by $50 million, agreed to make 30 million new documents public, and submitted to a nine-year ban on naming buildings, museum wings, and other charitable donations after themselves.

"We need documents, we need the story told," Massachusetts's Healey said, heralding the payout as "the most that individuals have ever paid for breaking the law." But with a payment schedule spread out over nine or ten years—and calculating interest likely to be earned from their investments—the family was likely to walk away even richer than they were now.

The loudest voice remaining among the hold-out states was Purdue's home-state attorney general, Connecticut's William Tong. "Unless Tong can pull a rabbit out of his hat, we're in big trouble," Ed Bisch told the group. Maryland and Washington State were also staunch objectors.

Barbara Van Rooyan, who'd spent years begging the FDA—to no avail—to restrict OxyContin prescriptions for severe pain following her son's death in 2004, felt the same way. "Every once in a while, you get this glimmer of hope that 'Oh my God, maybe the fat lady hasn't sung yet,' but I'm trying not to get my hopes up anymore," she said. For nearly two decades, Van Rooyan had been testifying before Congress and petitioning the

FDA. In 2007, she'd flown from California to march outside the federal courthouse in Abingdon, Virginia, to protest the terms of the company's first guilty plea.

When she stumbled across Ed Bisch's website soon after her son's death—then called OxyAbuseKills.com—it "saved my life and gave me hope that the grief could be used for good." She wasn't so sure about that anymore.

But a few states and the aching relatives of the dead weren't the only ones still opposing the settlement. In a statement, Biden's Department of Justice blasted it, too. The US Trustee pronounced it both unconstitutional and illegal, and the US attorney from the Southern District of New York said it violated Americans' "constitutional right to due process"—arguments that paralleled Quinn's earlier objections almost to the word. Why should a judge in White Plains get to tell a grieving mother in Ohio that she has no right to sue the Sacklers?

When it came time for creditors to vote on the confirmation plan, the DOJ fell short of blocking the settlement and abstained from voting altogether. Over Zoom, Lipson, who sometimes met informally with OxyJustice, went into teaching mode and explained the important minutiae of the DOJ's political entanglements:

In the final days of the Trump administration, the DOJ had negotiated a criminal plea agreement with Purdue Pharma. It was déjà vu for the parents and activists who'd witnessed the 2007 plea. But this time, the bankruptcy made things more complicated: Trump's DOJ tied the plea agreement to the confirmation plan. Lipson explained that Biden's new attorney general, Merrick Garland, was unlikely to renege on the 2020 deal, wherein Sackler family members would pay $225 million in civil penalties while Purdue pleaded guilty to felony charges of defrauding federal health agencies and violating anti-kickback laws. Purdue was fined $8.3 billion, but that fine was a fiction and a campaign headline-grabber because the company was then only worth about a billion. ("That $8.3 billion is 100 percent show," Mike Moore ranted. There's no $8.3 billion, and there never will be!")

Lipson saw the Biden DOJ's objections as "a partial reneging," he said, hopefully. "The prior administration can't completely bind the next one, but it matters," he told the group. "So the fact that these guys didn't vote at all, it's extraordinary." He was sure that if Trump's DOJ were still in charge, they would have voted for the bankruptcy plan and made no objection at all.

The DOJ could still prosecute the Sacklers after confirmation of the bankruptcy plan, but the states wanted and needed the money the Sacklers were about to send their way—which the Sacklers were sure to stop paying the moment a criminal case was filed. It was a game of mutual assured destruction, Lipson said.

"They need the money?" Nan Goldin asked.

"The states want the money, that's right," Lipson said.

He told the group, "I certainly think the more noise you make, the harder it will be for the DOJ to ignore it."

Quinn hoped to go out swinging, but earlier in the week Goldin's PAIN had discussed staging another protest and decided against it. The bankruptcy confirmation seemed to be a fait accompli. It was best, they thought, to return to focusing on the museums—they were plotting more swipes to get "The Sackler Wing" name removed from the Met.

If the bankruptcy plan were to be confirmed, the Sacklers, as well as 1,000 of their employees, subcontractors, corporate associates, and family trusts, would be shielded from civil suits related to the company's opioid products—forever. The list of entities released from future litigation was twenty-four pages long, single-spaced.

Bisch urged the group to gather outside Drain's courthouse in White Plains, but Goldin reminded them, "The last time we did it there, there were like fifteen people." Putting together a tight, press-worthy action usually took a month at minimum, and the hearing started in just two weeks.

Bisch was itching to protest and begged the group not to give up. He had already brought his sign, the one from the 2007 Abingdon hearing, out of storage. It had a picture of his eighteen-year-old son with the words *Eddie Bisch (9/22/82–2/9/01)*, now framed in yellowed tape. On the back, he added: "WRONG COURT. DOJ MUST PROSECUTE SACKLER CARTEL."

When the confirmation hearing began mid-August, Bisch wanted news organizations to have fresh photos to accompany their stories—a physical landscape that represented the more than half-million dead. Bisch wanted to recruit actor and musician Courtney Love because Love, formerly addicted to OxyContin herself, loved to bash the Sacklers, and especially David's wife, Joss. Love and Joss Sackler had gotten into a social media kerfuffle over Joss's fashion line, LBV, when Love refused to attend Joss's fashion show wearing a custom-made LBV dress embroidered with 24-carat-gold thread. Even after Joss offered to pay Love $100,000 to wear the dress, Love still refused, writing on Instagram: "Your. People. Killed. My. People."

"Take this for what it's worth," Bisch told the group. "But I had a dream last night, and Courtney Love was doing a kettlebell workout in a parking lot, and she was built! Someone asked her, 'Are you preparing for a fight?' And she didn't answer 'em."

"Ed, man, you gotta publish your dreams," Goldin said. "That's beautiful!"

Within a few days, PAIN came around to Bisch's idea to protest in White Plains on the eve of the confirmation hearing. Bisch reached out to a friend of his—a Florida businessman who'd also lost a son to OxyContin—to donate money to provide vans to drive the activists to White Plains.

*　　*　　*

The SACKLER Act was stalled, if not dead in the water, despite Congresswoman Maloney's push for a second Congressional Oversight Committee hearing in June featuring the *New Yorker* writer (and lawyer) Patrick Radden Keefe. Breathtaking in scope, Keefe's *Empire of Pain* had entered the *New York Times* best-seller list near the top in April 2021, raising important questions about the lack of guardrails between government and industry, and detailing exactly how the Sacklers used their wealth to avoid accountability. But as methodical and airtight as Keefe's articulation of his case was, the hearing at which he testified quickly devolved into a three-and-a-half-hour sideshow.

Congressman James Comer, a Republican from Kentucky, kicked it off by calling out Keefe for donating money to Democratic campaigns, arguing that the journalist was only appearing now to inflate sales of his book. Keefe told me that he once gave $250 to Stacey Abrams's voting rights organization, Fair Fight Action.

Comer repeatedly steered the hearing away from the SACKLER Act and toward the flow of illicit fentanyl coming into the country from Mexico, which he argued the Biden administration was failing to address. That same week, Vice President Kamala Harris was being pounded by Fox News for visiting Mexico without going to the border.

Comer wasn't wrong about fentanyl being a scourge. Black and Brown Americans were dying from it at alarming rates. Benzodiazepines, heroin, cocaine, and so-called dirty thirties (fake oxycodone pills) were all being routinely contaminated or replaced with the dangerous synthetic. The pain-pill-as-killer narrative was passé, Comer asserted; it was illicit fentanyl and methamphetamine, not OxyContin, that now drove most of the present harms and overdose deaths.

In recent years, law enforcement agencies, the CDC, and other medical authorities had overreacted to the first wave of the opioid crisis by clamping down too hard on opioid-prescribing. In fact, it is dangerous to force-taper or cut off pain patients, which often sends them to the fentanyl-infiltrated black market and/or suicide, without *at the same time* liberalizing the use of bupe, methadone, and other treatment modalities for pain and addiction, which often overlap.

Some doctors responded to the revised 2016 CDC opioid-prescribing guideline—and their fear of DEA prosecution—by declaring draconian caps and essentially abandoning their patients rather than offering pathways to compassionate pain management for those dependent on opioids, or addiction treatment for those addicted. People who needed opioids were refused access. Others with decades-long chronic conditions like extreme rheumatoid arthritis were abandoned by doctors and were now left bedbound. Some who were denied the opioids they'd been taking for decades attempted suicide or resorted to illegal drugs.

"They should have known that clamping down on pill mills and overprescribing would lead people to the black market," said Dan Vergano, the veteran science reporter. Between 2011 and 2020, opioid prescribing fell by 60 percent while overdose deaths doubled.

Vergano and I had both been criticized for drawing too much attention to overprescribed opioid pills by chronic pain patients who blamed us for ignoring their suffering. Many of their points were valid, if sometimes over-the-top and oblivious to the root causes of the crisis.

Purdue's exaggerated claims about the safety of OxyContin and opioids in general had created an overprescribing environment rife with widespread diversion that the company knowingly profited from. It not only harmed the people who got addicted by being overprescribed opioids—or after experimenting with leftover pills they'd swiped from the cabinet of a relative or neighbor who'd been overprescribed. But the flagrancy of their actions ensured that legitimate pain patients continue to be harmed today.

New prescribing guidelines aren't the font of today's current overdose wave, of course—the overprescribing pushed by Purdue and its ilk created OUD in many people, and that created the conditions for an explosion of overdoses. But the crackdowns pushed by law enforcement and misinterpretations of the voluntary 2016 CDC guideline were crude instruments that ended up denying medications to some legitimate patients while not always succeeding at restricting people from receiving opioids they didn't need.

Many of the prescription reductions ended up occurring among cancer, end-of-life, and post-surgery patients as well as people with progressive complex medical conditions—widely considered by most doctors to need opioids.

"Doctors are so concerned about being flagged, concerned about their license and their livelihood, they don't want to take [chronic pain patients] on, and so you end up with patient abandonment, and iatrogenic harms that can create a medically dangerous situation," said Dr. Beth Darnall, director of Stanford University School of Medicine's Pain Relief Innovations Lab, who studies best practices for voluntarily tapering patients from opioids.

Tapers should be consensual, conducted very slowly over many months, with patients given maximal control in their taper, including the ability to pause or stop their taper, or reverse it if their results are poor. Too often, she said, patients are only given psychological tools after medications have failed rather than offered support up front in combination with medical interventions.

"When someone's been taking opioids for thirty years, with stable behaviors and stable doses, that's a low-risk situation in which the patient is benefiting from their medication," Darnall said. In some instances, "literally, people who'd just had brain surgery could not get their prescriptions filled at pharmacies," she added.

The origins of the overdose crisis are multifaceted. Rampant OxyContin prescribing, set against a backdrop of economic devastation, had been the taproot of the epidemic, and fentanyl was the soil upon which it presently grew. It was also true that too many American doctors and dentists continued to prescribe opioids to new patients at unsafe rates, and that across-the-board reductions in opioid prescribing have not led to a reduced number of overdose deaths.

But the second meeting of the Congressional Committee on Oversight and Reform on the SACKLER Act was not the place for a nuanced discussion about this multiplicity of truths. "This hearing misses the point," Comer said, angrily. "It's so focused on the Sackler family that it forgets the ongoing epidemic affecting millions of Americans each day" caused by illicit fentanyl streaming into the country via Mexico.

Without directly addressing Keefe's arguments or Maloney's bill, Comer called for a hearing on "the border crisis" when most of the illicit-drug volume entering the United States is carried in via legitimate ports of entry on land and water, hidden in tractor-trailers, cars, and shipping containers.

The most effective speaker of the day by far was a mother from upstate New York. Alexis Pleus, fifty-one, had lost her son, Jeff, to a heroin overdose in 2014 and spent nearly every moment since agitating for accountability, fighting against tough-love/drug-war narratives, and doing gritty, on-the-ground harm-reduction work. As he did for the first SACKLER Act hearing, Mike Quinn helped Maloney's staffers line up speakers, including Pleus.

Pleus fields so many sorrowful calls from parents of the dead that she's developed a crippling fear of the ringer on her phone, she told the committee. As Pleus continued her story, Quinn sat next to her, silently holding up photos of her son: Jeff as a baby, Jeff with his brothers, Jeff right before the catastrophic football injury that had him taking prescribed OxyContin every four hours.

Pleus founded the nonprofit Truth Pharm six months after Jeff's death, around the time the Sackler family first hit the *Forbes* list of America's Richest Families. Since January 2015, the bodies have only continued to stack up, she told Congress. Her other two sons have lost six classmates to overdose, and her county now counted 303 people—including a thirteen-year-old—among the overdosed dead, the vast majority of whom had been incarcerated in local jails for addiction-related crime. One mother in her support network had lost all three of her children.

"And yet for the heads of that drug empire, they walk away unscathed," Pleus said.

Pleus said she often questions what she could have done differently to help her son. "And the only thing I can come back to is 'if he hadn't gotten addicted.' The other things are all a maybe. The fact that he was prescribed OxyContin, and the doctors didn't educate us on the risks—that's what started it all," she told the committee.

When it was former drug czar Jim Carroll's turn to testify, Comer and other committee Republicans repeatedly fed him questions about illegal fentanyl seeping across the border. Quinn seriously worried that Pleus would throw a chair across the room.

Pleus passed a note to Carroll pleading with him to stop. "They're using you as a distraction against this issue," she wrote. Privately, Carroll had told Pleus about his own family's trials with addiction with tears in his eyes.

She was tired of playing the role of "the token grieving mom." She was, in fact, a formidable force for treatment in Binghamton, New York, her hometown. Of the hundreds of people I've interviewed about the overdose crisis, Pleus, more than anyone, seemed to grasp all parts of the elephant. She'd held monthly educational seminars, challenged politicians to act, and advocated for treatment that wasn't solely abstinence-based. She gave out safe-use kits from her Truth Pharm office, and collaborated with an Ithaca-based nonprofit to offer low-barrier bupe both in person and via telehealth to several hundred patients in her region. When parents struggled with addicted kids, Pleus taught them the opposite of the tough-love trope about kicking them out of the house and letting them hit rock bottom that they'd been fed at most Families Anonymous meetings.

When she suspected that county officials weren't accurately reporting overdose counts, Pleus went directly to the mothers in her community and asked them to self-report overdoses to Truth Pharm. When it turned out that Pleus's hunch was right—that the overdose-death toll was four times higher than what officials were reporting—Truth Pharm held a press conference to announce the results, holding up corrugated-plastic tombstones to represent the uncounted lives lost. Like the VANDU founders, she made the politicians wear the deaths.

At a Trail of Truth die-in event she puts on annually, family members of the dead trace their bodies with sidewalk chalk and write memories of their loved ones inside the silhouettes. "By incorporating the people who are suffering into our work, it empowers them and gives them a place to put their grief and anger and frustration, and then they go out and help educate the rest of the community," Pleus said.

When I first interviewed her in mid-2020, Pleus said her success didn't stem from being a grieving mother. It was the fact that she was a grieving mother *and an engineer*. Having managed construction sites for decades, she was used to pushback, used to shrugging off dismissive, chauvinistic comments. "So it's like, 'Okay, you hate me, *whatever*,'" she said. Also, at six feet tall and with a mane of blond hair, she literally stands out in a crowd, especially when she and fellow Truth Pharmers show up to protests as they did for Nan Goldin's Guggenheim action—wearing matching turquoise shirts that say PHUCK BIG PHARMA.

Pleus applied that same *whatever* to politicians and slow-moving bureaucrats, especially those who work SAMHSA-funded community mental health centers. They were do-gooders for the most part, but it infuriated her when they concentrated more on being polite to avoid funding disruptions than advocating for the largely voiceless people who use drugs.

Such rigidity had long infuriated me, too. A few months before her death in 2017, my young friend Tess tried to arrange treatment for herself through our local clinic, called Blue Ridge Behavioral Health. But harsh policies that were not based in science prevented her from accessing lifesaving medications. At a time when fentanyl was infiltrating all corners of America, Tess could only get a bupe prescription if she tried their counseling program first *and failed.* That policy had since improved, but how many people died in the interim? And how many state agencies were still operating under archaic tough-love rules because of rigid bureaucrats nearing retirement who were too scared to read the latest data and change their minds, then challenge others to do the same?

"People doing this work—and this is the key—you literally cannot give a shit about what other people think of you," Pleus said.

Her thick skin came in handy when local health department officials took to Facebook to say that Pleus didn't know what she was talking about regarding methadone and bupe. "One said, 'This is why your son is dead!' And: 'People need to suffer before they can get well to learn their lesson. We can't medicate people through detox.'

"I kept telling [county health and social service officials], 'But this is archaic thinking. Bupe is the standard of care now in other countries.'"

In conservative Broome County, New York, Pleus's outspokenness had gotten Truth Pharm blacklisted from receiving funding from the county, and her own state senator no longer took meetings with her. So Pleus scraped together funding elsewhere, including from the Drug Policy Alliance, the Vera Institute, Ben & Jerry's Ice Cream, and a state-directed Medicaid grant for low-barrier care coordination.

At Goldin's Metropolitan Museum of Art protest in 2019, Truth Pharm volunteers, clad in their turquoise T-shirts, had been an integral part of the banner drop. Afterward, on the steps of the Met, Pleus gave a no-holds-barred speech, including the news that Richard Sackler had the audacity to patent a new form of bupe to treat addiction:

> *What matters to the Sacklers? Money. So what do we want back from them? Money. I want that money. I don't care if they go to jail, I don't care if they go to prison. I want their money. You know what else I want? I want that fucking patent [awarded to Richard Sackler in 2018] to the new Suboxone. And I want that Suboxone free for every single person who needs it...How dare they try to profit off this epidemic that they created?*

Though no Sacklers attended the second SACKLER Act hearing, Quinn went into it believing he'd scored an even better guest, one that had taken him days to line up: former US assistant attorney Rick Mountcastle, the tough-on-crime career prosecutor, now retired. Mountcastle's Virginia-based office had been the first to make a federal case against Purdue in 2007.

That case against Purdue culminated in a $600 million settlement in 2007, a single misbranding felony for the company, and misdemeanor charges that included $34 million in fines and probation for the company's top three executives—but no sanctions against any Sackler owners, whose lawyers and consultants had conveniently counseled them to step back from their posts in the early aughts just as Mountcastle's investigation was heating up.

Quinn hoped Mountcastle's appearance might be a game-changer. The prosecutor had made a practice of never, ever talking publicly about a settled case, as I well knew because he had never once given me an interview. But Quinn, somehow, got him to say what he really thought about the Sacklers, and not just to some reporter but to Congress. "He's just a good guy, and he's a cowboy," Quinn later enthused. "I can talk to cowboys!"

In video testimony, Mountcastle described launching his Purdue investigation. His staff had focused on the company's three top executives, hoping they would flip on their Sackler bosses. Instead, "their underlings took the fall," and were rewarded richly for it with millions of dollars, as later reporting revealed. Meanwhile, in the eleventh hour of that settlement negotiation, the George W. Bush administration's DOJ, under pressure from well-connected Sackler-hired hands including Rudy Giuliani and former federal prosecutor Mary Jo White, stymied Mountcastle's efforts to bring felony charges against the executives.

"I've now learned that, after 2007, the Sackler family didn't even read the pleadings," Mountcastle testified. "Using a different set of lieutenants, they doubled down...When they got caught again in 2020, the resolution came from the same political playbook, only worse. No one was charged, the company took the fall...And now the Sacklers appear to be gaming the system a third time, using a loophole.

"The Sackler family is the cartel of the opioid crisis. They used their company and their underlings to profit from repeated criminal conduct while escaping accountability. It would be a gross injustice to allow them to game a bankruptcy loophole to keep those profits. I urge passage of the SACKLER Act."

But there was no backburn to contain this wildfire, not with actual wildfires and a Congressional investigation into the January 6 insurrection stealing the headlines; not with needle exchanges being shut down not only in West Virginia but also in Scott County, Indiana; Atlantic City, New Jersey; and Eureka, California. The press, the public, and politicians shrugged at what Mountcastle had to say, if they heard him at all.

On the phone after the hearing, Quinn said, "Washington feels like it's all just two dialogues passing over each other all the time. I think we're in the last gasp of the empire. It's not good."

I began thinking the same thing, especially when a doctor friend of mine—a mild-mannered guy, not at all prone to hyperbole—told me, "I think we're heading for a civil war." At a rural Virginia grocery store where I sometimes shop, customers chat about whether the county might secede, after 170 years, back into red-state West Virginia, "where it belongs!" (Never mind that West Virginia had sprung from Virginia during the Civil War.) Down a favorite scenic Virginia byway, Trump supporters went to the trouble to cut Vice President Michael Pence's name out of the 2020 election signs that still dotted the landscape, a neighbor made a lawn ornament of Bigfoot holding Biden's severed head, and another plastered a sign on his barn taking aim at our governor, declaring, "Northam Is A Idiot."

Meanwhile Richard Sackler's side of the family had compiled the many reporting errors committed on a website called Judge-foryourselves.info. One of their lawyers, Tom Clare, pointed me to the website in an e-mail, as he warned me to avoid making "any errors or false statements about my clients and the opioid crisis generally in your upcoming [Hulu] series."

Clare's summer was a busy one. In July, he defended the

Israeli firm NSO Group after its Pegasus spyware was exposed in the *Washington Post* as a democracy-threatening tool widely used to surveil the smartphones of reporters, activists, and government officials. "Elegantly nasty," one critic described it. Clare's defense of NSO was ironic, considering that Richard Sackler and other Purdue executives had once patented a "Self-Destructing Document and Email Messaging System," their own wonky and ultimately useless attempt at ass-covering.

And yet Tom Clare and the Sacklers continued to assert that, although some Purdue employees may have committed multiple federal crimes, the Sacklers have always "acted ethically and lawfully." Their defense was all posted on the website Judgefor-yourselves.info.

John Oliver had needled the family for cheaping out on the .info domain name and bought judgeforyourselves.com himself, filling it with actual documents, letters from victims filed on the bankruptcy docket, and a repository placeholder for future documents resulting from the case.

"I just wrote a book about the ways in which [the Sacklers] were very, very, *very* involved," Keefe told me. "But I'm afraid our system is designed in a way that tends to insulate people like that from liability, and the Sacklers have played that system like a harp."

Keefe was exhausted and dismayed by the hearing. At the very least, he hoped that his *Empire of Pain* would serve as a historical account of the personal and regulatory mistakes that conspired to create the opioid crisis, and a warning. With more than a half-million people dead, perhaps the Sacklers would not be able to outrun the truth forever.

On August 17, 2021, Richard Sackler was asked during a bankruptcy confirmation hearing whether he understood how many Americans had died from opioid overdose. It was believed to be the first time a member of the family had appeared in open court.

"I do not know," he responded.

There was a lot he claimed not to know. In the first two hours of his testimony, one mother on the Ad Hoc Committee counted the number of times Sackler answered a question with either "I don't recall," "I don't remember," or "I don't recollect."

Fifty-seven.

I couldn't decide if my personal favorite dodge of his was when the assistant attorney general of Maryland asked him if he remembered a particularly pernicious marketing campaign devised under his watch, and Sackler replied, "I can't recall what I don't recall, but there may have been."

Or when he claimed to know nothing about the website Judgeforyourselves.info—after his own side of the clan had gone to the trouble of copyrighting it at the bottom of the site. Throughout the morning, the scion of OxyContin walked a razor's edge between frailty ("I have laryngitis," "I'm doing the best I can with my voice")—and picking apart the opposing attorneys' questions with clipped acuity.

Pleus tried not to get her hopes up, but she was beginning to think that all the protests and hearings might finally be adding up to something. A few days before the confirmation hearing began, Bisch got his wish for a protest, and the activists converged outside of Drain's courthouse in White Plains.

Pleus's group transformed the court's shrubbery garden into a cemetery by planting scores of black corrugated-plastic tombstones. The artist Fernando Alvarez brought a twenty-foot-tall likeness of "Robert Drain, the devil judge," complete with neon-red eyes, and the caption: "Iron curtain of the Sackler massacre."

Nan Goldin's lieutenants held a banner that read "Judge Drain's Morally Bankrupt Bankruptcy Court," and threw out their blood-splattered OxyContin dollars and fake prescription bottles. And fifty or so people shouted a call-and-response:

What do we want? Justice!
When do we want it? Now!

Pleus, Goldin, and Bisch gave fiery speeches, then Pleus led a die-in that closed with participants drawing chalk silhouettes around their bodies to represent the dead. "We want Drain to see this," Pleus said. "We want him to know what this family's done." The high-quality chalk (two dollars a stick) would remain outside Drain's courthouse office even after a few rains.

I didn't participate in the protest, but afterward I added Tess Henry's name to Pleus's silhouette and drew a sand dollar because Tess was known as "the queen sand dollar finder" in her family. Four years after her death, her murder remained unsolved, though private detectives hired by her mom claim to be working on it. In her mid-sixties, Patricia Mehrmann was raising Tess's six-year-old son alone while working as a hospital cardiac-care nurse. (A wealthy relative paid for his education.) We saw each other a few times a year—I took her flowers for Mother's Day, or little trinkets I found that reminded me of Tess—and we had pizza and beer on the deck of her house in the Blue Ridge Mountains. In between, we texted.

Recently she told me about a sick septuagenarian she'd tended at the hospital. Doctors couldn't figure out why the woman kept complaining of shortness of breath, thrashing around in her bed, and saying, "I just need to get out of my skin." But when Patricia talked to her and checked her medical records the doctors hadn't—she realized she hadn't been getting her daily Lortab dose in the hospital. She'd been taking the prescribed opioid for back pain for seven years.

The patient was dopesick, and Patricia was the only one to catch it. When the Lortab was reinstated, she immediately relaxed. After all these years, doctors were still clueless, she said, "the unfortunate reality of opioids and medical naïveté."

249

*　　*　　*

The night before the White Plains protest, Truth Pharmers and PAIN activists plastered the small city's downtown with fake prescriptions signed by Richard Sackler and written out to Judge Robert Drain featuring a now-infamous exchange between Richard and an underling: If OxyContin was uncontrolled outside the United States, the drug's inventor warned, it was highly likely that it would eventually be abused. To which Richard responded: "How substantially will it improve your sales?"

Bisch didn't participate in the late-night stunt. "I'm not getting arrested," he told me. But Goldin's and Pleus's volunteers were all in. Around midnight, police detained a Truth Pharm volunteer for defacing public property and held her for a few hours in the local jail, handcuffed to a bench. Police may have mistaken the arrestee, with her curly red hair, for Nan Goldin.

The week before, Drain said he had "some concerns about the breadth" of the third-party releases. The settlement presently called for granting blanket immunity to 1,000 names—Sackler family members, employees, trusts, consultants, and the like. Some entities were so obscure that Richard's cousin and former Purdue board member Mortimer D. A. Sackler told the court he didn't know who many of them were.

The attorney had gone into negotiations asking for the moon, of course, knowing Drain could feel smug about narrowing the list down in the final deal.

Charlotte Bismuth, the lawyer who'd begun interpreting the bankruptcy for PAIN on her kids' drawing pad two years before, was lifted by the hard-hitting questions asked during the hearing by Washington assistant attorney general Tad Robinson O'Neill, who represented one of the remaining nine states still objecting to the plan. By probing the Sacklers' involvement in an extended-release ADHD medication called Adhansia XR, approved in 2019, O'Neill was pointing out the folly of forever immunizing the Sacklers and everyone else on the twenty-four-page list. Like OxyContin, Adhansia is so strong it carries a black box warning about its high potential for dependence and abuse. Chances are, some teenager who hasn't even been diagnosed with ADHD could end up getting their hands on that drug, spend five seconds on the Internet learning how to subvert its time-release mechanism, and die. And no person or company would be held liable because of the plethora of legal releases.

Should no one be held liable for future harms caused by the company's drugs, even its non-opioids? O'Neill's questions had gone over my head and those of most of the activists listening in. But O'Neill was laying groundwork for future appeals, Bismuth explained. Throughout the trial, whenever Drain thought a lawyer's argument wasn't up to snuff, the judge made an art of petulantly rolling his eyes (as in *give me a break*), thumping his fist (angrily), rubbing his hands together while shaking his head (*idiots!*), and resting his chin under his palm with a squinty half-smile (bored, skeptical).

But Drain was both silent and stone-faced during the trial's most telling moment. Near the end of its first day, O'Neill had closed by asking Richard Sackler three questions:

"Mr. Sackler, do you have any responsibility for the opioid crisis in the United States?"

No.

"Does the Sackler family have any responsibility for the opioid crisis in the United States?"

No.

"Does Purdue Pharma have any responsibility for the opioid crisis in the United States?"

No.

When the stories of Richard Sackler's full-throated denial hit the press, they were accompanied by photos taken earlier in the week from the August 9 courthouse protest—exactly as Ed Bisch had envisioned it. Of the fifty or so people at the protest, about a quarter were press.

In the *Wall Street Journal*, the photo featured a Truth Pharm activist, clad in a turquoise shirt, erecting tombstones in the front lawn of Judge Drain's court. Associated Press photos included PAIN's banner with a winking Judge Drain, a close-up of the group's faux OxyContin bottles and faux OxyCash, and a chalk-printed message from Grace Bisch to her husband's long-dead son: "EDDIE B WE MISS YOU."

At the end of the next day's hearing, Judge Drain finally paused to acknowledge the more than half-million lives extinguished by opioids.

He brought up two letters recently added to the docket. "I have received letters from people that…" he paused…"speak eloquently and bravely about the impact. And if anyone doubts…their effect"—Drain paused again, his voice beginning to crack—"…you should read them…Not as advocacy pieces, but simply as evidence of the effect of this company's products."

Lipson, who occasionally translated the bankruptcy process for the Ad Hoc Committee, noted the irony in the judge's words: "The whole point of a court, even a bankruptcy court, is advocacy. Judge Drain may be moved by these letters, but not enough to do anything about it."

One letter had been sent by a Minneapolis woman with stage-four cancer who lost her firefighter husband in 2020 to addiction-related suicide. Troy Lubinski's descent had begun with an OxyContin prescription, "and that was the end of Troy," Stephanie Lubinski wrote. She wouldn't likely qualify for the settlement's minimum personal-injury payout of $3,500 because she couldn't access Troy's medical records—they'd divorced in 2018 after he bankrupted the family to buy painkillers. At the height of his addiction, he was consuming forty pain pills a day.

Troy had even sold their son's high-school football championship rings to buy drugs. Stephanie spent years paying off his rehab bill and was still crawling out of debt.

She told me she'd filed a victim claim on behalf of her two children when Troy, fifty-nine, was still alive. They were still friends, and Troy told his mother days before he took his life that he hoped they'd get back together. But Stephanie had to amend her personal-injury claim after Troy's suicide, writing in her letter to the judge:

"I may only have another year or two to live, and only want for my children to have some satisfaction in knowing the Sackler family will suffer a morsel of what we have," she wrote. "And I believe the Sackler family should know what their greed has caused. They should know the name, Troy Lubinski, and the many, many others who have lost their lives to OxyContin."

Troy Lubinski had been an avid hunter, a championship fisherman, a teetotaler, and a very funny guy who adored his family. In his final years he was never apart from his Labrador retrievers, Boone and Scout, whose barking alerted the neighbors to Troy's death. "People heard his dogs. It's a small town. Troy's dogs never bark."

But Judge Drain, who had recently announced he was retiring from the bench less than halfway through his term, never got around to telling the Lubinskis' story or reading from the letter.

The mercurial judge put the letters down and, tears rolling down his face, stood up and walked away from the bench without adjourning or saying a word.

Chapter Thirteen

The War on People

Brooke Parker and Joe Solomon checking on participants, Charleston,
West Virginia.

N ear the gold dome of the stately West Virginia capitol, HIV cases soared while city leaders staunchly refused to reopen the needle exchanges that had been created to stem the spread of disease. In several conservative pockets of the country, politicians were busy amplifying NIMBYism and trumping up complaints of needle litter and vagrancy in order to close needle exchanges against the advice of health officials. But nowhere in America had those with SUD been hammered harder by their neighbors—and those charged with their protection—than in the hollows and homeless encampments of West Virginia.

Inside a federal courthouse in Charleston, drug distributors labored to construct impenetrable defenses in the first bellwether trial to emerge from the Multidistrict Litigation (MDL) opioid case agglomeration. But no one could hope to remain as untouchable as the Sacklers. Purdue Pharma and its owners had managed to escape the arena of civil litigation by filing for bankruptcy, and no other court would presume to offer worldwide, infinite civil immunity to individuals who weren't even parties to the case.

The difference between the two cases became even more stark when exhibits were introduced. In the bankruptcy, that just didn't happen; the public could only see the odds and ends that weren't subject to the court's broad protective order.

In the civil trial, on the other hand, it wasn't long before bombshells began to drop. While West Virginia's overdoses climbed by a third during COVID, a song was entered as evidence of how pharma executives felt about the West Virginians upon whose graves their prosperity was built. The newly unearthed song came from a 2011 e-mail circulated at AmerisourceBergen, a riff on the theme song to *The Beverly Hillbillies*:

> *Come and listen to a story about a man named Jed,*
> *A poor mountaineer barely kept his habit fed,*
> *Then one day he was looking at some tube,*
> *And saw Florida had a lax attitude,*
> *About pills, that is. Hillbilly Heroin. OC.*

At the time, people from across the nation were carpooling to booming Florida pill mills, but AmerisourceBergen executives paused to chuckle at the song parody, including another rhyme referring to eastern Kentucky as "OxyContinville." When new regulations were introduced in that state, an executive chortled in an e-mail: "One of the hillbilly's [sic] must have learned how to read ?."

No wonder Richard Sackler wanted his e-mails to self-destruct. And that's *hillbillies*, asshole.

The mocking e-mails emerged as evidence in the Charleston courtroom more than a decade after they were sent. In court, AmerisourceBergen denied its employees had written the parody, though senior vice president Chris Zimmerman admitted forwarding it to the company's lobbyists, his underlings, and to the national distributor trade group. Tracking information about pill diversion was all part of the job, he explained. "It was in a joking manner," he said.

And: "The culture at [AmerisourceBergen] is of the highest caliber."

All told, that high-caliber culture resulted in the three distributors and one drugmaker agreeing to a $260 million settlement with two Ohio counties—while insisting, like the Sacklers, that they had done nothing wrong.

But anyone with walking-around sense now understood that shipping 100 million opioid doses to a county with a population of just 90,000 was not acting in the best interests of that community. Huntington, a small city an hour west of Charleston, had the highest overdose-death rate of any community in the nation. An Allegiant airline flight that flew from Huntington to Florida even had a nickname—the Pill Express.

In 2016, Huntington-based EMS workers had responded to twenty-six heroin overdoses *in less than four hours*. One in five babies born at the local hospital was exposed to addictive substances. Foster-care placements doubled, and the school system had to install a twenty-four-hour hotline so that the police and schools could communicate about students living in homes where parents had SUD. The high school now has a dedicated space where traumatized teens can go if they need to talk to an adult or just be alone, no questions asked. "The trauma these kids have experienced in many cases from the moment they have a memory is just staggering," said Amanda Coleman, a housing activist.

And still the companies "hammered the abusers," as Richard Sackler put it, as well as the bands of drug couriers, illegal syndicates, overprescribing doctors, and carpoolers hightailing it to Florida on the Flamingo Express. The distributors also tried to deflect the blame back onto Purdue, claiming it was really the OxyContin makers, aided by prescription-happy doctors and a bungling DEA, who were most at fault.

"We are a mirror on what happens in health care," a lawyer for Cardinal explained. "We reflect it, we don't drive it."

Charleston journalist Eric Eyre was not hopeful about the outcome of the trial taking place in his city. He'd already exposed how those same distributors flooded opioids into nearby counties already suffering from some of the nation's highest overdose rates. Over a decade, the distributors shipped 20.8 million oxycodone and hydrocodone painkillers to the small town of Williamson (population 2,900 and rapidly declining), without an alarm bell being rung—until Eyre rang it.

The companies and their lobbyists, it turned out, had essentially stripped the DEA of its ability to aggressively monitor suspicious pill orders by convincing Congress to agree to a more industry-friendly law. Political action committees representing Big Pharma had contributed at least $1.5 million to the twenty-three lawmakers who supported the law, former DEA lawyer D. Linden Barber had helped draft an earlier version of the law, and Barack Obama signed it without paying much attention to the fine print.

Barber was among dozens of top DEA officials who left the agency to work for the better-paying companies they had once regulated—not unlike the FDA's Curtis Wright, who approved OxyContin before landing at Purdue. So-called suspicious orders were supposed to be red flags, but policing such orders was now handled by a kind of honor system, left to corporations that had given up honor in favor of enhanced shareholder value long ago.

As Eyre predicted in an op-ed: "AmerisourceBergen will deny wrongdoing. Lawyers will scoop up a third of the cash. Politicians will steer the bulk of the money to fill budget holes wrought by the coronavirus shutdown. Only a small percentage, I fear, will be allocated to help West Virginians get through opioid-use-disorder treatment, which can take three to five years."

Suffering from a moderate stage of Parkinson's disease, Eyre had left the *Charleston Gazette-Mail* and was working for a scrappy online news start-up, *Mountain State Spotlight*. He spent most days of the three-month trial holed up in the court's overflow room, coaching younger coworkers on how to cover the story and occasionally writing or co-writing stories. The tremors from his Parkinson's made typing increasingly difficult.

During a June break in the trial, he shared his skepticism with me over a supper of Thai takeout. We were sitting with his wife, Lori, on the same front porch where the damning documents first landed in their broken mailbox, tipping Eyre off to revelatory data showing that huge pill shipments that flooded tiny West Virginia towns at a time when overdoses were already soaring. The newspaper series that resulted from those documents won Eyre a 2017 Pulitzer Prize. Lori bought a replacement mailbox, but for posterity Eyre insisted they use the old one, which was still missing its lid.

Eyre feared that the West Virginia lawyers didn't stand a chance against the distributors' guards. Far bigger than Purdue, the wholesalers were among the fifteen largest companies in the United States. They had throngs of corporate defense lawyers from New York City who flew in on private jets and interrupted the local lawyers constantly with objections.

Their rudeness rankled Eyre and set him on edge. When plaintiffs' attorney Paul Farrell talked in his closing arguments about the impacts of the crisis on West Virginia and how many of his own friends had died, Eyre found himself tearing up.

Weeks later, the day the defense wrapped, Eyre watched the defense attorneys high-fiving each other in the parking garage of the courthouse. "They think it's a slam dunk, and they're gonna win," he said.

A young reporter in Huntington who'd spent part of her childhood in foster care told me she had no understanding of Big Pharma's role in her life until she began covering the trial. At thirty, Courtney Hessler remembered her impaired mother driving ninety miles an hour down the interstate while nodding out. In 2017, Hessler was reporting on the first rumblings of the court cases when a doctor diagnosed her with PTSD. "I was having nightmares and flashbacks from childhood," she told me. "He said it was comparable to what combat veterans go through."

The diagnosis was a weight off her shoulders, she said, but covering the trial was sometimes triggering. When her stories ran in the *Huntington Herald Dispatch*, she got vehement reader feedback of the "let them die!" sort. "People here are so traumatized themselves," she said.

"There's not a person in Huntington who hasn't had something stolen from them by a person who needed money for drugs," Hessler said. "You can have the copper pipes taken out of your house while you're sleeping." The pain and anger of the family members and neighbors harmed by the addicted people in their lives often blocked their capacity for sympathy.

A few years ago, Hessler covered a story about a couple who overdosed in their car at a city park; the vehicle hadn't been placed in park, and as their heads slumped, their bodies slack and their lungs retreating into cozy submission, their car rolled onto a playground where children were playing. "Nobody was hurt, but mentally kids were hurt. They saw the car rolling at them, and the two people overdosing, and the EMS administering Narcan. That's traumatic," Hessler said.

"They say we're going to lose a generation if we don't do something. I say we've already lost that generation."

An older sister helped Hessler go away to college. But with $50,000 in student-loan debt, she struggles to get by. Her insurance deductible is so high—her psychiatrist visit was $200, the only time she went—that she can't afford regular counseling for her PTSD.

Eyre and Hessler weren't the only skeptical West Virginians. Asked to decipher the mood among her readers, *Charleston Gazette-Mail* reporter Caity Coyne told me, "Everyone just assumes it won't work out to our benefit."

Coyne was immersed in covering the city's worsening HIV crisis, including new city and state laws that restricted needle exchanges to the point of shutting most of them down. As of late June 2021, the county had confirmed sixty-eight HIV cases in two and a half years, almost half among Black Charlestonians. Eight months later, the number of confirmed cases topped 100. More than half of people with full-blown AIDS weren't in treatment at all. CDC outreach workers had recently flown in from Atlanta and spent a month interviewing people who use drugs, learning pretty much the same things I'd been hearing from drug users everywhere:

- It was almost impossible for them to access lifesaving addiction medicines.
- Clean needles were notoriously hard to come by.
- The one exchange still operating in Charleston only gave out one new needle in exchange for every used needle turned in by a drug user—a practice called one-for-one—and it required official identification, which most homeless users no longer had. "They're not accepting...and they make you feel like

you're a bad person," one participant told a researcher about Charleston's remaining one-for-one exchange.

- Hospital employees rarely tested people who use drugs for HIV, though a lone spitfire outreach worker combed the city's homeless encampments daily.
- Few people who use drugs wanted to go to the hospital because they were routinely stigmatized by hospital staffers when they did.

The CDC report on Charleston's crisis showed patients were being seen in hospitals eight to ten times before anyone ever tested them for HIV, an unthinkable shortcoming in a region with such a severe outbreak.

Though the state legislature had basically criminalized need-based needle exchange, SOAR and the many other syringe programs in the state were still doing what Lill Prosperino had been doing for years: quietly delivering safe-use supplies underground, no one-for-one rules and no questions asked. Prosperino was viewed by naysayers as a "terrorist" who "isn't from here," Coyne told me, even though they live an hour south of Charleston and grew up in Appalachia.

Coyne and other reporters told me that Charleston mayor Amy Schuler Goodwin was pro–harm reduction but too politically astute to say so publicly now in city council meetings because, they assumed, she was plotting her next campaign. One city councilor was so worried that Coyne's reporting would paint Charleston as the nation's HIV capital—when that horse had long ago trotted out of the barn—that she tried to get the young reporter fired by telling Coyne's publisher that she volunteered for SOAR and therefore had a conflict of interest in the story.

"I offered to give up my interview recordings!" Coyne said. "They actually called [SOAR leaders] to double-check" that Coyne had never been a volunteer.

On a stiflingly hot Saturday in late June, SOAR activists and their allies donned matching red T-shirts to spell out the words "HIV SOS" next to Charleston's Kanawha River. In a set of fiery speeches, they called on city leaders to declare the HIV crisis a public health emergency.

City leaders did not answer SOAR's call. The lone councilor who voted against the new restrictive law requiring one-for-one exchange and identification was the only one of the twenty-six members of city council to attend the SOAR event.

The following Monday, at the request of the West Virginia ACLU, a federal judge in Huntington issued a restraining order against the enforcement of a new state law which effectively banned most harm-reduction programs in the state. Charleston-based ACLU lawyer Loree Stark filed the lawsuit in the jurisdiction of a Huntington judge, arguing that the law was so vaguely written as to be unconstitutional. (The state law carried a civil penalty for violators of up to $10,000.)

"You could say I judge-shopped, yes," Stark said. She'd filed her case in Huntington rather than in the Charleston capitol where she worked. "There's only one federal judge there, and he's reasonable," she told me, smiling.

For the region's gay and lesbian community, Charleston's HIV epidemic brought up horrific memories. "Our gay allies are now calling the [anti-needle-exchange] naysayers out," Stark told me. "They're telling officials, 'You can't be for us and against people who are addicted.' The mayor and city council don't want to lose their seats. But there has to be an issue that's worth losing your seat for, and this is it."

A Huntington-based investigative journalist compared the Charleston politicians to Trump. "Their way of staying relevant and powerful is acknowledging that real problems exist here, but rather than solve them they create new problems they claim to have the solutions to," Kyle Vass said.

The political legerdemain of Charleston's anti-harm-reduction elected officials echoed the government's early inaction on HIV/AIDS. When ACT UP occupied Grand Central Station in 1991 and held up signs demanding "Money for AIDS, Not for War," the protest was "a response to profound oppression," as the HIV historian and author Sarah Schulman has said. Too often pundits and government officials criticized the tactics of the protesters to deflect attention from the greater problem, in this case the government's failure to protect the lives of those suffering from the effects of HIV/AIDS.

"That's the standard structure," Schulman told the *New York Times* podcaster Ezra Klein. "You see that in families, you see it in cliques, communities, religious groups, national groups—where the response is the thing that gets blamed, and the originating action, no one takes responsibility for."

The needle litter was the real problem in Charleston, the naysayers believed, not the burgeoning HIV/AIDS crisis. The "junkies" were the problem, not the doctors or health systems that refused to treat people who use drugs as human beings.

Similarly, the naysayers insisted, the immigrants bringing in illicit fentanyl were the real problems at the border—not the Sacklers or AmerisourceBergen and the like—who created and delivered the drugs, and, against all red flags to the contrary, kept pushing the demand.

Brooke Parker and I spent most of a chaotic afternoon hunting down four people in Charleston who had recently tested positive for HIV but hadn't yet been notified of their status. With a hospital badge dangling from the waist of her jeans, Brooke worked her way through homeless encampments wearing sandals, jeans, and a black, sleeveless T-shirt that said, "Pick Flowers & Fights." She was thirty-six, in recovery for thirteen years, and the week before she'd lost three of her clients to fatal overdose.

Officially, she's a "retention coordinator" for the hospital's federally funded Ryan White program, named for the young hemophiliac who contracted HIV through a blood transfusion in 1984 and then spent the rest of his short life rallying against the discrimination of people with AIDS. Most days, Brooke's goal is to test residents who use drugs, notify them of their results, then get them into treatment—for HIV and, if they're willing, for the co-occurring SUD and mental health disorders underlying it.

None of which ever, ever transpires in a linear fashion.

Instead, patients move between the time Brooke tests them and returns to notify them of their status. Brooke spends her days driving her Honda Fit from one bando or tent encampment to the next, asking around and trying to build trust. Some people are rude, like the man who only ever answers her with a heap of side-eye and "*Bitch, please!*" which both irks her and cracks her up.

Among most of the harm-reductionists I followed, on-the-job laughs are rare, and Brooke uses dark humor as a coping tool. It can take weeks to convince her patients to go to the hospital for help, only to have the nursing staff treat them like shit when they finally do. "I had one client get discharged with a chest tube back to a trap house, where I'm pretty sure she was being trafficked," she told me, fuming.

"You're sending her home to die!" Brooke told the doctor, then checked her out and took her to a domestic violence shelter.

The day before my visit, Brooke spent several hours driving an HIV-positive man named Henry an hour away to rehab—abstinence-based, at his request—only to learn later that the rehab had almost immediately sent him back to a hospital in Charleston due to a minor wound on his leg. (He'd been burned badly a few weeks before when the tent he was living in caught fire.)

Henry hadn't eaten all day, so we took him a Wendy's cheeseburger at the ER waiting room, where Brooke convinced him to stay until she could find him a bed in a treatment facility, which she did, in Morgantown. His goal was to get sober before he started his HIV meds.

Brooke takes trash bags to the homeless encampments where she spends most of her time. Every person she serves is hungry and thirsty; they all need help getting rid of their trash. She uses food and water as an entrée to convince people to enter care because, as she says, "I've done street work for twenty years, and I've never seen people so vulnerable and so on guard and mistrusting as they are now."

Some patients threaten to kill themselves after learning they're HIV-positive; others want to kill the person who gave it to them. Many dissociate and "ditch and dodge," unable to process the news—not just because it's painful information but also because their HIV-positive status is so far down their priority list. Before they can deal with having HIV, they need housing. They need their daily dose of dope so they won't find themselves alone in an ER shitting their pants under the judgmental eye of a snippy hospital worker.

They need help navigating each one of the disconnected bureaucracies that serve as their only portals to care.

"They need a *damn walk-in clinic*," Brooke says, sighing.

It's easier for people who use drugs to refuse being tested, which is why Brooke carries gift cards to Family Dollar as incentives, though she knows that some trade the gift cards for drugs. Recently, she allowed an HIV-positive patient named Charlie to borrow her cell phone for a three-hour disability interview. The only way he could manage explaining every traumatic moment in his life to the SSI (Supplemental Security Income) interviewer over the phone was to sit outside next to Brooke and chain-smoke. So they sat outside together next to the powerless shed where he was living. And they smoked.

They'd met months before at a SOAR health fair, where Brooke tested him and then funneled him to treatment when his test came back positive. "He said, 'Y'all literally saved my life.' If he hadn't had clean syringes [from the SOAR event], he would've had to tell his friends he was HIV-positive, and they would have killed him—they literally would have beaten him to death." Weeks later, another of Brooke's patients was murdered as retribution for having passed HIV to her drug dealer via a shared needle.

Charlie was now in sober living, taking bupe, and, after completing the HIV treatment regimen that Brooke arranged, had an undetectable viral load.

The phrase for that is U=U, for "Undetectable Equals Untransmittable."

"He gives me so much hope," she said, choking back tears. "We almost have an ID for him now."

But the truth, as I was beginning to comprehend it, was that Charlie's success remained a complete and total outlier in most of America, as rare as it was—and, ultimately, short-lived.

We spent most of the afternoon looking for Marie, a thirty-six-year-old sex worker who'd tested positive the week before. After several stops, we found her in an encampment she shared with her father near a truck stop and an Econolodge. Marie wore thigh-high boots, bright-red lipstick, and had "Daddy's Little Girl" tattooed on her forearm. Brooke talked to Marie and her dad for ten minutes about their mutual friend, Camille, who was currently in the hospital for complications caused by a drug called "crocodile" that had eaten the flesh off her forearm. To shame Camille, the Charleston Has Had Enough! Facebook group posted a picture of her open wounds on its page.

Marie seemed unmoved by the news of her HIV-positive status, after Brooke delivered the news privately, behind a tree. Brooke volunteered to pick her up the following week to get her viral load tested, a precursor to starting her on HIV meds. "I'll come back Tuesday to remind you," Brooke said. By the time Tuesday rolled around, Brooke predicted, Marie would have ditched and dodged, which was exactly what transpired. "Marie is still MIA," she texted me a week later. "I'm looking for her dad to do a test soon as he had a needle-stick injury from one of her points and is worried."

At an encampment behind a nearby IHOP, Brooke scanned the grounds for the remaining three positives on her list. But her search came to a halt when she spotted Kyle, a forty-five-year-old man in a wheelchair who needed her immediate help.

He'd picked maggots from his feet earlier in the day. Not only was Kyle in pain from the severe injection-related infections on his lower legs and feet, he was also dopesick. Brooke texted a picture of his wounds to a coworker and physician's assistant, who confirmed that Kyle's infection wouldn't clear without IV antibiotics. Kyle needed to be admitted to the hospital.

But when Brooke offered to take him, he shook his head. He'd spent eighteen hours in the hospital's ER for the same infections a week earlier, and "they did nothing for me."

Brooke sighed and apologized, then sighed some more. She squatted at Kyle's feet, put on rubber gloves, and spent the next half-hour applying packet after packet of triple-antibiotic ointment on Kyle's legs and feet. "Oh baby, I'm so sorry," she said, every time he winced.

Kyle wept openly as a friend of his, a woman in a short skirt with smeared red lipstick, walked up and handed him a Pepsi.

"That ointment ain't gonna cut it, honey," she told Brooke. "I was an LPN [licensed practicing nurse] for seventeen years."

Kyle's friend paused for dramatic effect.

"And then I got married," she said, spreading her arms with the timing of a stand-up comedienne. "And hence—a homeless hooker."

She squeezed Kyle's shoulder, bowed dramatically as she took her leave, and returned to her tent.

*   *   *

If a couple of things hadn't gone wrong for her—if she'd married a halfway decent man, for starters—she might be the hospital nurse taking care of Kyle, Brooke pointed out later, back in the car.

In all her interactions, Brooke tries to remind herself of this about her patients: At one point in their lives, most of them had kids and a house.

She pulled up a cell phone picture of another client, who'd been found dead by the river, still foaming at the mouth from overdose—one of the three she'd lost in the past week.

Brooke hit her vape pen.

"This is stressful shit," she said. "Most of the time I don't even realize I've been holding my breath all day."

As she finished rubbing the ointment on Kyle's feet and legs, two Charleston police officers walked up. They carried stacks of eviction notices, which they proceeded to affix to the chain-link fences and trees. Kyle and his friends now had two weeks to clear out of the encampment. The fliers listed numbers they could call for help with housing, but Brooke said that placements are rare and take at least six months to arrange.

"What are you doing here?" an officer asked Brooke.

"I'm a social worker," she said, politely showing her hospital badge.

The officer handed Kyle a flier and walked off.

Kyle folded it in half and sent it cartwheeling to the ground.

This is how Kyle, his friend the homeless sex worker, and a dozen or so others living in that encampment learned they would lose their home. Two weeks later, Brooke sent me a photo of what was left behind—clothes scattered everywhere, toiletries and pillows, a job application for Texas Roadhouse.

Health officers were talking about putting up fliers about HIV at the truck stop—to warn truckers not to carry the disease home to their families. "Like they did for syphilis in the 1980s," Brooke said. "But syphilis is curable, and I think all that will happen is that we end up with a lot of dead sex workers."

When I told Brooke that I couldn't do what she does without having a nervous breakdown, she shared her self-care ritual: she hangs out with her girlfriend, does yoga, sprawls on her living room floor so her cat can crawl over her, and eats a lot of grilled peanut butter and jelly sandwiches. She was trying to say "no" to outside work, even to helping with SOAR—though she backtracked on that pledge a month later and began ferrying clients to evening SOAR meetings in her Honda. Inspired by VANDU in Vancouver, Joe Solomon and other SOAR leaders were launching a series of monthly drug-user meetings, hoping to spark civil disobedience that would pressure city leaders to deal with its HIV/ AIDS crisis. VANDU founder Ann Livingston had stressed to Solomon that he should pay people who use drugs for their time (ten dollars per meeting), feed them (spaghetti), and let *them* direct the agenda.

I sat in on one meeting over Zoom, and the chief complaint among those who came wasn't the paucity of treatment, as organizers expected, but rather police brutality. A woman named Snow who already helped SOAR with secondary distro—passing out SOAR's needles to her friends—offered that most people who use drugs crave a place to shower and want to interact more with "people who will not only see the negative in us." They wanted friends.

I could tell you more hair-raising details about the structural violence and trauma Brooke sees every day. I could tell you how, a month after my visit, Brooke's number one success story, her patient Charlie, lost his housing after he was caught running a bike repair shop out of his sober-living home. Charlie moved back into his sister's shed and later relapsed. Despite all that Brooke did for him, it was nowhere near enough. Eventually he became verbally abusive to her, and she had to tell him he could call her but only when he was ready to treat her with respect again.

Brooke was now seeing five to ten new HIV-positive cases a month, most of them under the age of thirty. Kyle's abscesses were likely to kill him, and he still refused to return to the hospital. She had run into Marie several times, but whenever they arranged an appointment for care she always ditched and dodged. At her encampment Marie had posted a sign made of crayon and cardboard: *STOP. You have no reason to go any further am sick of assholes stealing from me I got traps that will hurt you and I will hunt you down. This camp belongs to Marie and her old man.*

With encampment evictions, unhoused people were becoming more protective of their outdoor space. "They're in survival mode, on high alert, and they're just so scared," Brooke said.

I worried about Brooke. She had recently gotten into an argument with a methadone clinic director who outed one of her patients for being HIV-positive in front of the entire waiting room—breaking every confidentiality law in the book and making Brooke so angry that she threatened to "literally destroy" him, leading to a lecture from a supervisor on the perils of being overly assertive.

"Bitch, please!" I said, just to make her laugh. It had become our shorthand for:

This is sad. Our country is so fucked.

Brooke was so stressed she found herself contemplating heroin for the first time in her life—her drugs of choice had always been alcohol and benzos.

"The urge to use is so strong, it isn't even funny," she told me. "I need some boundaries with all this right now." Her clients were worried about her, too.

"I'm a harm-reductionist first, then a case manager, and then I end up being people's friend, which is what I want but not always what I need. And it's not always what *they* need, and I hate that,"

Brooke said. Like Wendy and James in Surry County, she needed more structural support. But those in charge of the systems she navigated could barely comprehend what Brooke saw out in the field every day, let alone help her with it, and they had to wrestle with political constraints.

I gently chided her for volunteering for SOAR after vowing not to. For the third nighttime meeting of Solomon's nascent drug-user union, Brooke had driven four people (and their cat) from a tent city. "It ended up being perfect timing," she wrote. "I had unexpectedly found one of my people dead in his hotel room that afternoon and didn't need to be alone that night...I leaned on SOAR a lot this week."

I might need better boundaries, too. But if you can figure out how to witness what Brooke and Tim Nolan do every day; if you can figure out how to parachute in and out of their lives without being deeply moved by them and their work and without also wanting to roll a few stones—I'm all ears.

An hour west of Charleston, in the smaller city of Huntington, that "damn walk-in clinic" Brooke craved so desperately was already in operation.

The clinic was a collaboration with public health experts, three hospitals, and the mayor's office. No appointments were necessary, they were soon to launch evening hours, and the crux of the clinic's mission was to provide treatment triage including therapy (family, individual, group), addiction medications via an on-site pharmacy, spiritual care, job services, and peer recovery coaching.

How bittersweet that some people are now rediscovering what Jerome Jaffe came up with fifty years ago.

No one gets turned away, and, ironically, the program is housed in a former CVS building. The Huntington model is called PROACT, short for Provider Response Organization for Addiction Care & Treatment. Under the strong suggestion of the

Marshall University president who announced that everyone at his college, from researchers to student interns, should engage in helping their neighbors with SUD, and with considerable prodding from Jan Rader, Huntington's formidable fire chief—the word *badass* may be overused, but it's apt here—the people who designed PROACT made sure it could be replicated elsewhere by sharing their grant applications with other communities, including tips on fostering cross-pollination among competing groups and health care systems.

Even more meaningfully, across town is a homeless shelter called Harmony House run by Amanda Coleman, a medical anthropologist whose credo is that housing and medical care should be basic human rights. Most of Coleman's staff are peers in recovery, and they arrange housing and support services for roughly half of the unhoused people in the region, the large majority of them people who use drugs.

Overdoses in Huntington and surrounding Cabell County decreased 25 percent from 2017 to 2018, after the opening of PROACT. The decline continued as initiatives begun at PROACT developed further in 2018. But the decreases didn't last when COVID hit in 2020 and deaths shot up nationwide, including a doubling in Cabell County from the previous year.

Cabell County is smaller than Kanawha County, and, with Huntington being a college town, it's more politically progressive than Charleston. When the new statewide needle exchange restrictions went into law, PROACT and Harmony House served as a buffer for local efforts against harm reduction. Also, the shock of twenty-six overdoses happening in one day in Cabell County—and making international news for it—ensured that most of the region's leaders checked their egos at the door.

"We spend a lot of time talking about the biology of overdose and the treatment, but it's the politics that make the problem so uniquely bad in this country," explained Dr. Joshua Sharfstein, the Johns Hopkins addiction scholar. Sharfstein coauthored a set of principles designed to make sure that litigation money would be spent on evidence-based interventions—not fixing potholes and not abstinence-only treatment—with buy-in from a diverse coalition ranging from the liberal Drug Policy Alliance to the conservative American Medical Association. In the absence of clear guidelines, he told me, "making money available is a recipe for following the biases of the moment and not necessarily the evidence."

Responding to the state's new syringe laws, Cabell County's harm-reductionists tightened up residency and needle-return requirements and maintained a quiet, low-profile approach, said Lyn O'Connell, associate director of Marshall University Medical School's Division of Addiction Sciences. She suspected that most complaints about needle litter had been trumped up by naysayers—including people running for office on anti-harm-reduction platforms. The new restrictions weren't ideal, but they were politically necessary to keep the doors open.

"Cabell's health officer played the game a bit, survived, and got back to low-barrier," the journalist Kyle Vass explained. "Kanawha's refused to make changes that would harm patients, it got shut down, and now they're hurting bad."

Politics matter, just as Jerome Jaffe warned me. So does culture. When outsiders and experts charge into West Virginia saying things like "It works in New York and San Francisco," locals want to do the opposite.

For more than a century, rural Americans have been talked down to while their opportunities for work and upward mobility have been blocked. "When people are driven by fear, facts don't matter," O'Connell said. "We cannot scare people into a public health approach."

Shifting political acceptance is best accomplished through a combination of loud and moderate voices, said Dr. Stefan Kertesz, an addiction and pain-management scholar who teaches at the University of Alabama at Birmingham. "It's helpful to have strong voices that create tension and are willing to put in tons of labor for free. But you also need other voices who speak the local language in a gently assertive way and can find a way to work with people they're in disagreement with," he said.

It takes time to soften people who are traumatized, the Kentucky activist Robert Gipe said. "There's still a lot of anger mixed in with the grief when it comes to the SUD sufferers in a family," he said. "Yes, SUD is a disease, but those with that disease don't just cough and sneeze and ask you to bring them a glass of water. They steal and lie and fuck up Thanksgiving and break our hearts."

As the welter of opioid litigation spiraled to conclusion, the communities poised to spend settlement dollars on solutions were those with established infrastructures and the bandwidth to put resources at the points of frustration—sending an outreach worker to pick up dirty needles when neighbors complained about needle litter, for instance. One innovation began with a simple whiteboard in Mount Airy and horrific shouts of "Let 'em die and take their organs!" while the seed of another started with the tragedy of EMTs responding to twenty-six overdoses in four hours in the West Virginia hills.

Nikki King, the wily Indiana hospital administrator, figured out that the key to making health care actors and criminal justice systems collaborate was to incentivize wellness and cost-savings instead of simply continuing to jail people in the name of morality.

But too many stone-rollers still divide themselves between tough-love twelve-step models and the harm-reduction model of meeting people where they are with medicine, compassion, and tiny packets of triple-antibiotic ointment. Too many still universalize their own personal experiences instead of embracing the pluralistic approach that one size never fits all when it comes to addiction.

This moment is an historic opportunity to radically rethink addiction care, to do more than give lip service to the throwaway line—*addiction is a disease*—and to treat it like one. Lacking creative collaborations and strong leadership, the opioid-litigation money will likely end up being funneled into a patchwork of disparate state agencies that has never been up to the task of delivering care to the addicted, let alone listening to people who use drugs.

People with SUD are still ignored by policy makers when they often have the most knowledge to offer about their conditions, said Baltimore addiction specialist Yngvild Olsen, who cited a recent survey of 900 people with SUD. Their top three goals, in order, were: staying alive, reducing harmful substance use, and improving mental health. "Completely stopping substance use was not in their top three," Olsen said.

But too many well-meaning bureaucrats, politicians, and health care providers don't realize that they are active participants in a stigmatized structure born of racism, rent-seeking behaviors, and wrong-headed notions about a drug-free society that will never, ever exist.

As the bioethicist Carl Erik Fisher writes: "We will not end addiction, but we must find ways of working with it: ways that are sometimes gentle, and sometimes vigorous, but never warlike, because it is futile to wage a war on our own nature."

In the ongoing catastrophe that the crisis had devolved into, I had to keep reminding myself that the overdose crisis is not actually an unsolvable problem. Doctors helped get us into this mess, and they *could* help get us out. Bought-off politicians, limpid regulators, and a timorous Department of Justice that twice failed to punish the creators of the overdose epidemic had failed the nation, too.

When President Biden talked about putting over a trillion

dollars into an infrastructure bill last year, I wanted him to tour Mount Airy, where the largest employer now flies in employees from Puerto Rico, houses them, transports them to work, sees that they go to a doctor when they need one, and even offers retention bonuses. A jail in a neighboring county reached out to the chicken processing plant manager recently to see about employing inmates upon their release. The Surry County jail is just five minutes from the plant, but "nothing's gonna happen here until their new jail is built," said Mark Willis, who hopes the opioid settlement money will allow him to one day employ a peer recovery specialist inside the jail to connect people with treatment and jobs.

When I first began reporting on Mount Airy, the county had 700 job openings they couldn't fill. Now, three years later, the number was more than 1,500. "It goes up every time I check it," Willis said. A recent report fairly screamed the news with a bold subhead exclaiming, "The opioid epidemic is stealing prime-age men from the labor market," causing a 40-percent decline in the number of working-age men.

Mark Willis had not only mobilized a small army of peers and drivers to ferry the addicted to treatment; he was also, as of late 2021, on the verge of creating a pipeline from the jail to the workplace.

Of all the interventions his team had made, just under a third had followed through and entered treatment. Around 90 of the county's estimated 4,000 people with SUD had been officially connected to care. Approximately half the people using his Road to Recovery transportation network ended up being at home when Willis's drivers arrived to take them to treatment.

"You can drive a dump truck with $100 dollar bills and put it on our lawn, but that doesn't mean it's going to result in anything—if the infrastructure isn't there," Willis said. "The belief that you build this big, gleaming treatment center, and everyone lines up and six months later comes out of it—that ain't the way it works." More than one-third of the counties in his state hadn't yet appointed a point person assigned to abate the overdose crisis.

Before we can start rebuilding our nation's crumbling bridges and roads, we'll need to significantly shrink the nation's 88 percent treatment gap. The infrastructure we most need is the one that gets Americans treated and housed, the one that cares for the patient.

The abandonment of people who use drugs, fueled by stigma that was baked long ago into every aspect of society, explains why the treatment gap has barely budged, despite federal infusions of well over $10 billion in funding since 2016. It's rigid bupe regulations that require nine hours of weekly therapy, sheriffs who claim they don't have room to administer medicines, and bureaucrats who don't understand that it's a lot easier to recover from SUD when people have a roof (or even a tree) over their heads.

It's snippy health care providers who insist on seeing your insurance card *first*, and the continued refusal of most emergency departments in America to funnel the overdosed into evidence-based care. It's the 90 percent of American physicians who still refuse to prescribe addiction medicines because they don't want "those people in my waiting room," when—guess what?—they're already in their waiting rooms. The lucky ones, anyway.

It's the more than half the surveyed emergency room, family medicine, and internal medicine providers who—falsely—still believe that OUD is not treatable.

It's the fact that there are so many more $1,792-an-hour lawyers flying around in private jets than there are Tim Nolans voluntarily meeting the unseen where they are at night, after rolling stones all day at work.

"A half-million people are dead who should not be dead," the economist Angus Deaton first warned the country in 2015, refer-ring to deaths of despair. Back then, experts predicted that the overdose crisis would peak in 2018. Now, seven years hence, more than a million people are dead who should not be dead, and that's only counting drug-overdose deaths. And we are nowhere close to reversing life-expectancy declines.

If I live to be a hundred, I will never forget the image of Brooke Parker, sitting at the infected feet of a calmly weeping man while police officers went about the business of stapling up eviction notices. It was like we weren't even there, like the earth that we, too, walked on belonged solely to the politicians and bureaucrats and people who were still falling for Richard Sackler's "hammer the abusers" scam.

Epilogue

Brooke Parker searching for clients, Charleston, West Virginia.

I kept obsessively circling my subjects, returning to them time and again. I kept searching out magic wands and solutions, but the bricks from the crumbling drug war just kept falling.

My sources were all still out there working, their programs held together by tape and glue, reliant on GoFundMe and T-shirt sales and homemade salves. I knew operations were flimsier than ever when my dear friend Sister Beth Davies, a Catholic nun and drug counselor in Pennington Gap, Virginia, asked me to donate to her Addiction Education Center, where I'd gone years ago to interview Purdue's first victims. Sister Beth had never asked me for help, but her largest donor recently died of cancer. "Oh, how I hate to ask," she e-mailed. One of her patients, an LPN in recovery, had lost eight of her ten siblings to prison or opioid-related death. Another patient was the one who thought the government might be "trying to get rid of all the lowlifes" when Oxy first infiltrated Virginia's coalfields. We often e-mailed about them.

In 2007, when Purdue pleaded guilty to criminally marketing OxyContin—the first time, that is—it was Sister Beth who organized the parents of the dead outside the courthouse and carried the taped-up poster of Ed Bisch's son.

Since the crisis began, Sister Beth Davies has epitomized the best of what a servant-leader should be. Hers should be one of the most stable organizations in the entire recovery movement. But she is eighty-eight years old, works too many fucking hours, and is in danger of getting her lights cut off while the Sacklers' light bill is paid for a thousand years in advance.

It was Bisch's idea to start a GoFundMe campaign on her center's behalf. And if I know Ed Bisch, who has learned more about bankruptcy than a third-year law student, he will never stop advocating for families of the dead and people like Sister Beth.

The value of his son's life, according to the Drain-approved victim compensation formula: either zero (because the OxyContin that killed Eddie wasn't prescribed to him) or $3,500 at most.

"The AGs like to say no amount of money will bring back our loved ones," he said. "But I say no amount of money was worth giving the Sacklers and their accomplices immunity."

In mid-November of 2021, hoping to amplify the attention that Hulu's *Dopesick* brought to the recidivist crimes of Purdue and the family that had micromanaged the company, Bisch began planning a December 3 rally in front of the Department of Justice. Featured speakers would include Hulu show runner Danny Strong, the real-life former federal prosecutor Rick Mountcastle (portrayed in the show by Peter Sarsgaard), and former DOJ fraud section chief Paul Pelletier.

Mountcastle and Pelletier had never spoken at a protest, let alone one that brought together some 200 parents of the dead who'd traveled to Washington, DC, from as far away as Florida and Hawaii. While they chanted, the artist Fernando Alvarez unveiled another two-story curtain, this one with an Uncle Sam version of Deputy Attorney General Lisa Monaco and the message: "DON'T SHIELD THE SACKLER CARTEL!"

As Pelletier put it in a fiery speech, "Has there ever, ever been a crime in American history with more destruction, more victims, more death, more harm than this one? So how do you get justice? You prosecute the perpetrators; that's what the Department of Justice is supposed to do. And how do you find out who the perpetrators are? You follow the money!"

As the crowd chanted, Mike Quinn was back home in New York working his contacts, trying for a redo of the 2020 DOJ settlement arranged during the last gasps of the Trump administration. After writing four letters to request a meeting with the DOJ, a few hours after Bisch's protest, Quinn finally got a call from the US attorney responsible for the Purdue criminal case. The DOJ agreed to meet with Quinn's Ad Hoc Committee, the *so-called* committee, as Drain liked to call it.

With the bankruptcy now in appeal, US district court judge Colleen McMahon was asking tough questions that Judge Drain hadn't wished to entertain, like whether the Sacklers had abused the bankruptcy system by buying personal releases with a fraction of the fortune the family extracted from Purdue during the years leading up to the bankruptcy.

Public pressure continued to mount from all sides. The following week, the Metropolitan Museum of Art finally removed the name "The Sackler Wing"—home of the famous Temple of Dendur—and all other references to the Mortimer and Raymond Sackler families from its building. For a letter they wrote to the Met's board urging removal, PAIN had garnered the signatures of dozens of the most important artists in the world—including William Kentridge, Ai Weiwei, and Laurie Anderson. Nearly four years after lobbing fake OxyContin bottles into the reflecting pool, Nan Goldin and her lieutenants had finally erased the Oxy Sacklers from America's most famous museum.

A week later, in a startling rebuke to Judge Drain, Judge McMahon overturned the bankruptcy, explaining that bankruptcy courts lacked the authority to shield third parties like the Sacklers from liability.

Quinn was feverish from COVID and quarantining upstate in his family home but well enough, even late at night, to text me passages he'd highlighted from McMahon's 140-page ruling. He particularly liked it when she called Purdue's purported acceptance of responsibility "a charade" given the Sacklers' $10.4 billion draining of the company, much of it "deposited into spendthrift trusts that could not be reached in bankruptcy and off-shore entities located in places like the Bailiwick of Jersey."

The family's greed had finally reared back to bite them in the ass, if only temporarily. Had the Sacklers offered another billion, Quinn believes, none of the states would have appealed. Lawyers for Purdue and the Sacklers were already appealing McMahon's ruling, and negotiations would be ordered again by Drain, so the legal saga was far from finished.

A statement issued by Attorney General Garland proved to Quinn that he had seeded more than just grass in the thorny, never-ending case. The Justice Department wasn't just "pleased" with McMahon's decision; the DOJ flat-out rejected the notion that a bankruptcy judge had the authority to deprive victims of their right to sue the Sacklers.

Quinn, Bisch, and the other bankruptcy watchers were elated, but they also knew there was no point in trying to read too much into the statement—so many lawyers had carefully arranged the tea leaves. But had any of the influential DOJ attorneys been moved by the past year of briefs, protests, press, hearings, and even television shows to actually pursue criminal indictments?

Most of the activists hesitated to get their hopes up, only to be disappointed again. More prudent to consign the Sacklers' souls to the mercy of a higher power who, they prayed, would not shy away from judgment.

Not Bisch, of course. During a Zoom debrief following an appellate argument, his faith was as unwavering as his Philly accent.

"Hey guys!" he said, trying to buoy the group. "Like Tug McGraw said, 'Ya gotta believe.'"

In early March, the Sacklers added another billion dollars to the settlement pot, and the last of the attorney general holdouts caved. That left just the US Trustee's office and three hold-out victims as the only objectors in the case. Quinn stepped in to represent one of them, a Virginia woman named Ellen Isaacs, who'd lost her son, Ryan, after a seventeen-year battle with opioids that had started with a single OxyContin prescription. The appeals weren't resolved as of this writing, but Quinn was still working his contacts and still writing impassioned pleadings, vowing to take Isaac's case to the Supreme Court.

The Sacklers agreed to pay up to $6 billion, though their lawyers got the payment schedule extended from nine to eighteen years. They'd conceded to stop fighting the removal of the family name from the walls and endowments of institutions, and, soon after, the Guggenheim became the next to cut ties.

You can judge for yourselves whether their family statement, labored over by multiple lawyers, constituted a real apology. While the Sacklers still refused to admit to wrongdoing or accept personal responsibility, the family did acknowledge that "OxyContin, a prescription medicine that continues to help people suffering from chronic pain, unexpectedly became part of an opioid crisis that has brought grief and loss to far too many families and communities."

They also agreed to comply with an unusual hearing request in mid-March in which twenty-six victims took to Zoom to tell three Sacklers exactly how the Sacklers' drug had ruined their lives. The victims included Nan Goldin, Ed Bisch, Ryan Hampton, and an Indiana couple who began by playing a recording of a chilling 911 call in which the mother frantically screamed that she had just found her unresponsive son. "Four-thousand, eight-hundred and four. That is how many days have gone by since I made that horrifying phone call—a call that I never dreamed of making," Kristy Nelson told the Sacklers. "A call that I would not have had to make if it weren't for your unlawful behavior and obsessive greed."

For the first time, the Sacklers no longer had their lawyers or McKinsey consultants to shield them from wailing parents and pictures of the dead. The hours-long hearing felt primitive—more like a verbal stoning than an authentic form of justice.

Dame Theresa Sackler, a longtime member of the Purdue board, sat listening stoically and not responding, as did David Sackler, Richard's son. Inexplicably, Richard Sackler was permitted to participate via telephone instead of on camera. (His attorney confirmed that he was listening.) Other than to acknowledge that he was there, he never said a word or showed his face—a coward till the very end.

As Drain's courtroom door thudded shut, questions still hung in the air: Would future victims of corporate fraud stand a chance against wealthy wrongdoers? What would prevent another billionaire-run company from cashing in on the destruction of American lives, knowing full well that when the lawsuits landed they could simply sneak through an escape hatch they'd constructed in the nation's courts?

When I get scared, I still turn to the words of Mister Rogers: When times are dark, he said, look for the helpers. Wherever there are helpers, there is hope.

The last night I shadowed Tim Nolan, we met a dump-truck

driver in an Arby's parking lot in Hickory. Tim prescribed bupe for the guy while his girlfriend's kids played in the back seat of his truck and told me about their pretty new schoolteachers. It was almost fall and getting dark early, and Tim's wife still rightly worried about his driving at night.

Later, in a nearby trailer park, Tim passed out needles and tried his best to give hep A vaccines to those who were willing to take it—"as long as that ain't a damn COVID shot!" one man said.

The crickets were full-on chorusing by the time his Prius arrived at the end of a dirt road on the outskirts of Hildebran, a tiny town where the per capita income is $15,835. Tim was there to check on Daniel and Kristina, two of his favorite new patients. In their thirties, they, too, had begun hosting hepatitis C–testing gatherings, but not tonight because they were pretty sure they had COVID.

I stayed on the front stoop while Tim masked up and marched into their tiny, falling-down trailer, which they shared with two kittens, a dog, and "an unknown animal under the couch, possibly a baby possum," Kristina said. Tim gave them sterile needles and antidiarrheal meds for Daniel. It was supposed to be our last stop of the night.

The couple asked Tim to check on their friend, Tumbler, a newish patient who lived a few blocks away. Tim remembered that he had news to share from Tumbler's blood work, so off we left for an enclave of shotgun homes built for the mill workers who first peopled the town.

As he drove, Tim filled me in on patients from our previous trips. He was still seeing Julie most weeks at a gas station near the tent where she lived. Sam had fully disappeared after repeatedly selling his bupe to buy heroin. Kicking him out of the program weighed on Tim, but the front-desk clerk, Nicole—the one whose salary came nowhere near reflecting how much she ran the place—had put her foot down: "Tim, he's playing you."

Brenda, the steel-mill supervisor, was devastated when her job of eight years was eliminated. After she relapsed, Tim prescribed an antidepressant on top of her bupe and referred her to a counselor, but Tim doubted she'd followed up. The next time he reached out to her, his text bounced back.

Mary Jo was in a custody battle for her daughter, whom she was only able to speak to on the phone. She was still taking low-barrier bupe, but these days she rarely returned Tim's texts. "I'll go by her damn house if I need to," he said.

Alisha, the poisoned-cheesecake survivor, was doing great. The only illicit drug in her urine these days was marijuana—and, if you had seen her before she met Tim, you would understand what a goddamn miracle that was.

"This hollow is full of injectors," Tim said, as he twice pulled into the wrong driveway, trying to find the garage where Tumbler lived.

Tumbler wasn't home, but a neighbor pointed us up the street. Tim spotted him on the sidewalk, his lumbering frame silhouetted under a streetlamp. His legs were still swollen, but Tim told him his blood work had come back fine—no diabetes, no hepatitis. "I think it's your heart," Tim said of the man's swollen legs, promising to return the next week with a blood-pressure cuff.

But when he arrived at the appointed hour, Tumbler wasn't there. He was forty-two, and he hadn't been to a doctor in twenty-seven years.

As we drove back to my car, I asked Tim if he'd ever felt in danger, and the answer was an immediate no, never—although once a man mistook him for a dealer he was on the outs with and charged at him with a crowbar but dropped it as soon as he saw it was Tim.

Michelle Mathis was writing a grant so that Tim might one day do low-barrier medicine with a staff and from a bigger vehicle—anything but a van, which they both despised. Vans tipped off police that "drug users live here!" Mathis said. She preferred her nondescript grandma car, a Nissan.

With the help of a therapist, a peer, a case manager—maybe even one of them would drive?—the team would operate within the context of harm reduction and syringe service.

"The needles are the carrot, right?" I asked.

"The needles are always the carrot," Tim said. "I've known that going back to HIV in the eighties. You don't just walk into a homeless space and say, 'Who wants to be tested?' You offer them health care. They get a bad cold in the winter, you give them Sudafed, then you go, 'How about an HIV test?' Then, the carrots become bigger, like Suboxone."

And the sticks?

The good Lord willing, you break the sticks.

Five years ago, I was so depressed when I finished writing *Dopesick* that a minister friend felt he had to remind me that "not everyone is a heroin user, Beth." That was true. There are slivers of the country that remain untouched by the overdose crisis.

Nonetheless, even the most switched-off Americans know that rare is the ZIP code that hasn't been slammed by overdose deaths, and mortality rates continue to worsen every year. Government researchers recently recalculated the cost of overdose deaths in health expenses, reduced productivity, and other losses, and came up with a staggering *$1 trillion* per year—the equivalent of roughly half of America's economic growth last year.

And for the first time in a decade, teenage overdose deaths were on a precipitous rise, as even non-addicted recreational drug users and experimenters faced the possibility of encountering an increasingly poisoned drug supply. Fewer teens were using drugs, but those who did now ran the risk of overdose, with fentanyl present in not just fake Xanax bars and counterfeit Adderall pills but also in cocaine and methamphetamine.

But the vast majority of overdose deaths still occur among people who are opioid-addicted, said Columbia University professor

Dr. Andrew Kolodny. Stopping the flow of illicit fentanyl is important, but interdiction won't make a dent in deaths until the U.S. also addresses the demand for treatment by making it free and easily accessible.

"Just like Congress did when it came up with Ryan White Act funding for treatment of HIV on demand," Kolodny said. "What's most needed now doesn't exist. We have very few programs that offer patients low-threshold access."

I want to believe that we can all agree that no human being deserves to die abandoned and alone. I want to believe that, but in a world where people who use drugs, rather than go to a hospital where they've already been treated poorly, choose to die alone at home or next to a riverbank—I'm not so sure. America remains the only developed country on the planet where it's easier to get high than it is to get help.

When crises pile on top of each other, human beings tend to dissociate—it's hard to think about the climate crisis when you're worried about paying your electric bill. The more emotionally depleted we are, the more we revert to our lizard brains, and the more inured we become to the suffering of others.

I got traps that will hurt you and I will hunt you down.

Lizard brain warps our sense of self, it undercuts our health, and it literally turns us into victims of our own toxic individualism. "Americans are drowning in the lack of grace, the lack of humility, the complete inability to assume well about others," my friend, the trauma expert Laura van Dernoot Lipsky, said. She advised me to end *Raising Lazarus* by outlining action items—things we can do going forward "other than just escaping and pouring ourselves a huge gin and tonic."

The United States of America will not reverse its declining life expectancy until we replace our current system of corporate socialism with one that puts the health and happiness of regular people ahead of billionaires. Health care and housing should be basic human rights, full stop. Medicaid expansion is the lowest of low-hanging fruit and should be enacted in every state, with the goal of eventually adopting Medicare for All.

As Nikki King put it during a recent all-holler rant, "Treatment in America is like a big old quilt, and every time a new hole rips, the government tries to throw a patch on it, to the point where you can't even tell it's a quilt anymore." Because most people with mental health problems and SUDs are on Medicaid, which is administered by their individual states, policies are too often left "to the whims of crazy people," by which she means state and local politicians who wrongly blame suffering people for their own demise.

Federal leaders should adopt Medicare for All so that basic health care, SUD treatment, and mental health treatment with an emphasis on childhood trauma—arguably the biggest driver of SUD—can't be so easily politicized. The American Academy of Child and Adolescent Psychiatry has said there should be forty-seven child and adolescent psychiatrists for every 100,000 young people in America, but the national average is only eleven such doctors. "The beauty of federally guided policies is the people who control it don't live in anybody's backyard, so it's not quite as prone to weird politics," Nikki King said.

Not long ago, an Indiana state senator accused King of "killing God." In the wake of a thwarted school shooting, Nikki King, now thirty, was lobbying for a bill that required all state schools to have licensed therapists on staff. But the senator accused her of trying to get between people and their children. "This person who votes for funding in Indiana literally believes that I murdered God as a middle manager!" Nikki said.

The opioid-litigation dollars, when they finally trickle down, should first go to the struggling nonprofits that are meeting people who use drugs where they are—in jail cells, under bridges, next to McDonald's dumpsters. Our institutions, if they choose to, can learn a lot from the grounded, service-oriented kind of harm reduction embodied in the work being done right now by the people in these pages and so many like them.

But their work is simply not sustainable. Individuals, no matter how inspiring or selfless, cannot solve a systemic problem without sustained institutional/governmental support that replicates their heroic innovations.

It is a worrisome paradox that our nation, which leads the world in medical research spending, has among the world's worst outcomes for addiction and mental health. President Biden and every governor should use their bully pulpits and powers of the purse to reverse overdose deaths and other deaths of despair. Governors with medical schools under their authority should make state funding contingent on curricula that ensure all graduating physicians know how to recognize and treat addiction and pain. Right now, the typical doctor has between one and four hours of training in those areas, and many leave residencies without the benefit of clinical practice.

President Biden should do the same with federally funded medical-residency programs. The federal government presently puts $10 billion a year into them—when most are still producing doctors who don't know how to treat a disease that takes the lives of more than 100,000 people annually. Instead of just saying he supports harm reduction, Biden should lead efforts to end the ban on the federal funding of syringes. Patient caps and waiver restrictions for prescribing buprenorphine should be eliminated.

Politicians should use their platforms to ensure that SAMHSA-funded monies being funneled into disparate state-directed agencies no longer end up dependent on the whims of local boards who subscribe to abstinence-only, anti-medication models. Every taxpayer and every insurance dollar spent on treatment and prevention should go to evidence-based models emphasizing medication initiation and retention without requiring jumping through extra hoops.

"Unlike other epidemics, opioid addiction has been with us for many generations, and an entrenched addiction-treatment apparatus was already in place preceding the decades of doom the Sacklers thrust upon us," said Arthur Robin Williams, the Columbia professor. "Historical inertia has impeded progress for too long." At a time when middle managers are accused of murdering God, regulatory reform and federal leadership are critical. We need more innovative thinking from our leaders.

Biden should elevate the drug czar job to a cabinet-level position, as it was during Jerome Jaffe's tenure. The drug czar should use his megaphone to encourage all providers and hospital emergency rooms to treat addiction with medicines that dramatically improve outcomes. As cases grow less acute, patients transition from emergency or low-barrier care to outpatient care—ideally paired with peers, counseling services, housing, and other social supports.

As for us, the people, sometimes even learning bankruptcy law can be an act of protest—or love. We help each other by paying attention, educating ourselves and each other, giving time, sharing what we have.

Those of us privileged enough to have social capital should urge gatekeepers in government, health care, and law enforcement to study initiatives that are working elsewhere.

The War on Drugs is a war on Black people and the poor. It's Old Testament lizard brain. It should be abolished.

Until it is, initiatives that bridge law enforcement and medicine can help the 40 percent of addicted people who don't get treatment because they're just not ready to stop using drugs. Nikki King's CADS model should be widely replicated, as should Sheriff Stacey Kincaid's Fairfax County jail program. While bureaucracies are slow by design, Mark Willis's whiteboard contains multiple implementation innovations and could be a template for other distressed communities trying to reduce the number of overdose deaths. (In his heart, Andy Griffith was a harm-reductionist, and so, now, is Mark Willis.)

The low-barrier model of meeting people who use drugs where they are, including in trap houses and under bridges, is best exemplified in these pages by Tim Nolan's mobile bupe and hep C clinics, and by Brooke Parker's street outreach, as well as in a handful of walk-in clinics and sobering centers now operating from Houston to Huntington.

Such models should be replicated and expanded into a nation-wide system of clinics that provide mental health and addiction care—not unlike what Jaffe designed in just six or seven days at President Nixon's command. "We could have hundreds of [walk-in clinics or sobering centers] with the opioid-litigation money, but right now we have maybe twenty," said Greg Williams, a recovery activist and health-policy consultant. "We can't wait for ten years of evidence-based research like we did with bupe. We need to build things right now that meet people where they are in moments of crisis."

Above all, we need to listen not just to the on-the-ground helpers but also to the people they are seeking to help. It took me more than a decade to fully grasp this, but people who use drugs are the real experts.

Seven years ago, my friend Tess imagined a system in which she might one day be treated for SUD as easily as she had been overprescribed painkillers at our local urgent care center. She knew exactly what she needed. So did Snow, the homeless drug user who joined the nascent CANDU drug-users union in Charleston—and ended up helping kill a city council bill designed to outlaw sleeping on public property.

"Snow literally took the microphone and said, 'How dare you do this?!'" Joe Solomon told me. "Lill was there. They spoke.

The hill witch even put on a suit!" They celebrated at the next CANDU meeting with cake, "and we killed that cake like we killed the bill," he added.

It is cruel and scientifically backward to make treatment contingent on stopping drug use. The real magic wand is to give up on the rigid notion that a single fix exists.

Call that harm reduction, if you will, or call it caring for the patient.

The opioid-litigation money is a once-in-a-generation opportunity. The Sacklers willfully created the opioid crisis. They shamelessly lied to the health care community and enlisted their aid in carrying out a murderous rampage that has victimized hundreds of thousands of people in this country.

History will judge them for that. History may forgive those who thought they were doing the right thing but were misled by those they'd been trained to trust.

But how we respond to the horrors that have resulted will determine how *we* are judged. Best not to give up too quickly on a neighbor; best not to judge a stone too heavy to roll.

Only by endeavoring to help in the face of so much suffering can we bear witness to the miracle of raising Lazarus.

Author's Note and Glossary

Stigma fuels the harmful misperception of addiction as solely being a matter of personal choice rather than an affliction or a disease. In *Raising Lazarus*, I write about "drug users," "patients," and "people who use drugs" (the preferred person-first language) rather than *addicts* or *substance abusers*.

Also, I'd like to elaborate on a handful of key terms and acronyms used throughout this book:

- SUD: substance use disorder, referring to the problematic use of drugs, from opioids and stimulants like methamphetamines to alcohol and tobacco.
- OUD: opioid use disorder, referring to people who are addicted to opioid pills and/or heroin or fentanyl and other synthetic opioids.
- MOUD: medicines for opioid use disorder; in this book, I am largely referring to buprenorphine or methadone, the gold-standard medicines used to treat OUD. In my earlier works about the opioid crisis, I referred to those medicines as MAT, for medication-assisted treatment, as was standard at the time. But, as one researcher corrected me during a speech I was giving at her university: "Call it *medicine*, just like insulin is a medicine for diabetes!"

- Suboxone: the brand name for the drug formula of buprenor-phine and naloxone; many drug users and clinicians alike refer to it as "bupe" for short, which is mostly what I call it in these pages.
- Naloxone: the overdose-reversal drug, often referred to gener-ally by the better-known brand name, Narcan.
- FQHCs: federally qualified health centers; operating on a slid-ing fee scale, these clinics are among the federal government's best avenues for providing affordable bupe to uninsured people on the margins. But barriers remain even at FQHCs, especially in states that have resisted Medicaid expansion.

The majority of those I interviewed gave me consent to use their stories and, in all but a few cases, permission to use their full names. When I have omitted or used first names only, it is to preserve the safety or freedom of those whose stories I tell.

Acknowledgments

This book grew out of my 2018 book *Dopesick*. It sprang from the gut-wrenching stories I heard and the tough questions I was asked by hundreds of readers who reached out to me at presentations I gave and via my social media accounts. Then as now, the story of the overdose crisis remains a moving target. It's tricky to write a book about the near past—cases are appealed, politics change, variants emerge, numbers shift.

Some days it feels like America itself has relapsed.

In late 2019, agent Dorian Karchmar and editor Vanessa Mobley helped me conceptualize this project in myriad conversations, guiding me and challenging me but also—and this was key—patiently trusting that all my driving around and interviewing people and calling them back repeatedly over many months would add up to something universal and true, even as it veered far from our proposed plan of attack. And then a pandemic landed on top of an epidemic.

Now in my fourth decade as a journalist, I have always done my best storytelling when I follow what moves me, warts and all, relying on the long game to illuminate what the great Robert Caro means when he says, "Time equals truth."

I'm so grateful to the people in this book for trusting me and for teaching me so many unexpected things—Michelle Mathis for living her tattoo, Tim Nolan for his early-morning updates about "our peeps," Mike Quinn for cheerful lawyering and lawn care, Brooke Parker for well-placed f-bombs, Wendy Odum for reminding me to "just tell it like it is" (even when it didn't suit her cause), Mark Willis for stepping out of retirement and into the fray, Lill Prosperino for sheer fearlessness, Alexis Pleus for understanding all angles of the elephant, Mike Moore for never giving up on people, Nikki King for foot-tapping impatience, Sonya Cheek for her mastery of the chrome phone, Billie Campbell and James Stroud for finding hope in a trap house, Patricia Mehrmann for always reminding me of "our poet," and to Ed Bisch, for never, ever quitting.

Scholars, lawyers, medical professionals, and journalist/authors who read and offered helpful notes on segments or earlier drafts—or just listened to me process what I was seeing—include Brian Alexander, Charlotte Bismuth, Anne C. Case, Angus Deaton, Dr. Beth Darnall, Brandon del Pozo, Dr. Carl Erik Fisher, Joseph Friedman, Robert Gipe, Ryan Hampton, Cheri Hartman, David Herzberg, Jonathan Lipson, Dr. Steve Loyd, Dr. Yngvild Olsen, Travis Rieder, Dr. Joshua Sharfstein, Judge Duane Slone, Sam Snodgrass, Laura van Dernoot Lipsky, Dan Vergano, and Dr. Robin Arthur Williams. Research assistance by Caroline Perkins, Tadhg Hylier Stevens, and Kyle Vass was invaluable. Thanks, too, for the continued support of the entire *Dopesick* team at Hulu, especially Danny Strong, Ben Rubin, and Warren Littlefield.

At Little, Brown & Company, I am so lucky to have worked on two books with the incredibly supportive Vanessa Mobley, who brooks no shortcuts, sees the big picture better than I do, and knows what to cut. For their collegiality and publishing pluck, many thanks to Terry Adams, Anna Brill, Sabrina Callahan, Judy Clain, Mariah Dwyer, Mike Fleming, Jean Garnett, Lauren Harms, Lauren Hesse, Lena Little, Louisa McCullough, Bruce Nichols, Michael Noon, Elisa M. Rivlin, and Craig Young.

Acknowledgments

Editors at *The Atlantic* and the *New York Times* who helped sharpen my thinking in previous essays and articles that informed this work include Denise Wills, Honor Jones, and Sarah Wildman. Thanks especially to Carole Tarrant, who assigned me this topic in 2012 when we were both still working at the *Roanoke Times* and who is still willing to meet at a moment's notice to suss out storylines—newspaper or not, we are always each other's journalism tribe.

For their steadfast support and advice, I'm grateful to Dorian Karchmar, Jill Gillett, Kirk Schroder, and Tom Neilssen and Carolyn Kelly at BrightSight Speakers. I hope to continue roaming the streets talking stories with my longtime collaborator Josh Meltzer, who shot nearly all the photographs for this book and for *Dopesick*, for another two decades *at least*. When the walls in my home office grew too small, the Virginia Center for the Creative Arts and dear friends Scott and Jean Whitaker gave me wonderful spaces to write.

Lastly, the support of my friends and family—especially my husband, Tom Landon—is a balm whether we are fretting about the state of the world, walking through the Blue Ridge Mountains, or doing yoga over Zoom. Martha Bebinger, Jen Brothers, Angela Charlton, Mary Margaret Isbell, Chris Landon, Max Landon, Willis Landon, Sue Lindsey, Andrea Pitzer, Meredith and Tommy Roller, and Mindy Shively—thanks for your love and grace, and for always listening.

Notes

PROLOGUE

xii   *super high:* Sam (last name withheld), author interview, March 25, 2021. The rest of this encounter I personally observed on March 17, 2021.

xii   *"I'm trying to get me a car":* Jordan Hayes, author interview, March 17, 2021.

xii   *his usual array:* Tim Nolan, author interviews in person, over the phone, text, and e-mail: January–August 2021. The exchange with Sam—who asked me not to use his last name—occurred at the Icard, NC, McDonald's on March 17, 2021.

xiii   *The CDC estimates:* "Drug Overdose Deaths," Centers for Disease Control and Prevention, March 3, 2021, cdc.gov/drugoverdose/data /statedeaths.html; the estimate of more than a million Americans was calculated using CDC WONDER data and was confirmed by the University of Pittsburgh's Donald S. Burke on December 14, 2021.

xiii   *quintupled:* In 2000, 17,000 Americans died of overdoses; as of April 2021, the CDC figure topped 100,000 deaths.

xiii   *more than a century:* Mark S. Gold, "The Role of Alcohol, Drugs, and Deaths of Despair in the U.S.'s Falling Life Expectancy," *Journal of the Missouri State Medical Association* (March-April 2020); predicted recovery time comes from Steven Woolf and Heidi Schoomaker, *Journal of American Medicine* (2019), https://www.ncbi.nlm.nih.gov /pubmed/31769830.

301

xiii *50 to 100 times more potent:* "Fentanyl," National Institute on Drug Abuse.

xiii *29 percent higher:* "Opioid overdoses 29% higher in 2020 than before the pandemic: Study," *ABC News*, https://abcnews.go.com/Health/opioid -overdoses-29-higher-2020-pandemic-study/story?id=75785104.

xiii *almost a third:* Justin McCarthy, "Drugs Have Been a Problem in Family for 32 percent of Americans," *Gallup News*, November 11, 2021. Reports of family drug issues increased from an average of 18 percent in 1995. A majority of families, 64 percent, believe the nation's drug problem is extremely or very serious.

xiii *a dozen of their former classmates:* Jan Rader, fire chief of Huntington, West Virginia, author interview, November 7, 2021.

xiv *most complicated in American history:* Paul Hanly, author interview, August 12, 2020.

xiv *the company:* Jan Hoffman and Mary Williams Walsh, "Purdue Pharma, Maker of OxyContin, Files for Bankruptcy," *New York Times*, September 15, 2019.

xiv *trusting big law:* Adam Levitin, "Purdue Continues to Peddle Malarkey about Why It's in White Plains," *Credit Slips: A Discussion on Credit, Finance, and Bankruptcy*, July 29, 2021.

xiv *Judge shopping:* Jonathan Randles, "Companies Lease Offices in New York Suburb to Pick Bankruptcy Judge," *Wall Street Journal*, August 13, 2020.

xiv *swap out:* Brian Mann, "Justice Department Blasts Purdue Pharma's Bankruptcy Plan," NPR, July 19, 2021.

xiv *favor those, too:* Drain said in an early hearing in the Purdue case that third-party releases were the only way to bring "true peace," February 21, 2020.

xiv *3 million Americans:* Mohammadereza Azadford et al., "Opioid Addiction," August 26, 2021, ncbi.nlm.nih.gov/books/NBK448203.

xiv *$10 billion:* Madeline Holcombe, "The Sackler family withdrew more than $10 billion from Purdue Pharma during the country's opioid crisis," CNN, October 21, 2020.

xv *It sounded good:* Scott Higham and Lenny Bernstein, "The Drug Industry's Triumph Over the DEA," *Washington Post*, October 15, 2017.

xv *to curry favor:* "Purdue and other painkiller producers, along with their associated nonprofits, spent nearly nine hundred million dollars on lobbying and political contributions," Patrick Radden Keefe, "The Family That Built an Empire of Pain," *New Yorker*, October 23, 2017.

xv *plied lobbyists:* Olivier J. Wouters, "Lobbying Expenditures and Campaign Contributions by the Pharmaceutical and Health Product Industry in the United States, 1999–2018," *JAMA Internal Medicine*, May 2020.

xv–xvi *"virtually every senator and congressman":* Deposition of Richard Sackler, Case No. 17-md-2804, in the MDL No. 2804, "U.S. District Court of the Northern District of Ohio, Eastern Division," March 8, 2018, 315.

xvi *1 million overdose-death count is predicted to double:* This number, confirmed by the University of Pittsburgh's Donald S. Burke, is compiled by calculating all overdose deaths from 1996 through 2020, using CDC WONDER data. The figure is 1,044,528 deaths. Burke told me that "if we stay on the same exponential growth curve that we have been on for forty years, we will reach 2 million by 2029—that is, by the end of this decade" (e-mail to author, December 14, 2021).

xvi *rose most among Black Americans:* The rate of opioid deaths among Black people increased by 38 percent from 2018 to 2019; see: Marc R. Larochelle et al., "Disparities in Opioid Overdose Death Trends by Race/Ethnicity, 2018–2019, From the HEALing Communities Study," *American Journal of Public Health* (October 8, 2021).

xvi *(Native Americans claimed the highest overdose-death):* Claire Galofaro, "As COVID fueled the drug crisis, Native Americans hit worst," Associated Press, December 22, 2021.

xvi *(no group has seen a larger increase than Black men):* John Gramlich, "Recent surge in U.S. drug overdose deaths has hit Black men the hardest," *Pew Research Center,* January 19, 2022. The overdose-death rate among Black men has more than tripled since 2015 while rates among other racial or ethnic groups also increased but at a much slower pace.

xvii *kept breaking records:* Lenny Bernstein and Joel Achenbach, "Drug overdose deaths soared to a record 93,000 last year," *Washington Post*, July 14, 2021.

xvii *spends five times more to incarcerate:* One full year of methadone medication-assisted treatment costs $4,700 per patient, whereas one full year of imprisonment costs $24,000 per person. Also, every dollar invested in addiction treatment yields a return of between $4 to $7 in reduced drug-related crime, criminal justice, and theft; see: https://www.drugabuse.gov/publications/principles-drug -addiction-treatment-research-based-guide-third-edition/frequently -asked-questions/drug-addiction-treatment-worth-its-cost.

xvii   *18.9 million Americans in need of treatment:* United States Government Accountability Office, "Substance Use Disorder: Reliable Data Needed for Substance Abuse Prevention and Treatment Block Grant Program," December 2020, gao.gov/assets/gao-21-58.pdf, 3, citing 2020 Substance Abuse and Mental Health Services Administration data. Black patients are 77 percent less likely to be prescribed bupe and more likely to be prescribed methadone, which is more restricted and harder to get, according to Dr. Scott Nolen, who directs the Addiction and Health Equity Program at the Open Society Institute of Baltimore, Pew Center; see: "African Americans Often Face Challenges Accessing Substance Use Treatment," March 26, 2020. Other barriers for Black people include lack of insurance, not being guaranteed access to treatment in the criminal justice system, and the near-daily transportation requirements for receiving methadone.

xvii   *Black patients were far less likely than Whites:* Pooja A. Lagisetty et al., "Buprenorphine Treatment Divide by Race/Ethnicity and Payment," *JAMA Psychiatry, Research Letter,* May 8, 2019.

xvii   *"a drop of water":* Dr. Joe Wright, author interview, September 24, 2020.

xviii   *We have to hammer:* Joshua Miller, "Mass. Attorney General Maura Healey sues opioid maker Purdue Pharma," *Boston Globe,* June 12, 2018.

xix   *"El Chapo got":* Transcript of December 17, 2020 hearing; see: https://www.rev.com/blog/transcripts/the-role-of-purdue-pharma -and-the-sackler-family-in-the-opioid-epidemic-full-hearing-transcript.

xix   *A theory began circulating: Vox* reporter German Lopez, author interview, October 11, 2019; and bioethicist and author Travis Rieder, author interview, October 19, 2019. Journalist Michael Massing makes a similar point in "The Real Scandal in the Fight Against Opioids," *Politico,* July 21, 2018.

xix   *"sucks up":* Corey S. Davis, author interview, February 9, 2021.

xx   *a group of Indiana sheriffs:* My speech was to the Indiana Sheriff's Association, January 29, 2020.

xx   *sparking a 1,500 percent increase:* See: "HIV Diagnoses by County,

West Virginia, 2018–2021, https://oeps.wv.gov/hiv-aids/documents /data/WV_HIV_2018-2020.pdf. Data analysis by West Virginia treatment provider Joe Solomon; author interview, December 6, 2020; updated to count intravenous HIV cases from 2019 (fewer than five) to 2021 (85), November 2021, with the caveat that testing is limited and therefore this is an undercount.

xx   *mostly looked the other way:* The exception here is Dan Vergano, "West Virginia Is Trying to Block Needle Exchanges amid the Worst HIV Outbreak in the US," *BuzzFeed*, March 19, 2021.

xx   *have done successfully:* Dan Baum, "Legalize It All," *Harper's*, April 2016.

xxi   *"they create new problems":* Kyle Vass, author interview, June 26, 2021.

xxi   *"need therapy":* Sarah Stone, author interview, April 24, 2021.

xxii   *"tell it like it is":* Wendy Odum, author interview, January 5, 2021.

xxii   *"more devoted to 'order' than justice:"* King's "Letter from Birmingham Jail," April 16, 1963.

xxii   *"It's important to respect people who are out there":* Robert Gipe, author interview, September 20, 2019.

xxii   *Patricia retrace:* Beth Macy, "Finding Tess: A Mother's Search for Answers in a Dopesick America," Audible, November 2019. https://www .audible.com/pd/Finding-Tess-Audiobook/B07SZJ35BW.

xxii   *most of us continue blaming:* Associated Press–NORC Center for Public Affairs Research, "Americans Recognize the Growing Problem of Opioid Addiction," 2018.

xxiii   *$50 billion bureaucracy:* This figure includes $34.6 billion spent annually from the federal budget, an increase (adjusted for inflation) of 1,090 percent; see: Nathaniel Lee, "America has spent over a trillion dollars fighting the war on drugs. 50 years later, drug use in the U.S. is climbing again," CNBC.com, June 17, 2021. The Drug Policy Alliance and ACLU estimated the annual amount of War on Drugs spending to be $51 billion, as drug possession continues to be the number one arrest in the United States; see: Matt Sutton, "On 50th Anniversary of 'War on Drugs,' New Poll Shows Majority of Voters Support Ending Criminal Penalties for Drug Possession, Think Drug War Is a Failure," drugpolicy.org, June 9, 2021. Also see: Derek Hawkins and William Wan, "Health agencies' fund cuts challenge coronavirus response," *Washington Post,* March 8, 2020.

xxiv   *"secret of the care":* Dr. Francis Peabody, from a lecture given to Harvard Medical School students, October 21, 1926.

xxiv   *three thousand jobs:* Michael Hyland, "Apple to bring 3,000 jobs to Wake County, build RTP campus, invest more than $1 billion in NC," CBS17.com, April 26, 2021.

xxv   *shot in the head:* Chrissy Murphy, "Man in custody, crossbow shooting remains under investigation," *Hickory Record*, May 13, 2020.

CHAPTER ONE

3   *a mark of shame:* Rob Kyff, "Stigmas, or Stigmata?" *Hartford Courant*, November 20, 2007, https://www.courant.com/news/connecticut /hc-xpm-2007-11-20-0711190402-story.html; " 'Stigma'—Where the Word Comes From and What It Means," *PoetsIN,* https://www .poetsin.com/poetsin/the-word-stigma-where-it-comes-from-and-what -it-means/.

4   *Description of social death versus stigma:* Joe Wright, MD, "Only Your Calamity: The Beginnings of Activism by and for People with AIDS," *American Journal of Public Health* (April 7, 2013).

4   *Stigma theories:* Sam Snodgrass, author interview, April 25, 2019, backed up by research including: Steve Matthews, Robyn Dwyer, and Anke Snoek, "Stigma and Self-Stigma in Addiction," *Journal of Bioethical Inquiry* 14, no. 2 (May 3, 2017): 275–86, https://www.ncbi.nlm.nih.gov/pmc/articles/PMC5527047/.

4   *"Do shit":* Michelle Mathis, author interview, February 4, 2021.

5   *then claimed:* Kaitlin Miller, "Surry County Now No. 2 in Country for Opioid Overdoses per Capita," Spectrum Local News, August 27, 2019.

5   *"For some, taking off":* Michelle Mathis, author interview, May 2, 2021.

7   *"What's important is":* Karen Lowe, author interview, July 9, 2019.

8   *three times as likely:* CDC, Syringe Services Programs (SSPs) FAQS, https://www.cdc.gov/ssp/syringe-services-programs-faq.html.

8   *Mathis was organizing:* Michelle Mathis, author interviews, June 20, 2019, July 9, 2019, and August 22, 2020.

8   *"adolescents who are mad at their parents":* Keith Humphreys, author interview, January 20, 2020.

9   *"I find trap houses":* Michelle Mathis, author interview, January 21, 2021.

9   *effectively outlawed:* Technically, Charleston's health administrator shut the program down after the police chief revised and restricted rules

around the needle program; see: Kyle Vass, "Syringe Distribution Meets City Roadblock Amid Ordinance Concerns," West Virginia Public Broadcasting, December 4, 2020.

9 *"tell me the stories":* Michelle Mathis, author interview, February 4, 2021.

10 *"I know I stunk":* Garry Dolin, author interview, October 7, 2020.

11 *the county jail was filled:* When I visited the Surry County Jail on February 13, 2020, there were 202 inmates in a facility approved for 125. An additional 51 inmates were being housed, at the county's expense, in a jail at the other end of the state.

11 *McPeak had one client:* Emily McPeak, author interview, June 19, 2019.

12 *$750,000 annually:* Mark Willis, e-mail to author, October 26, 2020.

13 *"It's drugs, period":* Capt. Scott Hudson and Lt. Randy Shelton, author interviews, February 13, 2020.

14 *"we should let 'em die":* Opioid response director's meeting to form transportation network, Surry County Service Center, Dobson, NC, July 9, 2019.

14 *'I don't like the dirt':* Lesly-Marie Buer, author interview, October 23, 2020.

15 *White people use those drugs:* Human Rights Watch, "The Human Toll of Criminalizing Drug Use in the United States," October 12, 2016, https://www.hrw.org/report/2016/10/12/every-25-seconds/human-toll-criminalizing-drug-use-united-states.

15 *the ones who complain:* Alec McGillis, "Who Turned My Blue State Red?" *New York Times*, November 20, 2015, https://www.nytimes.com/2015/11/22/opinion/sunday/who-turned-my-blue-state-red.html.

15 *"worn out":* Jennifer M. Silva, author interview, June 4, 2021.

15 *"the heart of the heart of the heart":* Joe Solomon, author interview, January 26, 2021.

16 *"ABC stores will deliver":* Mark Willis, author interview, April 23, 2020.

16 *"wasp dope":* April M. Young, "Emergence of wasp dope in Appalachian Kentucky," *Addiction* 116, no. 7 (July 2021), https://onlinelibrary.wiley.com/doi/epdf/10.1111/add.15291.

16–17 *drug deaths continued their upward:* Josh Katz, Abby Goodnough, and Margot Sanger-Katz, "In Shadow of Pandemic, U.S. Drug Overdose Deaths Resurge to Record," *New York Times*, July 15, 2020.

17 *even CAVEs:* Stacy Stanford, National Association of County and City Health Officials, author interview, February 10, 2020.

17 *"what we really need":* Nancy D. Campbell, author interview, May 18, 2020.

18 *Dayton's overdose-death reduction was chronicled beautifully by Abby Goodnough; see:* "This City's Overdose Deaths Have Plunged. Can Others Learn from It?" *New York Times*, November 20, 2018, https://www.nytimes.com/2018/11/25/health/opioid-overdose -deaths-dayton.html.

18 *shocked into action:* Nan Whaley, author interview, February 7, 2020.

18 *real-time data sharing:* Barb Marsh and Jodi Long, author interviews, August 6, 2020.

18 *they reuse upon reentry:* See: Paul J. Joudrey et al., "A conceptual model for understanding post-release opioid-related overdose risk," *Addiction Science & Clinical Practice* 14, no. 17 (2016), https://ascpjournal .biomedcentral.com/articles/10.1186/s13722-019-0145-5.

19 *Time magazine photo essay:* James Nachtwey, "The Opioid Diaries," *Time*, March 5, 2018.

19 *"Too often":* Barb Marsh, author interview, August 6, 2020.

19 *"'namby pamby jail'":* Montgomery County, Ohio, Sheriff Rob Streck, author interview, February 24, 2020.

20 *first time treating men:* Dr. Tami Olt, author interview, August 20, 2020.

20 *goodwill gesture:* Chris Schaffner, author interview, January 29, 2021.

20 *"our girls":* Kshe Barnard, author interview, September 17, 2020.

20 *"I can't imagine":* Cris Schaffner, author interview, January 29, 2021.

21 *"'My brother should not have died'":* Chris Atwood Foundation director Ginny Lovitt, author interviews, December 4 and 7, 2020.

22 *"21st Century Cures Act":* Mike Debonis, "Congress Passes 21st Centure Cures Act, boosting research and easing drug approvals," *Washington Post*, December 7, 2016.

22 *more than $300 million:* Office of Inspector General, "States' Use of Grant Funding for a Targeted Response to the Opioid Crisis," March 13, 2020, https://oig.hhs.gov/oei/reports/oei-BL-18-00460.asp.

22 *"stuck in an airport somewhere":* Dr. Andrew Kolodny, as quoted by Rachana Pradhan and Brianna Ehley, "Hundreds of millions in state opioid cash left unspent," *Politico*, March 19, 2018.

23 *"I'm reminded of a line":* Rev. Ray Morgan, author interview, October 22, 2020. The song is "Memories of East Texas."

23 *around 4,000 of them:* Mark Willis worked out this estimate using a CDC study that estimated that for every overdose death, there were approximately 115 substance users in a given region (e-mailed to author, October 15, 2020).

24   *"My dad in Wisconsin":* Stacy Stanford, author interview, February 10, 2020.

CHAPTER TWO

26   *late on a Saturday:* Masha Gessen, "Nan Goldin Leads a Protest at the Guggenheim Against the Sackler Family," *New Yorker*, February 10, 2019.

26   *a seasoned activist had coached her:* Megan Kapler, author interviews, August 3 and 5, 2020.

26   *a civil disobedience strategy:* See: Daniel Ross, "The Die-In: A Short History," *Active History*, June 29, 2015, http://activehistory.ca/2015 /06/the-die-in/.

26   *"it immobilizes you":* Nan Goldin, author interview, July 24, 2020.

26   *pure fentanyl:* Nan Goldin, e-mail to author via Megan Kapler, November 10, 2021.

27   *taking twenty pills a day:* Nan Goldin, author interviews, December 4, 2019, and July 20, 2020.

27   *"You have no skin":* Liz Jobey, "Nan Goldin on art, addiction and her battle with the Sacklers over opioids," *Financial Times*, November 8, 2019.

27   *"deep, deep,* deep *darkness":* Nan Goldin, author interview, November 15, 2021.

27   *she thought OxyContin was safer:* Nan Goldin and Megan Kapler, author interviews, November 11 and 15, 2021.

28   *"bury the competition":* Richard Sackler, as quoted in the Purdue Frederick Co. newsletter, Winter 1996, and cited in the Massachusetts filing against Purdue and the Sacklers: https://www.mass.gov/files/documents/2019 /07/17/_09%20Affidavit%20of%20Robert%20Cordy%20Exhibits% 20001-015%20filed%2007-16-2019.pdf.

28   *unsealed by a Massachusetts:* Martha Bebinger and Christine Willmsen, "Lawsuit Details How the Sacklers, Family Behind OxyContin, Made More than $4 Billion," WBUR, January 31, 2019.

28   *weren't in on the stunt:* Video of the Guggenheim die-in can be seen here: https://www.youtube.com/watch?v=q2A4Tb8cOxE.

29   *The Sacklers had donated $3.5 million:* Patrick Radden Keefe, *Empire of Pain: The Secret History of the Sackler Dynasty* (New York: Doubleday, 2021), 104–105.

29 *first-ever billion-dollar drug:* Arnie Cooper, "An Anxious History of Valium," *Wall Street Journal*, November 15, 2013, https://www.wsj.com /articles/an-anxious-history-of-valium-1384547451.

30 *years-long prescription Valium habit:* Nan Goldin via Megan Kapler, e-mail to author, November 10, 2021.

30 *"public outrage":* Nan Goldin, author interview, July 24, 2020.

30 *on a par with Sally Mann:* See: Thessaly La Force, "Nan Goldin Survived Overdose to Fight the Opioid Epidemic," *New York Times Style Magazine*, June 11, 2018, https://www.nytimes.com/2018/06/11/t-magazine/a -heroin-chic-photographers-new-project-tackling-the-opioid-epidemic .html; and Janna Malamud Smith, "Art, Drugs and Money: How to View the Complicated Legacy of Arthur M. Sackler," *WBUR Cognoscenti*, March 29, 2019, https://www.wbur.org/cognoscenti/2019/03 /29/sackler-oxycontin-opioid-crisis-art-janna-malamud-smith.

31 *bad-boy hijinks:* Mike Quinn, author interview, July 20, 2020.

31 *"make Nan stop":* PAIN meeting, author interviews, December 4, 2019.

32 *"I love journalists!":* Mike Quinn, author interview, February 17, 2021.

32 *"We are deeply in your debt":* La Force, "Nan Goldin Survived an Overdose.

33 *"very scary":* Nan Goldin said this in an OxyJustice meeting, October 22, 2020.

33 *spooked, by the presence:* Mike Quinn, author interview, January 11, 2021.

33 *took the Sackler name down:* Noami Rea, "The Louvre Museum Has Removed the Sackler Name from Its Walls and Website Following Protests by Nan Goldin's Activist Army," *Artnet News*, July 17, 2019, https://news.artnet.com/art-world/the-louvre-museum -has-removed-the-sackler-name-from-its-walls-and-website-1602979.

34 *country where the government:* See: "List of members of the Ordre des Arts et des Lettres," *Wiki 2*, https://wiki2.org/en/List_of _members_of_the_Ordre_des_Arts_et_des_Lettres.

34 *eschew future Sackler gifts:* Note that the Sackler Trust voluntarily withdrew a $1 million donation to the National Portrait Gallery, saying it might "deflect" the gallery from its important work; see: Dearbail Jordan, "Is this America's most hated family?" *BBC News*, March 22, 2019, https://www.bbc.com/news/business-47660040.

34 *"decadent architecture":* See: "Nan Goldin and P.A.I.N. Target Director Tristram Hunt during V&A Museum Protest," *Artforum*, November 18, 2019, https://www.artforum.com/news/nan-goldin-and-pain -call-out-tristram-hunt-during-v%26a-museum-protest-81315.

34 *"If museums don't stand"*: Jordan, "Is this America's most hated family?"

34 *trespassing arrest:* Goldin and Kapler were arrested, along with other activists from the group Housing Works; see: Hakim Bishara and Jasmine Weber, "Artist Nan Goldin Arrested in Protest Outside Governor Cuomo's NYC Office," *Hyperallergic*, August 28, 2019, https://hyperallergic.com/515015/artist-nan-goldin-arrested-in -protest-outside-governor-cuomos-office-in-nyc/.

34 *"feared as a tiger with claws"*: See: https://www.documentcloud.org /documents/6562741-04-Purdue-Docs-2-08-to-10.html.

36 *"crawl into the coffin"*: Joanne Peterson, author interview, November 20, 2020.

37 *"artist to another artist"*: Ad Hoc Committee on Accountability meeting, September 17, 2020.

38 *successfully petitioned:* Harry Cullen, author interview, July 15, 2020. Cullen asked for ninety days, Purdue countered with thirty, and the judge sided with Purdue.

CHAPTER THREE

39 *chronic, recurring acquired disease:* This is the leading theory of addiction, known as the neurobiological disease model; there is some disagreement about the particulars, but what is not controversial is that OUD involves changes to the brain's structure and function. (Bioethicist Travis Rieder, e-mails to author, December 14 and 23, 2021.)

39 *five days:* See: Anuj Shah, Corey J. Hayes, and Bradley C. Martin, "Characteristics of Initial Prescription Episodes and Likelihood of Long-Term Opioid Use—United States 2006–2015," Centers for Disease Control and Prevention, Morbidity and Mortality Weekly Report, March 17, 2017, https://www.cdc.gov/mmwr/volumes/66 /wr/mm6610a1.htm#F1_down.

40 *a person becomes desperate:* Sam Snodgrass, "Opioid Addiction and the Myth of Powerlessness," *Medium*, January 27, 2020, https://medium .com/@samphd87/opioid-addiction-and-the-myth-of-powerlessness-a12 8dc54d114.

40 starvation and desperation Sam Snodgrass, PhD, founder of Broken No More, multiple author interviews in 2020 and 2021.

40 *58 percent:* Seattle-pioneered Law Enforcement Assisted Diversion,

or LEAD, for low-level drug offenders reduced subsequent arrests by 58 percent; see: Sara Jane Green, "LEAD program for low-level drug criminals sees success," *Seattle Times*, April 8, 2015.

40   *critics:* Helen Redmond, "The LEAD Program Faces a Reckoning for Centering Police," *Filter*, September 17, 2020.

41   *recovery without the benefit of bupe:* Noa Krawczyk et al., "Opioid agonist treatment and fatal overdose risk in a statewide US population receiving opioid use disorder services," *Addiction*, February 24, 2020. People taking bupe or methadone had an 80 percent lower risk of dying from an opioid overdose than people in treatment without the use of medications, the authors reported.

41   *sober for more than two decades:* See: Gina Vivinetto, "Philip Seymour Hoffman's partner opens up about his tragic addiction," *Today*, December 13, 2017, https://www.today.com/popculture/philip-seymour -hoffman-s-partner-opens-about-his-tragic-overdose-t120028.

41   *"to get better on their own":* This phenomenon, called "natural recovery," is often cited among addiction reporters as well as in Carl Erik Fisher, *The Urge: Our History of Addiction* (New York: Penguin Press, 2022), 274, and Wilson M. Compton et al., "Prevalence, Correlates, Disability, and Comorbidity of DSM-IV Drug Abuse and Dependence in the United States," *Archives of General Psychiatry* 64, no. 5 (2007). But the economist Anne C. Case told me that overdose deaths that were once highest for people in their late 40s and early 50s pre-fentanyl are now much higher for people in their 20s and 30s.

41   *The tourism board:* Beth Macy, "Purdue Pharma and Johnson & Johnson opioid cases expose Big Pharma's addiction lies," NBCNews.com, August 27, 2019.

41   *one of the highest:* North Carolina Injury and Violence Prevention, "Opioid Overdose Emergency Department Visits: North Carolina, April 2018," May 15, 2018.

42   *"go to hell and walk out!":* Beth Macy, *Factory Man: How One Furniture Maker Battled Offshoring, Stayed Local—and Helped Save an American Town* (New York: Little Brown, and Company), 2014, 138.

42   *the largest employers became:* Surry County Economic Development Partnership, "Data and Demographics," (n.d.), https://www.surryedp .com/surry-county-demographics/.

42   *52 percent of the working-age population had jobs* and *500 job openings:* Mark Willis, author interview, November 14, 2019.

42 *55 million opioids:* "Drilling into the DEA's pain pill database," *Washington Post*, updated January 17, 2022, https://www.washington post.com/graphics/2019/investigations/dea-pain-pill-database/.

43 *perniciously entwined:* Alan B. Krueger, "Where Have All the Workers Gone? An Inquiry into the Decline of the U.S. Labor Force Participation Rate," *Brookings Papers on Economic Activity* (Fall 2017), https://www.ncbi.nlm.nih.gov/pmc/articles/PMC6364990/.

43 *foster care went up:* Kids Count Data Center, from 2010 to 2019.

43 *more than half:* Surry County 2020 NC Data Card, NC Child: The Voice for North Carolina's Children, 2017 data.

43 *EMS calls soared:* Surry County Emergency Medical Services, comparing 2010 to 2020. Job opening data came from Willis's office, courtesy of data analyst Jamie Edwards.

43 *43 percent of the decline in the nation's male labor force:* Krueger, "Where Have All the Workers Gone?," using data gathered between 1999 and 2015.

43 *"All our kids are dead":* Wendy Odum, author interview, October 9, 2020.

45 *socks matched his wingtips:* Wendy Odum, author interview, October 14, 2020.

46 *"handing out marijuana cigarettes":* Police Chief Tim Jones's earlier rejection of needle exchange was reported by Henri Gendreau, "Needle program backed by chief," *Roanoke Times*, April 14, 2019.

46 *"change has always been driven":* Dr. Sam Snodgrass, author interview, January 25, 2021.

46 *"Any positive change":* The Chicago School, "Any Positive Change," The Chicago School of Professional Psychology, February 21, 2019.

46 *it's irrefutable:* Dr. Tami Olt, author interview, August 20, 2021.

47 *"the only thing that kept assholes":* Chris Schaffner, author interview, September 17, 2020.

47 *(sites established in Canada):* Canadian harm reduction: See: Garth Mullins interview; also Mottie Quinn, "Safe Drug Injection Sites Are Coming to America. Canada Has Had Them for Years," *Governing*, April 10, 2019, https://www.governing.com/topics/health-human -services/gov-supervised-injection-site.html.

47 *happening underground:* Christine Vestal, "Philadelphia could become the first US city to host a safe injection site for drug users," *USA Today*, November 18, 2019, https://www.usatoday.com/story/news/health

/2019/11/18/philadelphia-kensington-opioid-safe-injection-sites-could
-coming/4227249002/.

48   *Rhode Island announced:* Julie Wernau, "Rhode Island Set to Be First
State to Pilot Safe-Injection Sites for Drug Users," *Wall Street Journal,*
October 24, 2021.

48   *green-lighted:* Amanda Eisenberg, "De Blasio administration pushes to
approve supervised injection sites," *Politico,* October 25, 2021."

48   *(In its first two weeks):* Mike Fritz, "Do safe drug consumption sites
save lives? Here's what we know about NYC's new venture," *PBS
NewsHour,* December 13, 2021.

48   *"spirit of humility":* Michelle Mathis, author interview, October
9, 2020.

48   *3,500 drug courts:* Office of Justice Programs, "Drug Courts," US
Department of Justice, August 2021, https://www.ojp.gov/pdffiles1
/nij/238527.pdf.

48   *even some conservative states:* Al Cross, "Ky. Has 59 operating syringe
exchanges and six in the wait," *Kentucky Health News,* July 15, 2019.

49   *"you don't just roll up":* Wendy Odum, author interview, January 5, 2021.

50   *"like being a teacher":* Mark Willis, author interview, July 22, 2019.

50   *Surrey County stood to gain:* The community calculator score is at
opioidnegotiationclass.com. Willis calculated his county's score from
the MDL lawsuit after deducting 15 percent for a special needs fund
and 10 percent for attorneys' fees. (Mark Willis, author interview,
June 14, 2021.)

CHAPTER FOUR

54   *estimated that thousands:* Many media outlets have reported that
250,000 Americans used unprescribed opioids and coca products in
the early 1900s, but some experts insist that number is unknow-
able, then and now (though the CDC estimates that 11 percent of
Americans are drug users). The firmest calculation through history,
according to historian David Herzberg, is that per capita sales of
pharmaceutical opioids were "nearly four times higher in the early
21st century than they were in the early 20th century." (E-mail to
author, November 12, 2021.)

54   *history is steeped in racism:* Maia Szalavitz, "One Hundred Years Ago,

Prohibition Began in Earnest—And We're Still Paying for It," *Pacific Standard*, June 14, 2017.

54 *Chinese laborers:* David Herzberg, *White Market Drugs: Big Pharma and the Hidden History of Addiction in America* (Chicago: University of Chicago Press, 2020).

55 *"Negro Cocaine Fiends":* Dr. Edward Huntington Williams, *New York Times*, February 8, 1914.

55 *writes physician and bioethicist:* Carl Erik Fisher, *The Urge: Our History of Addiction* (New York: Penguin Press, 2022), 129.

55 *could literally order:* Joe McKendry, "Sears Once Sold Heroin," *The Atlantic*, March 2019, https://www.theatlantic.com/magazine /archive/2019/03/sears-roebuck-bayer-heroin/580441/.

55 *forced by the new law:* David Herzberg, *White Market Drugs, Big Pharma and the Hidden History of Addiction in America* (Chicago: University of Chicago Press, 2020).

55 *battle over the Affordable Care Act:* Jennifer M. Silva, *We're Still Here: Pain and Politics in the Heart of America* (New York: Oxford University Press, 2019), 15.

56 *indirectly express:* Michelle Alexander, *The New Jim Crow: Mass Incarceration in the Age of Colorblindness* (New York: New Press, 2012), 69.

56 *"Prohibition policies":* David Herzberg, author interview, December 11, 2020.

56 *"Did we know we were lying":* John Ehrlichman described this "Southern strategy" to journalist Dan Baum in 1994, as recollected in "Legalize It All: How to Win the War on Drugs," *Harper's Magazine*, April 2016, https://harpers.org/archive/2016/04/legalize-it-all/.

56 *something to do that also helped her husband gin up support:* Michael Massing, *The Fix: Under the Nixon Administration, America Had an Effective Drug Policy* (New York: Simon & Schuster, 1998), 160.

57 *prescribed sedatives:* Nixon developed a sedative habit while in office, Fisher, *The Urge,* 237. Nancy Reagan habitually used tranquilizers, sleeping pills, and diuretics, according to her daughter, Patti Davis; see: Donnie Radcliffe, "Patti Davis Says Mother Popped Pills," *Washington Post*, April 30, 1992.

57 *John F. Kennedy's therapeutic approaches:* Dan Baum, *Smoke and Mirrors: The War on Drugs and the Politics of Failure* (New York: Little, Brown, 1996), 43.

57   *while working as a spokesman:* James P. Herzog, "Reagan Hit for Record on Medicare," Scripps-Howard, November 1, 1980.

57   *The AMA remains an opponent:* Danielle Carr, "Why Doctors Are Fighting Their Own Professional Organization Over Medicare for All," *The Nation,* February 24, 2020.

57   *widespread public support:* Bradley Jones, "Increasing share of Americans favor a single government program to provide health care coverage," *Pew Research Center,* September 29, 2020.

57   *a little-known story:* Massing, *The Fix,* 131.

57   *"in the face of so much brass":* Ibid., 110.

58   *national system:* Ibid.,119.

58   *crime related to it plunged:* Michael Massing, author interview, January 21, 2021, and Massing, "The Real Scandal in the Fight Against Opioids," *Politico,* https://www.politico.com/magazine/story/2018/07/21/opioids-treatment-politicians-media-219023.

58   *not the other way around:* Massing, *The Fix,* 133.

58   *"best available answer":* Fisher, *The Urge,* 233.

58   *"I'm not faulting":* Dr. Jerome Jaffe, author interview, October 23, 2020.

59   *literally 100 times harsher:* Carl Hart, *Drug Use for Grown-Ups* (New York: Penguin Press, 2021), 93 and 203.

59   *pharmacologically, the drugs are the same:* Dr. Dan Ciccarone, author interview, January 19, 2021.

59   *more Black men:* Scott Grammer, "Study Finds That War on Drugs Kept Black Men from Higher Education," *Prison Legal News,* November 6, 2019, quoting the work of University of California, Berkeley, professor Tolani Britton.

59   *direct-action protest by the grassroots group ACT UP:* For the history of HIV/AIDS activism, I recommend David France's documentary *How to Survive a Plague,* Independent Lens, January 2012.

60   *65 percent of the FDA's drug-approval budget:* C. Michael White, "Why is the FDA funded in part by the companies it regulates?" *The Conversation,* May 13, 2021. More than a third of the overall FDA budget comes from user fees, but a larger percentage, 65 percent, of the funding for regulatory activities derives from user fees: "Fact Sheet: FDA at a Glance," FDA, November 2021.

60   *largest lobbying industry:* Olivier J. Wouters, "Lobbying Expenditures and Campaign Contributions by the Pharmaceutical and Health

Product Industry in the United States, 1999–2018," *JAMA Internal Medicine*, May 2020.

60   *the OxyContin medical review:* "Internal Memorandum: Proposed Indictment of Purdue Pharma L.P.," written by Kirk Ogrosky, Deputy Chief, Fraud, US Department of Justice, October 6, 2006.

60   *especially President Bill Clinton:* Donna Murch, "The Clintons' War on Drugs When Black Lives Didn't Matter," *New Republic*, February 9, 2016.

61   *federal drug budget:* "Drug Policy Facts," drugpolicyfacts.org, https://www.drugwarfacts.org/chapter/economics; Pew stats are here: "More Imprisonment Does Not Reduce State Drug Problems, *Pew Research Center*, https://www.pewtrusts.org/en/research-and-analysis/issue-briefs/2018/03/more-imprisonment-does-not-reduce-state-drug-problems.

61   *significantly longer sentences:* "More Imprisonment Does Not Reduce," Pew Research Center. To test this, Pew compared state drug imprisonment rates with three measures of drug problems—self-reported drug use (excluding marijuana), drug arrests, and overdose deaths—and found that higher rates of imprisonment didn't translate into lower rates of drug use, arrests, or overdose deaths.

61   *(Herzberg speculates):* David Herzberg, calculating the rise using morphine-equivalent sales data, e-mail to author, November 16, 2021.

61   *"disproportionately lock up people of color":* Daniel Ciccarone, author interviews, January 19, 2020, and January 18, 2021.

62   *most prolific jailer:* Wendy Sawyer and Peter Wagner, "Mass Incarceration: The Whole Pie 2020," Prison Policy Initiative, March 24, 2020, https://www.prisonpolicy.org/reports/pie2020.html.

62   *more than were enslaved:* Laura M. Maruschak and Todd D. Minton, "Correctional Populations in the United States, 2017–2018," US Department of Justice, Office of Justice Programs, https://www.bjs.gov/content/pub/pdf/cpus1718.pdf.

62   *No. 1 cause of accidental death:* Josh Katz and Margo Sanger-Katz, "'The Numbers Are So Staggering.' Overdose Deaths Set a Record Last Year," *New York Times*, November 29, 2018, https://www.nytimes.com/interactive/2018/11/29/upshot/fentanyl-drug-overdose-deaths.html.

62   *claiming more lives:* National Center for Biotechnology Information, "Trends in Opioid Use, Harms, and Treatment," National Academy of Sciences, 2017, https://www.ncbi.nlm.nih.gov/books/NBK458661/.

62 *tried to plunder:* Stephen Payne, "President Trump Again Proposes Massive Cuts to Student Aid," NAASFA.org, March 12, 2019. Jill Colvin's Mary 13, 2019, story for the Associated Press, "Trump targets Pell Grant money for NASA's budget boost," recounted Trump's idea to shift money from Pell Grants in order to return American astronauts to the moon by 2024.

62 *Michael Botticelli had begun to steer:* German Lopez, "America is in the middle of its deadliest drug crisis; Trump wants to gut the agency that can help," *Vox*, May 5, 2017.

63 *created tumult:* Sarah Karlin-Smith and Brianna Ehley, "Trump again targets drug policy office, proposing 95 percent budget cut," *Politico*, January 18, 2018.

63 *disorganized and ineffective:* Government Accountability Office, "The Office of National Drug Control Policy Should Develop Key Planning Elements to Meet Statutory Requirements," December 2019.

63 *"massive patchwork":* Dr. Joshua Sharfstein, author interview, April 6, 2021.

63 *slight decline:* Joan Stephenson, "Drug Overdose Deaths Head Toward Record Number in 2020, CDC Warns," *JAMA Health Forum* 1, no. 10 (October 20, 2020), https://jamanetwork.com/channels/health-forum/fullarticle/2772241.

64 *"Isolation is killing":* Dr. Steve Loyd, author interview, October 9, 2020.

64 *one family lost two:* Wendy Odum, author interview, October 28, 2020.

64 *hatchet wound:* Amy Gecan and Erin Shafto, author interviews, October 29, 2020.

64 *"they always treated her like shit":* Virginia Harm Reduction Coalition director Lawson Koeppel, author interview, November 25, 2020.

64 *nodding out in drug court:* Fairfax County Judge Penney Azcarate, author interview, March 2, 2021.

64 *"tidal wave is crashing":* Dr. Cheri Hartman, e-mail to author, June 23, 2020.

64 *18 percent increase:* "Vital Statistics Rapid Release—12 Month-ending Provisional Counts and Percent Change of Drug Overdose Deaths," Centers for Disease Control and Prevention, updated January 12, 2022, https://www.cdc.gov/nchs/nvss/vsrr/drug-overdose-data.htm#dashboard.

64 *$50 billion:* Derek Hawkins and William Wan, "Health agencies' fund cuts challenge coronavirus response," *Washington Post*, March 8, 2020.

65   *(coined by narcotics agents):* Anna King, "Is the word 'marijuana' racist?" *Salon*, August 26, 2013, https://www.salon.com/2013/08/06/weed_and_words_the_growth_of_dank_vocabulary_partner/.

65   *"When cannabis is on the ballot":* Jonah Engel Bromwich, "This Election, a Divided America Stands United on One Topic," *New York Times*, November 5, 2020.

65   *"seeped into all of us":* Ted Lewis, from "Should California Follow Oregon's Lead to Decriminalize Drugs and Fund Treatment?" (webcast), January 28, 2021.

66   *"ended up running a treatment":* Sami Alloy, author interview, February 19, 2021.

66   *Joe Biden pledged:* German Lopez, "Joe Biden's new plan to end the opioid epidemic is the most ambitious in the field," *Vox*, March 6, 2020, https://www.vox.com/policy-and-politics/2020/3/6/21167803/joe-biden-opioid-epidemic-plan-drug-overdoses.

66   *there was no mention:* Abraham Gutman, "Joe Biden and the Kinder, Gentler War on Drugs," *Newsday*, October 22, 2020, https://www.newsday.com/opinion/commentary/joe-biden-war-on-drugs-hunter-biden-addiction-program-opioids-1.50044352.

66   *It didn't go far enough:* Umme Hoque, "Buprenorphine X-Waiver Burden Eased under New Federal Rules," *Filter*, April 29, 2021.

66   *(The current cap):* SAMSHA guidelines, "Understanding the Final Rule for a Patient Limit of 275," Centers for Disease Control and Prevention, https://www.cdc.gov/nchs/nvss/vsrr/drug-overdose-data.htm#dashboard.

66   *"very few medications":* Dr. Arthur Robin Williams, author interview, October 1, 2021.

66–67   *remained hardest for minority:* Pooja A. Lagisetty et al., "Buprenorphine Treatment Divide by Race/Ethnicity and Payment," *JAMA Psychiatry*, May 8, 2019.

68   *"Not only is this wrong":* Carl Hart, *Drug Use for Grown-Ups* (New York: Penguin Press, 2021), 7 and 26.

68   *pulled her over:* Bland was pulled over on a so-called pretextual traffic stop, ibid., 159. See: Dan Solomon, "On 'Contempt of Cop,' Jailhouse Suicide, and Sandra Bland," *Texas Monthly*, July 24, 2015, https://www.texasmonthly.com/the-daily-post/on-contempt-of-cop-jailhouse-suicide-and-sandra-bland/.

68   *move to legalize simple possession:* "Governor Northam Proposes

Accelerating Marijuana Legalization in Virginia," press release, March 31, 2021.

69 *"I still run into people":* Paul Krugman, " 'Let's Talk About Personal Responsibility': A Year of Tough Conversations in the Comments," *New York Times*, December 30, 2020, https://www.nytimes.com /2020/12/30/opinion/2020-pandemic-election-comments.html.

69 *frame the comparison:* Anne C. Case and Angus Deaton, *Deaths of Despair and the Future of Capitalism* (Princeton, NJ: Princeton University Press, 2020), 130.

70 *The Hospital:* Brian Alexander, *The Hospital: Life, Death, and Dollars in a Small American Town* (New York: St. Martin's Press, 2021).

70 *American medicine transmogrified:* Brian Alexander, e-mail to author, November 12, 2021.

70 *left on their own to navigate it:* Ibid.

70 *relatively few deaths of despair:* Anne Case and Angus Deaton, "The Great Divide: Education, Despair and Death," National Bureau of Economic Research, September 2021.

70 *"killing the low-wage labor market":* Anne Case and Angus Deaton, author interviews, December 21, 2021.

71 *at rates three times higher:* Case and Deaton, "The Great Divide," citing D. G. Blanchflower and A. J. Oswald, "Trends in extreme distress in the United States, 1993–2019," *American Journal of Public Health* 100, 10 (2020): 1560–62.

71 *it favors Black people:* S. Woolhandler et al., "Public policy and health in the Trump era," *Lancet* 397, no. 10275 (2021).

71 *57.2 million people:* United States Government Accountability Office, "Substance Use Disorder: Reliable Data Needed for Substance Abuse Prevention and Treatment Block Grant Program," December 2020, https://www.gao.gov/assets/gao-21-58.pdf.

71 *outgrow their use:* Maia Szalavitz, "Most People with Addiction Simply Grow Out of It. Why Is This Widely Denied?" *Pacific Standard*, June 14, 2017.

72 *making its way to California:* Dennis Romero, "Cluster of California fentanyl overdoses alarms authorities," NBC News, January 17, 2019, https://www.nbcnews.com/news/us-news/cluster -california-fentanyl-overdoses-alarms-authorities-n959151.

72 *more than 60 percent:* Jesse C. Baumgartner and David C. Radley, "The

Drug Overdose Toll in 2020 and Near-Term Actions for Addressing It," The Commonwealth Fund, August 16, 2021.

72   *fentanyl and other synthetics were involved:* Jesse C. Baumgartner and David C. Radley, "Overdose Deaths Surged in the First Half of 2021, Underscoring Urgent Need for Action," The Commonwealth Fund, February 7, 2022.

72   *"Not bupe":* Daniel Ciccarone, author interview, January 19, 2021.

72   *racialized coin:* Fisher, *The Urge,* 202, analyzing Herzberg.

73   *centralized planning:* "The company that makes OxyContin could become a 'public trust'—what would that mean?" *The Conversation,* December 4, 2019, https://theconversation.com/the-company -that-makes-oxycontin-could-become-a-public-trust-what-would-that -mean-126981.

73   *"We can't get rid of":* United States Bankruptcy Court, Southern District of New York, In the Matter of Purdue Pharma L.P., November 17, 2020, transcript pp. 164–65.

74   *doctors kickbacks to prescribe:* German Lopez, "Purdue pharma admits to crimes for its OxyContin marketing. But no one is going to prison," *Vox,* October 21, 2020, https://www.vox.com/2020/10/21/21526868 /purdue-pharma-oxycontin-opioid-epidemic-department-of-justice; also United States Department of Justice, "Founder and Former Chairman of the Board of Insys Therapeutics Sentenced to 66 Months in Prison," press release, January 23, 2020.

74   *a lap dance:* German Lopez, "Some opioid executives are finally going to prison," *Vox,* January 24, 2020.

74   *culture of impunity:* Jesse Eisinger, "Why Only One Top Banker Went to Jail for the Financial Crisis," *New York Times,* April 30, 2014, https://www.nytimes.com/2014/05/04/magazine /only-one-top-banker-jail-financial-crisis.html.

74   *"mirage":* Ed Silverman, "A historian was cited to support making Purdue a public benefit company. He actually thinks it's a bad idea," *Stat,* December 11, 2020, https://www.statnews.com/pharmalot/2020/12 /11/purdue-sackler-bankruptcy-opioids-herzberg/.

74   *sadistic to me:* Ed Bisch, author interview, November 18, 2020.

75   David Herzberg and Joseph Gabriel, letter to Judge Robert Drain, filed December 10, 2020.

75   *among the largest drivers of life-expectancy:* University of Virginia public policy professor Christopher Ruhm, author interview, January 26, 2021.

75   *ten-dollar bag of dope:* Corey S. Davis, author interview, February 9, 2021.

76   *most high-profile case:* Edward Helmore, "'The Madoff of millennials'? Fyre Festival investors eye a court fight with organizer," *The Guardian,* May 17, 2017.

77   *"funhouse mirror":* Mike Quinn, author interview, September 28, 2021.

CHAPTER FIVE

82   *(Surry County's number):* See the *Washington Post* data set: https://www.washingtonpost.com/graphics/2019/investigations/dea-pain-pill-database/.

82   *crisis didn't surface:* My reporting on Ripley County and treatment innovator Nikki King between 2016 and early 2020 was published in *The Atlantic*: "America's Other Epidemic: A New Approach to Fighting the Opioid Crisis as It Quietly Rages On" (May 2020). Subsequent interviews since the publication of that piece are noted.

83   *quintupled:* Kids Count Data Center, comparing 2012 rates (6 percent) to 2017 (31.8 percent): https://datacenter.kidscount.org/data/tables/1130-child-abuse-and-neglect-rate-per-1000-children-under-age-18#detailed/5/2292-2383/false/871,870,573,869,36,868,867,133,38,35/any/2467.

83   *child abuse and neglect rate:* Indiana Prevention Resource Center, Indiana University, "County Epidemiological Data," 2020, https://iprc.iu.edu/epidemiological-data/. Ripley County's rate for child abuse and neglect was 19 percent; the state rate was 13.4. See also: Justin L. Mack, "Indiana has the second-highest child abuse rate in the nation, report says," *Indianapolis Star*, April 1, 2019.

83   *voted to shut it down:* Mitch Legan, "Indiana Needle Exchange That Helped Contain a Historic HIV Outbreak to Be Shut Down," National Public Radio, June 3, 2021.

83   *"No one should have to":* Dr. William Cooke, author interview, July 14, 2021.

83   *whose 2021 memoir:* William Cooke, *Canary in the Coal Mine* (Carol Stream, IL: Tyndale Momentum, 2021).

84   *more than doubling:* "Drug Overdose Deaths," Centers for

Disease Control and Prevention, March 2021, https://www.cdc.gov
/drugoverdose/data/statedeaths.html.

85   *rationing her vacation time:* Nikki King, author interview, December
30, 2016.

85   *decommissioned most of:* Michelle R. Smith, "50 years later, Kennedy's
vision for mental health not realized," Associated Press, October 21,
2013. Ninety percent of state-hospital beds were cut during this time,
leaving nowhere for the sickest people to turn, so they ended up
homeless, abusing substances, or in jail.

85   *"Ronald Reagan's ass":* Nikki King, author interview, May 24, 2021.

87   *44 percent:* US Census data, QuickFacts, July 1, 2019, estimate for
2015–2019 period: https://www.census.gov/quickfacts/letchercoun
tykentucky.

88   *one in four:* Clary Estes, "One in 4 Rural Hospitals Are at Risk
of Closures and the Problem Is Getting Worse," *Forbes*, February
24, 2020.

88   *our mother lay in hospice:* Beth Macy, "If I'd Stayed in My Hometown, Would I Be a Trump Voter?" *New York Times*, December
21, 2020.

89   *height of a severe COVID outbreak:* Abby Goodnough, "A Tiny Hospital Struggles to Treat a Burst of Coronavirus Patients," *New York
Times*, April 16, 2020.

89   *Fewer than half:* Hospital CEO Tim Putnam, author interview, May
24, 2021.

89   *"so suspicious of government":* Jennifer M. Silva, author interview, June
1, 2021.

89   *the gap between rural and urban death rates:* Sarah H. Cross et al.,
"Rural–Urban Disparity in Mortality in the US From 1999 to 2019,"
JAMA, June 8, 2021.

90   *insurance spending on addiction declined:* Fisher, *The Urge,* 262.

91   *may or may not understand:* Maia Szalavitz, "How America Overdosed
on Drug Courts," *Pacific Standard*, May 18, 2015.

91   *very often deadly:* 70 to 90 percent of OUD patients discharged
to medication-free residential or outpatient care quickly relapse and
face a high risk of overdose death; see: Dr. Arthur R. Williams and
Dr. Adam Bisaga, "From AIDS to Opioids—How to Combat an
Epidemic," *New England Journal of Medicine* (September 1, 2016).

91   *Fewer than a third:* Tamara Beetham et al., "Therapies Offered at

Residential Addiction Treatment Programs in the United States," *JAMA Network Research Letter*, August 25, 2020. According to the authors, just 29 percent of programs in a survey offered medicines for OUD to participants and "actively discouraged use" of those medicines to callers.

94   *data she collected:* Nikki King, "Outcomes and Factors Influencing Relapse and Recidivism in a Rural Substance Abuse Treatment Program Collaborative," Medical University of South Carolina, Doctor of Health Administration, April 30, 2021.

94   *soured on the story:* Tim Putnam, author interview, May 25, 2021.

95   *More than a quarter of the nation's newspapers:* Penelope Muse Abernathy, "The News Landscape in 2020," usnewsdeserts.com, 2020.

95   *recidivism rates 35 percent lower:* Nikki King, "Changing What's Possible," PhD dissertation, Medical University of South Carolina, April 15, 2021.

96   *"trapped into conspiracy theories":* Lindsey Gessendorf, author interview, May 24, 2021.

97   *all-holler interview:* Hari Sreenivasan, "How Nikki King Is Innovating Treatment for Opioid Addiction," *Amanpour & Company*, February 8, 2021.

98   *"doesn't exist":* Dr. Christopher Dull, author interviews, Nov. 19, 2019, and June 11, 2011.

99   *"absolutely no training":* Dr. Richard Turner, author interview, May 25, 2021.

CHAPTER SIX

100   *just one abortion clinic:* Holly Yan, "These 6 states have only 1 abortion clinic left. Missouri could become the first with zero," *CNN Health*, June 21, 2019, https://edition.cnn.com/2019/05/29/health/six-states-with-1-abortion-clinic-map-trnd/index.html.

100   *second-lowest voter:* "2020 November General Election Turnout Rates," United States Elections Project, updated December 7, 2020, http://www.electproject.org/2020g.

100   *soon participate in the January 6:* Derrick Evans was elected to serve as a delegate and stormed the capitol before he was sworn in. He was forced to resign when he was charged with misdemeanors, which

have since been raised to five felony counts. See: Brad McElhinny, "Derrick Evans faces two additional charges in Jan. 6 Capitol breach," *MetroNews*, May 4, 2021, https://wvmetronews.com/2021/05/04 /derrick-evans-faces-two-additional-charges-in-jan-6-capitol-breach/.

101 *drown his kids if they were gay:* Eric Porterfield, also a delegate, compared the LGBTQ+ community to the KKK and said if his one of his kids turned out to be gay he'd take him to a lake and "see if they can swim." See: Kristin Lam, "West Virginia lawmaker called to resign after comparing LGBTQ people to the Ku Klux Klan," *USA Today*, February 13, 2019, https://eu.usatoday.com/story/news/2019/02/13 /eric-porterfield-west-virginia-lawmaker-slammed-anti-gay-remarks/2 865439002/.

101 *that would outlaw needle exchange:* As of 2020, thirty-nine states had laws removing impediments to SSPs. See: Marcelo Fernández-Viña, "State Laws Governing Syringe Services Programs and Participant Syringe Possession, 2014–2019," *Sage Journals*, Public Health Reports, July 31, 2020.

103 *"This rail is flimsy":* Witnessed outside of Pies and Pints, following an author talk I gave with novelist Robert Gipe about harm reduction on November 7, 2021.

104 *"I've overdosed":* Kelli Keen, author interview, December 6, 2020. I interviewed the needle-exchange operator the same day and on November 25, 2020.

104 *1,500 percent:* "HIV diagnoses by county, West Virginia, 2018– 2021," West Virginia Office of Epidemiology and Prevention Services, September 16, 2021, https://oeps.wv.gov/hiv-aids/documents/data /WV_HIV_2018-2020.pdf.

104 *"mini-mall for junkies":* Kyle Vass, "Politics of Harm Reduction," *Dragline*, April 3, 2021.

104 *ample evidence:* "Needs-Based Distribution at Syringe Services Programs," Centers for Disease Control and Prevention, December 2020, https://www.cdc.gov/ssp/docs/CDC-SSP-Fact-Sheet-508.pdf.

104 *"most concerning":* Leslie Rubin, "This HIV outbreak is currently the most concerning in the United States," WCHS ABC Channel 8, February 11, 2021, https://wchstv.com/news/local/cdc-kanawha-hiv -outbreak-most-concerning-in-us-among-people-who-inject-drugs.

105 *centuries-old Appalachian:* David A. Taylor, "The Fight Against Ginseng Poach in the Great Smoky Mountains," *Smithsonian*, April

21, 2016, https://www.smithsonianmag.com/science-nature/fight
-against-ginseng-poaching-great-smoky-mountains-180958858/.

105   *Sharpied the hill:* Joe Solomon, author interview, January 21, 2021.

106   *"nothing like getting in fistfights":* Lill Prosperino, author interview,
April 17, 2021.

106   *Not all were people who:* Ayae Yamamoto, "Association between
Homelessness and Opioid Overdose and Opioid-related Hospital Ad-
missions/Emergency Department Visits," *Social Science & Medicine,*
December 2019.

107   *Charlotte Bismuth captured the scene:* Charlotte Bismuth, tweet, December 5, 2020.

108   *"their own death":* Richard Sackler from November 2020 transcript;
provided by Ryan Hampton, co-chair of the bankruptcy's Unsecured
Creditors Committee.

108   *virtual gathering:* The hearing was called "The Role of Purdue
Pharma and the Sackler Family in the Opioid Epidemic," December
17, 2020.

110   *"a setup since day one":* Ryan Hampton, text messages to author,
December 17, 2020.

111   *"The world is hearing us":* OxyJustice, Zoom meeting after the
December 17, 2020, hearing.

112   *2020 Department of Justice settlement:* Jan Hoffman and Katie Bren-
ner, "Purdue Pharma Pleads Guilty to Criminal Charges for Opioid
Sales," *New York Times,* October 21, 2020.

112   *hugely complicated:* Jonathan Lipson, author interviews, December 30
and 31, 2020.

112   *more damning documents:* "News organizations urge federal court to
unseal judicial records in Purdue Pharma bankruptcy case," Reporters Committee for Freedom of the Press, November 23, 2020,
https://www.rcfp.org/unseal-purdue-pharma-bankruptcy/.

112   *"WhatsApp conversations":* Documents first reported by Anand
Giridharadas here: "EXCLUSIVE: The Sacklers' group chat of pain,"
The Ink, December 19, 2020, https://the.ink/p/sacklers.

113   *PR consultant Davidson Goldin:* Davidson Goldin was hired November 2018, according to the documents, filed under bankruptcy case
under exhibit 2167_01.

113   *Purdue's poison pill:* Jonathan C. Lipson and Gerald Posner,
"The Sacklers' Last Poison Pill," *New York Times,* December

5, 2020, https://www.nytimes.com/2020/12/05/opinion/sackler-purdue
-pharma-doj.html?searchResultPosition=1. This piece also provides background on Davidson Goldin going to work for the Sacklers.

113 *since his hiring in 2018:* Exhibit No. 126 of the document trove
shows that Goldin was hired in November 2018. His monthly salary
amount was redacted in the documents.

114 *"tongue-lashing":* Ed Bisch, author interview, December 18, 2020.

114 *"manipulating the system":* Charlotte Bismuth, author interview, December 18, 2020.

114 *$50 million:* Mike Moore, author interview, March 11, 2021.

114 *kickbacks to doctors:* Jonathan Lipson, e-mail to author, January
12, 2021.

114 *"unrepentant and unremorseful":* Rep. Gerry Connolly, author interview, March 8, 2021.

115 *"put it inside something boring":* John Oliver, *Last Week Tonight with
John Oliver,* June 2, 2014.

115 *approve the release:* Rick Archer, "Sackler Family Can't Keep Names of
Its Businesses Secret," *Law360,* February 18, 2021.

115 *"game of chicken":* Jef Feeley and Jeremy Hill, "Purdue Talks Stall on
Demand for More Cash from Sacklers," Bloomberg News, January
27, 2021.

CHAPTER SEVEN

116 *only capable of minor tweaks:* Sarah Wakeman, "Fed up with baby
steps amid 'tsunami of overdose death,'" *Harvard Gazette,* December
1, 2021.

117 *less than a fourth:* Mike Moore, e-mail to author, November 16, 2021.

118 *"walking-around sense":* See: Bill Whitaker, "Opioid Crisis: The Lawsuits That Could Bankrupt Manufacturers and Distributors," *60
Minutes,* December 16, 2018.

118 *just three months:* Mike Moore, e-mail to author, February 15, 2021.

119 *a golf course:* Cezary Podkul, "Tobacco Settlement Funds Sprin-
klers, Golf Carts and a Grease Trap," *ProPublica,* October 24,
2014,   https://www.propublica.org/article/tobacco-settlement-funds
-sprinklers-golf-carts-and-a-grease-trap.

119 *production of tobacco:* Jim Estes, "How the Big Tobacco Deal Went Bad,"

New York Times, https://www.nytimes.com/2014/10/07/opinion/how -the-big-tobacco-deal-went-bad.html?searchResultPosition=2.

119 *raising the price of cigarettes:* Walter J. Jones and Gerard A. Silvestri, "The Master Settlement Agreement and Its Impact on Smoking 10 Years Later," *Chest* 137, no. 3 (March 2010), https://www.ncbi.nlm.nih.gov /pmc/articles/PMC3021365.

119 *British Petroleum paid:* Valerie Bauman, "BP Oil Spill Holds Settlement Payout Clues for Opioid Litigation," Bloomberg Law, September 25, 2019.

119 *(leaning toward donating):* Mike Moore, e-mail to author, November 18, 2021. "Not going to be huge numbers by the time it trickles down to me," he wrote. "The city and county lawyers will take 80 percent, I expect."

120 *"nobody really wants to talk":* Mike Moore, author interview, November 23, 2020.

120 *every two and a half minutes:* Nicholas Kristof, "Can Biden Save Americans Like My Old Pal Mike?" *New York Times*, February 14, 2021.

120 *the numbers had risen:* Roni Caryn Rabin, "Overdose Deaths Reached Record High as the Pandemic Spread," *New York Times*, November 17, 2021. The previous quarters' counts were 96,000 deaths annually and, before that, 93,000.

121 *"radically reenvisions":* Brandon del Pozo, author interview, December 8, 2020.

121 *"earth three times":* Jennifer Witt, "Don't Try to Settle the Score—The Real Cost of Fighting," Witt Law Group, October 20, 2019, https:// wittlegal.com/about-us/ebooks/author/590-jenniferwitt?start=50.

122 *just one patient:* David E. Weissman and David J. Haddox, "Opioid pseudoaddiction—an iatrogenic syndrome," *Pain* 36, no. 3 (March 1989), https://pubmed.ncbi.nlm.nih.gov/2710565/.

122 *referenced in legitimate:* Marion S. Greene and R. Andrew Chambers, "Pseudoaddiction: Fact or Fiction? An Investigation of the Medical Literature," *Currrent Addiction Reports* 2, no. 4 (October 2014), https://www.ncbi.nlm.nih.gov/pmc/articles/PMC4628053/.

123 *hadn't received much training:* Dr. Joshua Sharfstein, author interview, August 17, 2021, and Dr. Stefan Kertesz, author interview, September 1, 2021.

123 *first billion-dollar drug:* Arnie Cooper, "An Anxious History of Valium," *Wall Street Journal*, November 15, 2013, https://www.wsj.com /articles/SB10001424052702303289904579195872550052950.

123 *"there ain't another term for it":* Damian Sutherland, author interview, February 18, 2021.

124 *all-time record:* "Overdose Deaths Accelerating During COVID-19," press release, Centers for Disease Control and Prevention, December 17, 2020, https://www.cdc.gov/media/releases/2020/p1218-overdose -deaths-covid-19.html.

124 *$26 billion:* Amanda Bronstad, "Lawyers Suing Over Opioid Crisis Announce $26 B Proposed Settlement," Law.com, November 5, 2020.

124 *food fight:* Mike Moore, e-mail to author, February 18, 2021.

124 *(died at age 70):* Emily Langer, "Paul J. Hanly Jr., key lawyer in opioid litigation, dies at 70," *Washington Post*, May 24, 2021.

125 *"we are screwed":* Barry Meier, *Pain Killer: An Empire of Deceit and the Origin of America's Opioid Epidemic*, 2d ed. (New York: Penguin Random House, 2018), 163, footnoting a secret prosecution memo from the 2007 federal case. Meier has reported on the memo but has not publicly released it, saying it would be illegal to do so.

125 *an award-winning employee:* Sara won a service award from Purdue for Y2K preparedness, according to Hanly, who kept the award on his desk.

125 *Her description of the company's inner workings:* Maureen Sara deposition, May 19, 2004, in the US District Court for the Northern District of Alabama, Western Division: *Jerry Bodie v. The Purdue Pharma Company.* Hanly shared the deposition with me, saying it wasn't under seal.

125 *Self-Destructing Email:* Soo Youn, "One year after OxyContin launched, Purdue Pharma execs applied to patent 'self-destructing' emails," ABC News, May 28, 2019. "I thought it was interesting, but nothing came of it commercially," Richard Sackler said in a deposition in the MDL case.

125 *"Tom Hagen of modern pharmaceutical lawyering":* Paul Hanly, author interview, July 1, 2020.

126 *to get instant relief:* Sara deposition, p. 104. Sara was being questioned by Purdue lawyer Donald I. Strauber.

126 *escorted out of company:* Sara deposition, p. 39. "Sign it or you are fired," Sara described Purdue's lawyer telling her when she was fired, pp. 64–65.

126 *"not as a drug addict":* Barbara Ezepchick, e-mail to author, December 2, 2021.

127   *buried by Purdue influence peddlers:* Barry Meier, "A Secret Opioid Memo That Could Have Slowed an Epidemic," *New York Times*, April 16, 2019. A shorter version of that DOJ memo, written by the DOJ's deputy fraud chief Kirk Ogrosky in 2006, can be found here: https://www.posner.com/geraldposner/2020/08/just-unsealed-2006-doj-memo.

127   *future sales:* Jan Hoffman, "Sacklers Would Give Up Ownership of Purdue Pharma under Settlement Proposal," *New York Times*, August 27, 2019, https://www.nytimes.com/2019/08/27/health/sacklers-purdue-pharma-opioid-settlement.html.

127   *who were nowhere near bankrupt:* Gerald Posner, *Pharma: Greed, Lies, and the Poisoning of America* (New York: Simon & Schuster, 2020), 530.

127   *had found precedent:* The precedent is a 1985 case in which the A. H. Robins Company, makers of the Dalkon Shield, filed for bankruptcy protection, and the court shielded the family from liability: Gerald Posner and Ralph Brubaker, "The Sacklers Could Get Away With It," *New York Times*, July 22, 2020, https://www.nytimes.com/2020/07/22/opinion/sacklers-opioid-epidemic.html.

128   *"nearly impossible":* Paul Hanly, author interviews, July 1, 2020, and August 12, 2020.

128   *failed to disclose:* Jonathan Randles, "Purdue Lawyers Face Disclosure Questions Over Sackler Defense," *Wall Street Journal*, February 13, 2021.

129   *repeated delays:* Eric Eyre, "COVID-19 pushes back more opioid lawsuits in West Virginia," *Mountain State Spotlight*, October 14, 2020, https://mountainstatespotlight.org/2020/10/14/covid-19-pushes-back-more-opioid-lawsuits-in-west-virginia/.

129   *"there's this opioid fatigue":* Eric Eyre, author interview, February 10, 2020.

129   *"how heartless":* Former Purdue sales rep (name withheld because the rep fears retribution for speaking about the company), author interview, March 7, 2017.

129   *their wealth intact:* Posner and Brubaker, "The Sacklers Could Get Away With It."

129–30   *calling Posner a "numbskull":* Aaron Keller, "Purdue Pharma Judge Throttles 'Misinformed,' 'Numbskull' *New York Times* Opinion Writers," *Law & Crime*, July 29, 2020, https://lawandcrime.com/federal-court/purdue-pharma-judge-throttles-misinformed-numbskull-new-york-times-opinion-writers/.

130   *"Easter Island"*: Mike Quinn, author interview, February 17, 2021.

130   *against creditors' claims:* Alexandra Clough, "EXCLUSIVE: Sackler family company pays $7 million for mansion near Boca Raton," *Palm Beach Post*, October 25, 2019, https://www.palmbeachpost.com/news/20191 025/exclusive-sackler-family-company-pays-7-million-for-mansion-near -boca-raton.

130   *counted more rehabs:* Colton Wooten, "My Years in the Florida Shuffle of Drug Addiction," *New Yorker*, October 14, 2019.

130   *"I wish they'd hide elsewhere":* Hannah Morse, "Palm Beach County recovery advocates to Sackler family: You belong in jail," *Palm Beach Post*, October 21, 2020, https://www.palmbeachpost.com/story/news/local /2020/10/21/palm-beach-county-recovery-advocates-purdue-pharma -sackler-family-you-belong-jail/3716406001/.

132   *No. 1 tool:* Nicole Kravitz-Wirtz et al., "Association of Medicaid Expansion with Opioid Overdose Mortality in the United States," *JAMA Network* (January 10, 2020), https://jamanetwork.com /journals/jamanetworkopen/fullarticle/2758476; and Kendal Orgera and Jennifer Tolbert, "The Opioid Epidemic and Medic-aid's Role in Facilitating Access to Treatment," *KFF*, May 24, 2019, https://www.kff.org/medicaid/issue-brief/the-opioid-epidemic -and-medicaids-role-in-facilitating-access-to-treatment/.

132   *last or next to last:* "2018 Annual Report," *America's Health Rankings*, United Health Foundation, 2022, https://www.amer icashealthrankings.org/learn/reports/2018-annual-report/findings -state-rankings.

132   *cumbersome access barriers:* "Spotlight on Mississippi: Best Practices and Next Steps in the Opioid Epidemic," American Medical Association, May 2019, https://www.end-opioid-epidemic.org/wp -content/uploads/2019/05/AMA-Paper-Spotlight-on-Mississippi -May-2019_FOR-WEB.pdf.

133   *had overdosed and died:* Damian Sutherland, text message to author, February 18, 2021.

134   *address the harms of OxyContin:* Mike Spector, "U.S. states seek $2.2 trillion from OxyContin maker Purdue Pharma," Reuters, August 17, 2020.

134   *"You watch":* Sam Snodgrass, author interview, August 10, 2020.

134   *return to substance use:* John F. Kelly and William L. White, *Addiction Recovery Management: Theory, Research and Practice* (New York: Humana Press, 2011), chapter 16.

134   *"behind closed doors":* John Shinholser, author interview, January 30, 2021.

CHAPTER EIGHT

136   *25 percent:* Damon Centola, "The 25 Percent Tipping Point for Social Change," *Psychology Today,* May 28, 2019, https://www .psychologytoday.com/us/blog/how-behavior-spreads/201905/the-25 -percent-tipping-point-social-change. Centola's work is also featured in *Scientific American*: David Noonan, "The 25% Revolution: How Big Does a Minority Have to Be to Reshape Society?" June 8, 2018, https://www.scientificamerican.com/article/the-25-revolution -how-big-does-a-minority-have-to-be-to-reshape-society/.

136   *"None of that matters:"* Damon Centola, author interview, April 8, 2021.

137   *"so dangerous, and so harsh":* Shelly Young, author interview, March 2, 2021.

139   *If technology can be harnessed:* Author presentation from "Searching for Answers," Google technology conference on addiction, Washington, DC, November 13, 2018. Google presented best-practices information on this site afterward: https://recovertogether.withgoogle.com/.

140   *hard to describe how differently:* Noa Krawczyk et al., "Only One in Twenty Justice-Referred Adults in Specialty Treatment for Opioid Use Receive Methadone or Buprenorphine," *HealthAffairs,* December 2017. "The lack of adequate treatment in jails and prisons puts a vulnerable population of around 2.3 million people at risk," writes German Lopez, "How America's prisons and jails perpetuate the opioid epidemic," *Vox,* January 30, 2020.

141   *jail-cell window:* Sahana Karpoor, author interview, March 3, 2021.

141   *more than three times as many:* Surry had 250 of its 71,200 citizens in jail when I first visited; Fairfax had 600 of its population of 1.18 million.

141   *the Bible to Brené:* Daniel Adams, author interview, March 8, 2021. Adams wrote an essay about his crime for the Marshall Project: "I Killed My Wife. Now I Want to Help Prevent Domestic Violence," October 3, 2019.

142   *jailhouse mugshot:* Inside Nova, "Operation Dragon Slayer mugshot gallery," July 1, 2014.

144   *Rhode Island's prisons:* Traci C. Green et al., "Postincarceration Fatal Overdoses after Implementing Medications for Addiction Treatment in a Statewide Correctional System," *JAMA Psychiatry*, April 2018.

144   *three times less likely:* K. E. Moore, "Feasibility and effectiveness of continuing methadone maintenance treatment during incarceration compared with forced withdrawal," *Journal of Addiction Medicine* 12, no. 2 (2018), 156–62.

144   *two-thirds of the people in jail:* Bureau of Justice Statistics, 2014.

144   *"she was open to it":* Physician assistant Scott Haga, author interview, April 9, 2021.

145   *(used informally for therapeutic reasons):* Theodore J. Cicero et al., "Understanding the use of diverted buprenorphine," *Drug and Alcohol Dependence*, December 2018.

145   *"radical a shift":* Laura Yager and Sheriff Stacey A. Kincaid, author interviews, February 16, 2021.

146   *"how to get to yes":* Marissa Farina-Morse, author interview, March 25, 2021.

146   *Just 11 percent:* SUD treatment data is notoriously lagging in the United States, but several jail-based treatment experts provided this data. Author interviews: Drs. Jean Glossa and Shannon Robinson, Rich VanderHeuvel, Scott Haga, April 9, 2021.

146   *risk for people shortly after leaving incarceration:* Ingrid A. Binswanger et al., "Release from Prison—a High Risk of Death for Former Inmates," *New England Journal of Medicine* (January 11, 2007).

147   *"human beings are swayed":* Jennifer Potter, author interview, March 5, 2021.

148   *"War on Drugs that's caused the problem":* Ann Livingston, author interview, March 29, 2021.

149   *"so fucking tired":* Ann Livingston, author interview, March 20, 2021.

149   *hit a snag:* Gordon Katic and Sam Fenn, "In Surrey, 'Harm Reduction' Drug Approaches a Hard Sell," *The Tyee*, September 26, 2014.

CHAPTER NINE

151   *"worst mistake":* Norah O'Donnell, "Former FDA head: Opioid epidemic one of 'great mistakes of modern medicine,'" *CBS Evening News*, May 9, 2016.

151　*Woodcock continued approving:* Beth Macy, "He Lost His Son to an Overdose. Now He's Taking On the 'Top Drug Cop,'" *New York Times*, February 23, 2021.

151　*up to 4.275 billion:* Mike Spector, "Sacklers boost opioid settlement offer to $4.3 billion," Reuters, March 12, 2021.

152　*the SACKLER Act:* "Maloney, DeSaulnier Introduce SACKLER Act to Prevent Bad Actors from Evading Responsibility Through Bankruptcy Proceedings," House Committee on Oversight and Reform, March 19, 2021.

152　*"just get slid over to the side":* Mary Bono, author interview, March 19, 2021.

152　*Big Pharma's playbook:* Mary Bono, e-mail to author, March 31, 2021.

152　*nearly a billion:* Matthew Perrone and Ben Wieder, "Pro-painkiller echo chamber shaped policy amid drug epidemic," Associated Press, September 19, 2016.

152　*96,801 predicted overdose deaths:* "Statement from Acting Director Regina LaBelle on Today's CDC Overdose Death Data," press release, Whitehouse.gov, October 13, 2021. This figure calculates overdose deaths in the twelve-month period ending February 2021.

153　*former Purdue secretary:* Nancy Camp, author interview, October 5, 2020.

153　*Michael Jackson:* Richard Esposito, "Exclusive: Police Say Michael Jackson 'Heavily Addicted to OxyContin,'" *ABC News*, June 25, 2009.

153　*"didn't want to hear":* Nancy Camp, author interview, October 5, 2020.

154　*"Pablo Escobar of the new millennium":* Emma Ockerman, "A Friend Once Warned the Billionaire Behind OxyContin That He 'Could Become Pablo Escobar of the New Millennium,'" Vice.com, May 29, 2019.

154　*"the Sacklers' cathedral":* Michael S. Quinn, letter to United States Bankruptcy Court, "Limited Objection of the Ad Hoc Committee on Accountability to Debtors' Motion to Extend the Preliminary Injunction," Chapter 11, Case No. 12-23649, Southern District of New York, filed March 19, 2021.

154　*Quinn was nervous:* Mike Quinn, text to author, March 19, 2021.

154　*"a lot of things on my mind":* From bankruptcy hearing, March 19, 2021.

154　*Quinn's next brief:* Quinn, "Limited Objection of the Ad Hoc Committee," filed April 16, 2021.

155　*"held in contempt":* Charlotte Bismuth, author interview, May 6, 2021.

155   *not been recorded:* Libby Lewis, "The Swashbuckling Lawyer Who's Taking On the Sackler Family," *New Republic*, June 28, 2021.

155   *Warren was reportedly considering it:* Patrick Radden Keefe, author interview, April 12, 2021.

156   *According to billing records:* Matthew Cunningham-Cook, "As Purdue Pharma Sought Controversial Bankruptcy Settlement, It Spent Over $1.2 Million on Lobbying," *The Intercept*, August 13, 2021.

156   *peeled off nine Democratic senators so far:* ABI presentation, William A. Brandt Jr., minute 22:30, https://abi-sessions.s3.amazonaws.com /2021/NCBJ/NCBJ21_Lunch_Keynote.mp4.

156   *issue of nonconsensual releases:* Drain was listed among the speakers for a seminar called "Mass Tort Chapter 11 Cases Today," December 10, 2021, American Bankruptcy Institute.

157   *deaths remained significantly lower:* Abby E. Alpert et al., "Origins of the Opioid Crisis and Its Enduring Impacts," National Bureau of Economic Research, November 2019.

157   *"in and out of jail":* Dema Hadieh, author interview, March 3, 2021.

158   *Operation OxyFest:* Francis X. Clines, "Cancer Painkillers Pose New Abuse Threat," *New York Times*, February 9, 2001.

159   *Roberts doubted:* Brittany Roberts, e-mails to author, March 25, 2021.

159   *"past trauma":* Marissa Farina-Morse, author interview, April 25, 2021.

159   *still in touch:* Kristy Howard and Brittany Roberts, e-mails to author, April 12, 2021.

159   *through a jail intermediary:* Laura Yager, author interview, September 29, 2021.

160   *"a huge disadvantage":* John F. Kelly, e-mail to author, May 13, 2021; comments based on his paper, with M. Claire Greene, and Brandon G. Bergman, "Beyond Abstinence: Changes in Indices of Quality of Life with Time in Recovery in a Nationally Representative Sample of U.S. Adults," *Alcoholism: Clinical and Experimental Research* 42, no. 4 (April 2018).

160   *$337 million:* Debtors' Corporate Monthly Operating Report, January 2021, filed March 4, 2021, as cited in: Quinn, "Limited Objection of the Ad Hoc Committee," filed March 19, 2021. Keefe's book details the Sacklers' harassment of him: *Empire of Pain,* 435-37.

160   *immense price tag:* Jeremy Hill and Dawn McCarty, "With $2,300 Phone Calls, Purdue Runs Up Huge Bankruptcy Tab," Bloomberg News, May 11, 2021.

160 *tough-biceps emojis:* "Serpentine drops Sackler name following 're-branding,'" *Art Newspaper,* March 25, 2021.

161 *people in recovery:* "When covering painkiller crisis, don't blame the victims," *Poynter,* September 26, 2016.

161 *Obama's demotion:* Dan Diamond, Matt Viser, and Lenny Bernstein, "Manchin ally emerges as a frontrunner to be Biden's 'drug czar,'" *Washington Post,* March 17, 2021.

161 *overdoses were doubling:* Holly Hedegaard et al., "Drug Overdose Deaths in the United States, 1999–2018," CDC's NCHS Data Brief, No. 356, January 2020.

161 *fentanyl turned into:* Scott Higham, Sari Horwitz, and Katie Zezima, "The Fentanyl Failure," *Washington Post,* March 13, 2019.

162 *emergency-level surge:* Zachary Siegel, "Biden's Likely 'Drug Czar' Presided over Destruction of WV Syringe Program," *Filter,* March 17, 2021, https://filtermag.org/biden-drug-czar-gupta-syringes/.

162 *He remains under attack:* Robert Gebelhoff, "Needle exchanges need a champion. Will Biden's drug czar nominee be that person?" *Washington Post,* July 20, 2021.

162 *"still living with the wreckage":* Robin Pollini, author interview, April 6, 2021.

163 *increased seven-fold:* This is based on an increase from 11 IV-drug cases in 2014 to 84 cases in 2021 as of December 16, 2021; see: Department of Health and Human Resources, HIV Diagnoses by County, West Virginia, 2018–2021: https://oeps.wv.gov/hiv-aids /documents/data/WV_HIV_2018-2021.pdf; also "HIV Diagnoses by County, West Virginia, 2013–2017," https://oeps.wv.gov/hiv-aids /documents/data/WV_HIV_2013-2017.pdf.

163 *"crucible days":* Joe Solomon, e-mail to author, March 30, 2021.

163 *got the job:* Kyle Vass, "Critics say Biden's drug czar pick at odds with push for 'harm reduction' policies," *The Guardian,* November 5, 2021.

163 *"locked up until they're clean":* "The Generation Lost to the Opioid Crisis," VICE News, December 11, 2019.

163 *Pollini herself was physically threatened:* Dr. Robin Pollini, author interview, April 6, 2021.

163 *blocked from receiving funds:* West Virginia Public Radio reporter Kyle Vass, e-mail to author; Vass tweeted about it March 10, 2021. (E-mail confirmed it April 9, 2021.)

164 *"Why should I lose":* Twitter coverage of public meeting, @CaityCoyne, West Virginia *Gazette-Mail*, April 5, 2021.

164 *"that is concerning":* Caity Coyne, author interview, April 12, 2021.

164 *"full inquiry":* John Raby, "CDC inquiry sought on HIV outbreak in WVA's largest county," Associated Press, April 6, 2021.

164 *to buy drugs:* Rebecca Shabad et al., "Manchin privately raised concerns that parents would use child tax credit checks to buy drugs," *NBC News*, December 20, 2021.

164 *from corporations and billionaire business:* Donors to Manchin's PAC included American Express, Goldman Sachs, Lockheed Martin, health insurance companies, and natural gas company CNX Resources, as well as PACs tied to the coal and mining industries, according to Brian Schwartz and Jacob Pramuk, "Corporate donations to Sen. Joe Machin's PAC surged as he fought President Biden's agenda," CNBC.com, December 21, 2021.

165 *who'd gone on* Oprah: Scenes from the original *Oprah* show and an update she did in 2010 can be seen here: https://www.youtube.com/watch?v=WCDoTrCqgSY. Waters took up "people should not use drugs" rhetoric regularly in more recent years; see: Staff reports, "Protest to bring back needle exchange drawing mixed reactions," WCHS, October 15, 2019.

165 *came to regret:* "Oprah Returns to Williamson, West Virginia," September 15, 2010. "I was caught up in the mob mentality," Waters told Oprah during the follow-up episode.

165 *flying his drone:* Kyle Vass, "Without a Home Can You Be a Good Neighbor?" West Virginia Public Broadcasting, March 11, 2020, https://www.wvpublic.org/news/2020-03-11/without-a-home-can-you-be-a-good-neighbor. According to the reporter, Kyle Vass: "He took the video down after I arranged a somewhat gotcha meeting with him where I brought a copy of the aircraft ordinances from the state code and read it to him. I believed I asked him if he saw 'any irony in the fact that he had likely broken [the law] in an attempt to catch other people breaking the law.'"

165 *recent estimate:* Jill Kriesky, "Saving Lives and Saving Money: The Case For Harm Reduction in Kanawha County, WV," West Virginia Center on Budget and Policy, (n.d.; report analyzes data through 2020), https://wvpolicy.org/wp-content/uploads/2021/03/Harm-Reduction-Report-Final.pdf.

167   *recommended by the CDC:* "Needs-Based Syringe Distribution and Disposal at Syringe Services Programs," Centers for Disease Control and Prevention, September 2020, https://www.cdc.gov/ssp/docs/CDCSSP-FAQ_508.pdf.

167   *protest targeted owners:* Campbell Robertson, "Unpaid Miners Blocked a Coal Train in Protest. Weeks Later, They're Still There," *New York Times*, August 19, 2019.

168   Until the battle's won: Florence Reece, "Which Side Are You On?" (song written in 1931); see: https://www.youtube.com/watch?v=Jl0RPoGdCqo.

168   *demands were finally met:* $5.47 million was awarded in back wages in a bankruptcy settlement to the fired miners; see: Johnnie Lewis, "Harlan County, Kentucky, coal miners win $5 million," International Action Center, October 29, 2019.

168   *overdose deaths had gone up 45 percent:* Lauren Peace, "West Virginia Overdose Deaths Set New Record Amid Pandemic," *Mountain State Spotlight*, April 21, 2021. In 2020, 1,275 West Virginians died, up from 878 in 2019.

168   *fentanyl was finding fertile ground:* Thomas Fuller, "San Francisco Contends With a Different Sort of Epidemic: Drug Deaths," *New York Times*, April 23, 2021.

169   *Fauci was burned in effigy:* Ellen McCarthy and Ben Terris, "Anthony Fauci was ready for this. America was not." *Washington Post*, March 20, 2020.

169   *"schmuck behind the curtain":* From the David France documentary *How to Survive a Plague*, January 2012.

169   *fifteen years:* Stephanie Watson, "The History of HIV Treatment: Antiretroviral Therapy and More," WebMD, June 9, 2020.

169   *"speed dial":* Mike Moore, author interview, August 20, 2020, and former Purdue admin Nancy Camp, author interview, October 5, 2020.

169   *web camera:* Prosecution memo prepared by Assistant US Attorney Rick A. Mountcastle, "Memorandum for the United States Attorney Regarding the Investigation of Purdue Pharma L.P., et al.," September 28, 2006, 20.

169   *"can't just be the moms":* Dr. Joe Wright, author interview, September 24, 2020.

170   *"the more to the left":* Sarah Schulman said this on the *Ezra Klein Show* podcast, *New York Times*, June 22, 2021.

170 *MASH-style tents:* Martha Bebinger, "Tent Medicine to Treat Those with the Coronavirus in Boston's Homeless Community," WBUR, March 23, 2020; Deborah Becker, "Focus Remains on Troubled Boston Area Amid Concerns the Pandemic Is Worsening the Opioid Crisis," WBUR, November 19, 2020.

171 *"we had overdose teams":* Dr. David E. Smith, author interview, April 21, 2021.

171 *coined the phrase:* Smith has been given credit for the phrasing, but the World Health Organization in 1946 declared that "the enjoyment of the highest sustainable standard of health is one of the fundamental rights of every human being"; see: Julia Kaufman, "Health Care Is a Right, Not a Privilege," Kenan Institute for Ethics, August 10, 2018, https://kenan.ethics.duke.edu/health-care-is-a-right-not-a-privilege/.

172 *"I want you to celebrate them":* Dr. David E. Smith, author interview, April 21, 2021.

CHAPTER TEN

176 *unicorn-shaped erasers:* Karen Garcia, author interview, February 4, 2021.

179 *broken-heart tattoo:* Jessica Maloney, author interview, November 22, 2021.

180 *"'Dude, this was reported to us'":* Nebo testing night, author interviews, March 18, 2021.

180 *they were afflicted:* Tim Nolan (quoting Simone Weil), e-mail to author, April 27, 2021; see: https://iep.utm.edu/weil/.

181 *"see where it goes":* Tim Nolan, e-mails to author, patient updates in March and April 2021.

182 *"an encounter with the unseen":* Tim Nolan, e-mail to author, April 16, 2021.

182 *"'something for my nerves'":* Tim Nolan, e-mails to author, June 2 and 14, 2021.

183 *"had come so far":* Tim Nolan, e-mail to author, June 2, 2021.

183 "that's *the gift*": Tim Nolan, e-mail to author, May 12, 2021.

184 *"What we don't have":* Dr. Andrew Muir, author interview, April 6, 2021.

184 *tears running down your [their] legs:* Obituary, Debbie Jack

Silver, Beam Funeral Service, https://www.beamfuneralservice.com
/obituaries/debbie-deb-jack-silver, June 2017.

185 *learned of the death on Mother's Day:* Tim Nolan, e-mail to author,
April 7, 2021.

185 *decimated by budget cuts:* Christopher Rowland and Peter Whoriskey,
"U.S. health system is showing why it's not ready for a coronavirus
pandemic," *Washington Post,* March 4, 2020.

187 *40 percent:* SAMHSA, "Key Substance Use and Mental Health Indi-
cators in the United States: Results from the 2019 National Survey
on Drug Use and Health," September 2020, 54–55. Among adults in
the survey who felt they needed treatment for their SUD, 24 percent
said they didn't know where to go for help, and 21 percent reported
financial barriers (no insurance coverage and/or not being able to
afford treatment).

189 *Most patients still don't:* Caleb Banta-Green, "Buprenorphine utiliza-
tion among all Washington State residents based upon prescription
monitoring program data—Characteristics associated with two measures of retention and patterns of care over time," *Journal of Substance
Abuse Treatment* (May 25, 2021).

190 *glowing 2018 economic report:* "Report Examines Economic
Impact of Google Data Centers in N.C. and across U.S.,"
Economic Development Partnership of North Carolina, April 23,
2018, https://edpnc.com/report-examines-economic-impact-google
-data-centers-lenoir-n-c-across-u-s/.

190 *fewer than a third:* Government Accountability Office Studies, and Beth
Macy, "The Reality of Retraining," *Roanoke Times,* April 22, 2012.

190 *distributed 58 million:* Table Rock Pharmacy, Burke County, opioid
data mapping provided by the *Washington Post*: https://www.washington
post.com/graphics/2019/investigations/pharmacies-pain-pill-map/. AR-
COS data from the *Washington Post*: https://www.washingtonpost.com
/graphics/2019/investigations/dea-pain-pill-database/.

190 *more prescriptions than people:* Sharon McBrayer, "DEA opioid sources
released after court order," Morganton.com, August 6, 2019.

191 *In regions with higher rates:* Sujeong Park and David Powell, "Is the
Rise in Illicit Opioids Affecting Labor Supply and Disability Claiming
Rates?" National Bureau of Economic Research, September 2020.

191 *highest disability rate:* "2017 State Report for County-Level Data: Prevalence," Annual Disability Statistics Compendium, Institute on Disability,

University of New Hampshire, 2019, https://disabilitycompendium.org
/compendium/2017-state-report-for-county-level-data-prevalence/NC.

191   *Google server farm:* Jonathan Q. Morgan, "Using Economic Development Incentives: For Better or for Worse," *Popular Government*,
Winter 2009.

191   *woefully scant:* Tim Bartik, author interview, April 16, 2021.

192   *"create an environment":* China Schertz, author interview, May 27, 2021.

192   *Partners in Health:* Farmer was profiled by the journalist Tracy Kidder
in his majestic book, *Mountains Beyond Mountains: The Quest of Dr.
Paul Farmer, a Man Who Would Cure the World* (New York: Random
House, 2003).

192   *was a proponent:* Dr. Paul Farmer, "How Liberation Theology Can
Inform Public Health," PIH.org, December 23, 2013.

192   *"Of all the forms of inequality":* Martin Luther King Jr., convention
of the Medical Committee for Human Rights press conference,
Chicago, March 25, 1966.

193   *"go to the addicted":* Farmer, "How Liberation Theology Can Inform
Public Health."

193   *"dangerous":* Emma McGinty and Colleen Barry, "Stigma Reduction
to Combat the Addiction Crisis—Developing an Evidence Base,"
New England Journal of Medicine (April 2, 2020).

193   *told me her patients just assumed:* Dr. Yngvild Olsen, author interview,
August 17, 2021.

194   *study based in Fresno:* Robin Pollini, e-mail to author, April 15, 2021.

194   *("Nicole doesn't mess around"):* Tim Nolan, e-mail to author, July 17, 2021.

194   *"twenty-nine days clean":* Tim Nolan, e-mail to author, May 8, 2021. I
met Brenda at Mary Jo Silver's house on March 18, 2021.

CHAPTER ELEVEN

196   *"drug dwelling":* Mount Airy Police Reports, *Mount Airy News*, March
21, 2018.

196   *"something ain't right":* Billie Campbell, James Stroud, and Jacob (last
name withheld), author interviews, April 26, 2021.

197   *"killing the helpers":* Tracey Helton Mitchell, Twitter post, July
17, 2021.

197   *"refer people to us":* James Stroud, author interview, February 5, 2021.

198   *five times more likely:* "Summary of Information on the Safety and Effectiveness of Syringe Services Programs," Centers for Disease Control and Prevention, May 23, 2019, https://www.cdc.gov/ssp /syringe-services-programs-summary.html.

198   *outcry was so loud:* Tom Joyce, "Project Lazarus coordinator terminated," *Elkin Tribune,* July 23, 2017. Public health education specialist Karen Eberdt was dismissed from her job with the Surry County Health and Nutrition Center shortly after announcing plans to propose the opening of a needle exchange in Mount Airy.

198   *"politicians who have no clue":* Fred Brason, founder of Project Lazarus, author interviews, May 4 and June 15, 2021.

199   *benefit from closing the Medicaid coverage gap*: "North Carolina Still Has a Coverage Gap," North Carolina Community Health Center Association, using Kaiser Foundation data, 2019.

199   *provided free smartphones:* Emily McPeak, author interview, June 15, 2021.

200   *"just not evidence":* Dr. Carl Erik Fisher, author correspondence and interview, September 29, 2021.

200   *crystal clear:* Consensus Study Report, "Medications for Opioid Use Disorder Save Lives," National Academies of Sciences, Engineering, and Medicine, 2019, https://www.nap.edu/catalog/25310 /medications-for-opioid-use-disorder-save-lives.

200   *often ignored:* Dr. Arthur Robin Williams, e-mail to author, October 1, 2021.

200   *stepped-care model:* Kathleen M. Carroll and Roger D. Weiss, "The Role of Behavioral Interventions in Buprenorphine Maintenance Treatment: A Review," *American Journal of Psychiatry* 174, no. 8 (August 1, 2017): 738–47, https://doi.org/10/gf4nhr.

200   *alternative treatments:* Dr. Joshua Sharfstein, author interview, December 5, 2021.

200   *happening at harm-reduction organizations:* Abby Goodnough, "Helping Drug Users Survive, Not Abstain: 'Harm Reduction' Gains Federal Support," *New York Times,* June 28, 2021.

200   *"really traumatic":* Colin Miller, e-mail to author, June 21, 2021.

201   *"won't be sustainable":* Fred Brason, author interview, June 15, 2021.

201   *official count:* Mark Willis, author interview, June 14, 2021.

202   *"always brings new growth":* Wendy Odum, author interview, April 19, 2021.

202 *so he could sleep without worrying:* James Stroud, author interview, January 14, 2021.

203 *"That's the bullshit":* Wendy Odum, James Stroud, and Eric Snow, author interviews, January 5, 2021.

204 *"we'll transport them":* Mark Willis, author interview, June 14, 2021.

204 *leaps and bounds:* Mark Willis and data analyst Jamie Edwards, author interviews, March 19, 2021.

204 *high-production-value videos: Surry, The Road to Recovery* videos are all featured on Vimeo: https://vimeopro.com/nctta/surry-the-road -to-recovery/video/455059549.

205 *picked off the naysayers:* Judge Duane Slone, author interview, April 25, 2020.

205 *highest judicial honor:* "Tennessee judge receives highest judicial honor for his work on the opioid epidemic," Knoxcounty.org, November 26, 2019.

206 *Barbecue and Sweet Tea:* Donnie Varnell, author interview, February 16, 2021.

206 *less likely to get stuck:* Max Blau, "Southern states slowly embracing harm reduction to curb opioid epidemic," *PBS NewsHour,* April 17, 2019.

206 *changed their tune:* Dr. William Cooke, author interview, July 15, 2021, and "Boone County Jail becomes first in Indiana to administer subox-one for addiction treatment," News Channel 4, March 3, 2020.

207 *"really our relationships":* Angie Gray, author interview, January 8, 2019.

207 *"how can we not be"* Dr. John Burton, Author interview, January 17, 2019. Burton's turnaround is voiced in the *Finding Tess* Audible Original, 2019.

207 *"Any time I tried":* Mark Willis, author interview, September 17, 2021.

208 *"saying no":* Mark Willis, author interview, February 13, 2020.

209 *prescription for her psoriatic arthritis:* Sonya Cheek, author interview, September 24, 2021.

210–11 *"My passion":* Sonya Cheek, author interview, January 6, 2021.

211 *clothes on his back and that's it:* Dylan Goughery, author interview, June 22, 2021.

214 *"Jesused me out":* Billie Campbell, author interview, September 12, 2021.

216 *skepticism:* Tracey Helton Mitchell, e-mail to author, June 29, 2021.

217 *"I have qualms":* Dr. Anna Lembke, author interview, April 23, 2021.

217 *"When a disease is seen as treatable":* Dr. Joshua Sharfstein and Dr. Yngvild Olsen, author interview, August 17, 2021. I also interviewed Sharfstein separately on April 6, 2021.

218 *extrapolating from studies:* Carl Erik Fisher, author interview, September 29, 2021. Studies extrapolated from are gathered in New York State Office of Addiction Services and Supports Medical Advisory Panel, "Best Practices for Long-Term Maintenance with Medications for Patients with Opioid Use Disorder," December 9, 2020.

219 *only recently stopped experiencing:* Sonya Cheek, author interview, September 24, 2021.

219 *up a third from the same period:* Surry County data analyst Jamie Edwards, e-mail to author, September 20, 2021.

CHAPTER TWELVE

223 *Cops were complaining:* Tim Nolan, author interview, August 1, 2021.

224 *was MIA:* Mike Moore, author interview, August 4, 2021.

224 *"'You can come back from this'":* Sonya Cheek, author interview, September 24, 2021.

224 *everyone at Tabitha's House to pray:* Billie Campbell, author interview, September 27, 2021.

224 *"stomping on a snake":* Mark Willis, author interview, August 6, 2021.

224 *"You don't attack":* Michelle Mathis, author interview, July 31, 2021.

225 *naloxone shortage:* Meryl Kornfield, "Affordable naloxone is running out, creating a perfect storm for more overdose deaths, activists say," *Washington Post,* August 10, 2021.

225 *"bricks are falling":* Dan Vergano, author interview, August 16, 2021.

225 *Police initially said:* "Kittanning man pleads guilty in death of local teen," *Jeffersonian Democrat,* September 1, 2021.

225 *But Vergano later learned:* Dan Vergano, e-mail to author, September 1, 2021.

226 *"no billions":* John Oliver, "Opioids III: The Sacklers," *Last Week Tonight with John Oliver,"* August 9, 2021.

226 *near-silence on the radio:* Brian Mann, Twitter, August 12, 2021.

227 *often unlistenable:* Ibid.

227 *bristled whenever:* Quinn, "Limited Objection of the Ad Hoc Committee," filed June 16, 2021.

227 *almost half:* Jonathan Randles, "OxyContin Maker Purdue's Chapter 11 Trial to Test Limits of Bankruptcy Powers," *Wall Street Journal*, August 12, 2021.

227 *Broadly, the law was unsettled:* Jan Hoffman, "Sacklers Threaten to Pull Out of Opioid Settlement Without Broad Legal Immunity," *New York Times*, August 17, 2021.

228 *micromanager:* "Anything you could do to reduce the direct contact of Richard into the organization is appreciated," said a Purdue sales official, pleading with another higher-up for relief, as cited in *Commonwealth of Massachusetts v. Purdue Pharma et al.*, Super Court, C.A. No. 1884-cv-01808, January 31, 2019, https://www.mass.gov/files/documents/2019/01/31/Massachu setts%20AGO%20Amended%20Complaint%202019-01-31.pdf.

228 *aren't supposed to make decisions:* Judicial Code of Conduct, CANON 3(A)(1).

229 *"quirky, interesting guy":* Jonathan Lipson, author interview, June 21, 2021.

229 *a Yalie like Drain:* John Hersey wrote that Drain's work was "dense, adult, historical, and eccentric. Mr. Drain promises to be a notable storyteller," as quoted on the Amazon page for: Robert Drain, *The Great Work in the United States of America* (Pennsauken Township, NJ: BookBaby, 2013), https://www.amazon.com/Great -Work-United-States-America-ebook/dp/B00IIUWMGY.

229 *"load of hooey":* Jeremy Hill, "Purdue Backs Bankruptcy Examiner after Explosive Hearing," Bloomberg News, June 16, 2021. The berating exchange occurs on p. 33 of the hearing transcript and throughout.

230 *"Bright students":* Quinn, "Limited Objection of the Ad Hoc Committee," filed April 16, 2021.

230 *"We're like ninjas":* Mike Quinn, author interview, November 23, 2021.

230 *"simple guy from upstate":* Mike Quinn, author interview, May 14, 2021.

230 *he had friends:* Michael Quinn, text to author, August 13, 2021, and interview with author, February 11, 2022.

231 *arguably one of the key architects:* Keefe, *Empire of Pain*, 298–300. "Stuart had more power than anyone in the company, including the CEO," a former Purdue employee told Keefe.

231 *renewed his controlled-substance prescribing license:* State of Connecticut, CSP, approved June 10, 2021.

232 *funneling the scoop to a reporter:* Cunningham-Cook, "As Purdue Pharma Sought Controversial Bankruptcy Settlement."

232 *"the whole corruption":* Jonathan Randles, "Purdue Law Firms to Waive $1 Million in Fees over Sackler Defense Disclosures," *Wall Street Journal*, April 29, 2021.

232 *settled with the three firms:* United States Department of Justice, "Law Firms Representing Purdue Pharma Agree to Relinquish $1 Million in Settlement with U.S. Trustee Program," https://www.justice.gov/opa/pr/law-firms-representing-purdue-pharma-agree-relinquish-1-million-settlement-us-trustee-program, April 29, 2021.

233 *"the side effect of having courage":* Mike Quinn, author interview, June 17, 2021.

233 *In the final Zoom:* OxyJustice Zoom meeting, author's transcription, July 22, 2021.

233 *thirteen other nonconsenting states:* Brian Mann, "Fifteen States Drop Opposition to Controversial Purdue Pharma OxyContin Bankruptcy," National Public Radio, July 8, 2021.

233 *"We need documents":* "Healey: Purdue Settlement Will Unlock Sackler 'Secrets,'" WBUR, July 8, 2021.

234 *"grief could be used for good":* Barbara Van Rooyan, multiple author interviews, 2016–21, and Beth Macy, "The Four Ordinary People Who Took On Big Pharma," *New York Times*, July 20, 2019.

234 *Purdue pleaded guilty:* Jan Hoffman and Katie Benner, "Purdue Pharma Pleads Guilty to Criminal Charges for Opioid Sales," *New York Times*, October 21, 2020.

235 *("one hundred percent show"):* Mike Moore, author interview, November 23, 2020.

236 *feeling too defeated:* Megan Kapler, author interview, July 22, 2021.

236 *loved to bash:* Bridget Read, "Courtney Love Wants Nothing to Do with OxyContin Heiress," *The Cut*, September 9, 2019.

236 *"Your. People. Killed. My. People":* Mara Siegler, "Courtney Love and OxyContin heiress Sackler continue to war," *Page Six*, September 12, 2019. Joss Sackler accused Love of wanting more money, and Love said, "I asked for a stupid-ass amount—$250,000—to donate to charities."

237 *Stacey Abrams's voting rights organization:* Patrick Radden Keefe, text to author, June 8, 2021. "Go Stacey fucking Abrams!" Keefe texted, thoroughly wiped out and dispirited by the day's events.

237 *Black and Brown Americans:* National Institutes of Health, "Disparities in opioid overdose deaths continue to worsen for Black people, study

suggests," September 9, 2021, https://www.nih.gov/news-events/news
-releases/disparities-opioid-overdose-deaths-continue-worsen-black
-people-study-suggests.

237 *medical authorities had overreacted:* Jacob Sullum, "A New Study Finds
That Reducing Pain Medication Is Associated with an Increased Risk
of Overdose and Suicide," *Reason*, August 6, 2021.

238 *pathways to compassionate:* Brendan Saloner, "Commentary on Kertesz
& Gordon (2019): Don't abandon opioid prescription control efforts,
reform them," *Addiction*, September 18, 2018.

238 *fell by 60 percent:* Maia Szalavitz, "The Pain Was Unbearable. So Why
Did Doctors Push Her Away?" *Wired*, August 11, 2021.

239 *denying medications to some legitimate:* Mark Olfson et al., "Trends
in Opioid Prescribing and Self-Reported Pain Among US Adults,"
HealthAffairs, January 2020.

239 *widely considered by most doctors to need opioids:* Andrea C. Enzinger et
al., "US Trends in Opioid Access Among Patients With Poor Prognosis
Cancer Near End-of-Life," *Journal of Clinical Oncology* (July 22, 2021).

239 *tools to help them better control their pain:* Dr. Beth Darnall, "To treat
pain, study people in all their complexity," *Nature*, May 1, 2018

239 *only given psychological tools after medications have failed:* Aram Mar-
dian et al., "Engagement in Prescription Opioid Tapering Research:
The EMPOWER Study and a Coproduction Model of Success,"
Journal of General Internal Medicine (August 13, 2021).

239–40 *"people who'd just had brain surgery":* Dr. Beth Darnall, author interviews, December 1, 2021, and January 3, 2021.

240 *rates unsafe:* Brian Mann, "Doctors and Dentists Still Flooding U.S.
with Opioid Prescriptions," National Public Radio, July 17, 2020.

240 *most of the illicit:* Michael Sinclair, "The wicked problem of drug
trafficking in the Western Hemisphere," Brookings Institute, January
15, 2021.

240 *harm-reduction work:* Alexis Pleus, author interview, August 3, 2021.

240 *crippling fear of the ringer:* Alexis Pleus, testimony, "The SACKLER
Act and Other Policies to Promote Accountability for the Sackler
Family's Role in the Opioid Epidemic," US House Committee on
Oversight and Reform, June 8, 2021.

241 Forbes *list:* Alex Morrell, "The OxyContin Clan: The $14 Billion
Newcomer to *Forbes* 2015 List of Richest U.S. Families," *Forbes*,
July 1, 2015.

241 *would throw a chair:* Mike Quinn, author interview, June. 9, 2021.

241 *"token grieving mom":* Alexis Pleus, author interview, July 21, 2021.

242 *a grieving mother* and an engineer: Alexis Pleus, author interviews, September 11 and 14, 2020.

244 *audacity to patent:* David Armstrong, "OxyContin Maker Explored Expansion into 'Attractive' Anti-Addiction Market," *ProPublica,* January 30, 2019. Dr. Kathe Sackler said the new bupe product would make the company an "end-to-end pain provider." These details first surfaced in the Massachusetts case against Purdue and the Sacklers.

244 I want that money: Andrew Russeth, "'They Should Be in Jail': Nan Goldin, Anti-Sackler Opioid Activists Take Fight to Guggenheim, Met," *ARTnews,* February 10, 2019.

245 *later reporting revealed:* The company provided Howard Udell with a $5 million payout, Michael Friedman with $3 million, see: Keefe, *Empire of Pain,* 284. "Those three guys basically took the hit for the family, because the family was going to take care of them," former Purdue chemist Gary Ritchie told Keefe.

246 *"the last gasp of the empire":* Mike Quinn, author interview, August 9, 2021.

246 *"any errors":* Thomas A. Clare, letter to the author, June 9, 2021.

247 *democracy-threatening tool:* Dana Priest, Craig Timberg, and Souad Mekhennet, "Private Israeli spyware used to hack cell phones of journalists, activists worldwide," *Washington Post,* July 18, 2021.

247 *useless attempt:* Kathe Sackler deposition, April 1, 2019.

247 *"played that system like a harp":* Author interview on "After Words with Patrick Radden Keefe," C-SPAN, May 8, 2021.

247 *first time:* Jan Hoffman, "Sacklers Threaten to Pull Out of Opioid Settlement Without Broad Legal Immunity," *New York Times,* August 17, 2021.

248 *"I do not know":* I listened in to this hearing, August 18, 2021. (Journalists weren't permitted to make recordings, but I took notes.) Cynthia Munger counted the "I don't recall/remember/recollect" mentions.

248 *"I can't recall":* Bankruptcy confirmation hearing, August 18, 2021. The assistant AG was Brian Edmunds.

248 *bottom of the site:* Copyright 2021, "The Raymond Sackler Family. All Rights Reserved," judgeforyourelves.info (Richard mistakenly said it ended in "dot net").

248 *"Iron curtain"*: The piece was created by Fernando Alvarez: www.the
-curtains.com; the protest was on August 9, 2021.

249 *"medical naïveté"*: Patricia Mehrmann, author interview, August 6,
2021.

250 *"How substantially"*: Natalie Rahhal, "The Sackler family wanted
to sell OxyContin as an UNCONTROLLED substance—but the
drug's inventor told them that would be dangerous," *Daily Mail*,
January 19, 2019.

251 *trial's most telling moment*: Rick Archer, "Ex-Purdue Chair Denies
Blame for Opioid Crisis," *Law360*, August 18, 2021.

252 *send by a Minneapolis woman*: Stephanie Lubinski, January 6, 2021, to
Judge Robert D. Drain, Case No. 19-23649, submitted to the docket
July 8. "He no longer wanted to live with his addiction, and the pain
of what he had destroyed."

252 *sold their son's*: Stephanie Lubinski, author interview, August 25, 2021.

253 *walked away from the bench without saying a word*: "Whereupon these
proceedings were concluded at 4:34 p.m.," notes the court transcript,
August 19, 2021. UCC co-chair Ryan Hampton (who was watching
the proceedings via telecast) confirmed that Drain was crying and
abruptly walked away from his chair.

CHAPTER THIRTEEN

254 *against the advice of health officials*: Dan Vergano, "Atlantic City Wants
to Close Its Needle Exchange and Here's Why Opponents Say That's
a Terrible Idea," *BuzzFeed News*, November 4, 2021. Other examples
of politicians voting to close syringe exchanges occurred in Eureka,
California, and Scott County, Indiana, in 2020 and 2021.

255 *opioid case agglomeration*: Danny Hakim, William K. Rashbaum, and
Ronie Caryn Rabin, "The Giants at the Heart of the Opioid Crisis,"
New York Times, April 22, 2019.

255 Hillbilly Heroin. OC.: Eric Eyre, "Analysis: There's Nothing Funny
About an Addiction Crisis," *Mountain State Spotlight*, May 13, 2021.

256 *AmerisourceBergen denied*: Meryl Kornfield, "Drug distributor employees emailed a parody song about 'pillbillies,' documents show,"
Washington Post, May 23, 2020.

256 *$260 million*: AmerisourceBergen, Cardinal Health and McKesson

agreed to pay $215 million while the Israeli-based drugmaker Teva agreed to contribute $20 million in cash and $25 million worth of buprenorphine; see: Julie Carr Smyth and Geoff Mulvihill, "$260 million deal averts 1st federal trial on opioid crisis," Associated Press, October 21, 2019.

256   *highest overdose-death rate:* Paul Farrell, "In the United States District Court for the Southern District of West Virginia," Civil Action No. 3:17-01362, "Plaintiffs' Proposed Findings of Fact and Conclusions of Law," August 26, 2021.

256   *The Pill Express:* Ibid., 221.

256   *in less than four hours:* Andrew Joseph, "26 overdoses in just hours: Inside a community on the front lines of the opioid epidemic," *STAT*, August 22, 2016.

256   *One in five babies:* Kris Maher and Sara Randazzo, "Landmark Opioid Trial Opens in West Virginia," *Wall Street Journal*, May 3, 2021.

256   *a dedicated space:* Amanda Coleman, author interview, September 21, 2021.

257   *"just staggering":* Ibid.,

257   *"We reflect it":* Brendan Pierson, "Big three drug distributors blame doctors, regulators in trial over opioid epidemic," Reuters, May 3, 2021.

257   *20.8 million:* Eric Eyre, "Drug firms shipped 20.8M pain pills to WV town with 2,900 residents," *Charleston Gazette-Mail*, January 29, 2018.

257   *stripped the DEA:* Scott Higham and Lenny Bernstein, "The Drug Industry's Triumph over the DEA," *Washington Post*, October 15, 2017; and Scott Higham, Lenny Bernstein, Steven Rich, and Alice Crites, "Drug industry hired dozens of officials from the DEA as the agency tried to curb opioid abuse," *Washington Post*, December 22, 2016.

258   *"AmerisourceBergen will deny":* Eric Eyre, "Analysis: There's nothing funny about an addiction crisis."

258   *interrupted the local lawyers constantly:* Eric Eyre, author interview, June 25, 2021.

259   *high-fiving each other:* Eric Eyre, author interview, July 30, 2021.

259   *"so traumatized":* Courtney Hessler, author interview, June 23, 2021.

260   *"Everyone just assumes":* Catie Coyne, author interview, June 26, 2021.

260   *had confirmed:* Dr. Christine Teague, author interview, June 25, 2021.

260   *topped 100:* Brooke Parker, e-mail to author, February 22, 2022.

260   *More than half:* Brooke Parker, author interview, June 25, 2021.

261   *"bad person":* Sean T. Allen, "Understanding the public health conse-
      quences of suspending a rural syringe services program: A qualitative
      study of the experiences of people who inject drugs," *Harm Reduction
      Journal* 16, no. 33 (2019): 4–5.

261   *eight to ten times:* Christine Teague, as quoted by Kyle Vass, "HIV in the
      Mountain State: Mike Survives an Early AIDS Infection as Medications
      Improve," West Virginia Public Broadcasting, September 2, 2021.

261   *plotting her next campaign:* Christine Teague, author interview, June
      26, 2021.

262   *"only one federal judge":* Loree Stark, author interview, June 26, 2021.

262   *"new problems":* Kyle Vass, author interview, June 26, 2021.

263   *a response to profound oppression:* Sarah Schulman interviewed by Ezra
      Klein, "Sarah Schulman's Radical Approach to Conflict, Communi-
      cation, and Change," *The Ezra Klein Show, New York Times,* June
      22, 2021.

264   *"sending her home to die":* Brooke Parker, author interview, June
      25, 2021.

267   *Kyle:* All the first names used in this section have been changed at
      Brooke's request, due to fear of retribution.

269   *a place to shower:* "Snow," author interview, August 18, 2021.

270   *"in survival mode":* Brooke Parker, author interview, September
      30, 2021.

270   *"I need some boundaries":* Brooke Parker, author interview, August
      23, 2021.

271   *"didn't need to be alone that night":* Brooke Parker, e-mail to author,
      September 19, 2021.

272   *decreased 25 percent:* West Virginia Department of Health
      & Human Resources, "DHHR Data Suggests West Vir-
      ginia Overdose Deaths Appear to Be Declining," September
      5, 2019, https://dhhr.wv.gov/News/Pages/Gov.-Justice---DHHR-
      Data-Suggests-West-Virginia-Overdose-Deaths-Appear-to-be-Decl
      ining.aspx.

272   *including a doubling:* Courtney Hessler, "Record-breaking fatal over-
      doses reported in W.Va. in 2020 after years of decreases," *(Huntington)
      Herald Dispatch,* April 28, 2021.

272   *"but it's the politics":* Drs. Joshua Sharfstein and Yngvild Olsen, author
      interview, August 17, 2021.

273   *principles designed to:* Johns Hopkins Bloomberg School of Public Health, "Coalition Releases Principles to Guide State and Local Spending of Forthcomig Opioid Litigation Settlement Funds," January 27, 2021, https://publichealth.jhu.edu/2021/coalition-releases-principles-to-guide-state-and-local-spending-of-forthcoming-opioid-litigation-settlement-funds.

273   *tightened up residency:* Lyn O'Connell, author interview, August 30, 2021.

273   *"Kanawha's refused to make changes":* Kyle Vass, author interviews, September 27–30, 2021.

274   *"in a gently assertive way":* Dr. Stefan Kertesz, author interviews, September 1 and 2, 2021.

274   *"anger mixed in with the grief":* Robert Gipe, e-mail to author, September 20, 2021.

275   *recent survey of 900 people with SUD:* Community Catalyst, "Peers Speak Out: Priority Outcomes for Substance Use Treatment and Services," April 2021: https://www.communitycatalyst.org/resources/tools/peers-speak-out/pdf/Peers-Speak-Out.pdf.

275   *Fisher writes:* Fisher, *The Urge,* 300.

276   *infrastructure bill last year:* Madeleine Ngo, "Skilled Workers Are Scarce, Posing a Challenge for Biden's Infrastructure Plan," *New York Times,* September 9, 2021.

276   *declined by 40 percent:* Ron Hetrick et al., "The Demographic Drought," Emsi, 2021, https://www.economicmodeling.com/wp-content/uploads/2021/07/Demographic-Drought-V18.pdf, 16.

276   *just under a third:* Mark Willis, author interview, September 13, 2021. "About one in three referrals actually gets placed," he told me on September 17, 2021.

277   *well over $10 billion:* The funding amount combines figures from programs such as the 21st Century CURES Act, the State Targeted Response Grant, the State Opioid Response grant, and the Substance Abuse Block Grant, as gathered from these sources: SAMHSA, "HHS, to maintain funding formula for $1B opioid grant program," October 30, 2017, https://www.samhsa.gov/newsroom/press-announcements/201710300530; and "States' Use of Grant Funding for a Targeted Response to the Opioid Crisis," Oversight.gov, March 13, 2020, https://www.oversight.gov/report/hhsoig/states-use-grant-funding-targeted-response-opioid-crisis; and SAMHSA, "State

Opioid Response Grants," March 20, 2020, https://www.samhsa.gov /grants/grant-announcements/ti-20-012.

277 *90 percent* and *OUD is not treatable*: American Society of Addiction Medicine, "ASAM Advocacy Roadmap," February 2020, https://www.asam.org/docs/default-source/advocacy /asam_report_feb2020_final.pdf?sfvrsn=f73f51c2_2, Fisher, *The Urge,* 288; and Lisa Rapaport, "Few doctors can legally prescribe opioid-addiction drug," Reuters, January 6, 2020.

277–78 *more than a million:* I calculated this figure by starting with a half million in 2015, then conservatively extrapolating out 2017 numbers of 158,000 deaths of despair over the next five years, including the beginning of the pandemic. See: Roge Karma, "'Deaths of despair': The deadly epidemic that predated coronavirus," Vox.com, April 15, 2020. My calculation of 1,044,528 deaths from 1996 to late 2021 was confirmed by University of Pittsburgh public health researcher Donald S. Burke after consulting data he'd recently presented to the ONDCP, e-mail to author, December 14, 2021.

EPILOGUE

279–80 *"Oh, how I hate to ask":* Sister Beth Davies, e-mail to author, September 23, 2021.

280 *"no amount of money":* Ed Bisch, e-mail to author, September 30, 2021.

281 *"You follow the money!":* Paul Pelletier, speaking at December 3, 2021, rally in front of the Department of Justice organized by Relatives Against Purdue Pharma.

281 *finally removed:* Sarah Cascone, "In a Landmark Move, the Metropolitan Museum of Art Has Removed the Sackler Name from its Walls," *Artnet,* December 9, 2021.

282 *had finally erased:* Patrick Radden Keefe, "An Astounding List of Artists Helped Persuade the Met to Remove the Sackler Name," *New Yorker,* December 10, 2021. The Sackler name remains in two galleries named for Arthur Sackler, who died before OxyContin was introduced.

282 *"a charade":* Paul Pelletier and Beth Macy, "After 'startling rebuke' of multibillion-dollar bankruptcy settlement, 'these Sacklers don't deserve a pass—again," *STAT,* December 19, 2021. McMahon's ruling

can be found here: https://portal.ct.gov/-/media/AG/Press_Releases
/2021/Judge-McMahon-Decision-121621.pdf.

282   *flat-out rejected:* Department of Justice, "Statement from the Attorney General Merrick B. Garland Regarding Purdue Pharma
Bankruptcy," December 16, 2021, https://www.justice.gov/opa
/pr/statement-attorney-general-merrick-b-garland-regarding-purdue
-pharma-bankruptcy

283   *Zoom debrief:* Ad Hoc Committee for Accountability meeting, May
2, 2022.

283   *the last of the attorneys general caved:* Seamus McAvoy, "Purdue Pharma
to pay $6 billion in new opioid settlement": *Hartford Courant,* March
3, 2022.

284   *hearing felt primitive:* Meryl Kornfield, "Opioid victims confront Purdue Pharma's Sackler family: 'It will never end for me,'" *Washington
Post,* March 10, 2022.

286   *Mary Jo was:* Mary Jo Silver, author interview via Facebook, September
24, 2021. All other updates came from my last visit to see Tim Nolan
on September 16, 2021. Two months later, Brenda was reemployed,
"doing fantastic!" and reporting fifty-two days of sobriety, according
to Nolan via e-mail on November 8, 2021. Three months later,
Brenda had another job with decent benefits and was sober, and Mary
Jo was hosting hep C–testing gatherings for Tim again and trying to
win back custody of her daughter, as Tim was proud to report in an
e-mail to the author, November 29, 2021.

287   $1 trillion *per year:* RAND Corporation, "Commission on Combat-
ing Synthetic Opioid Trafficking," RAND.org, February 7, 2022.
In 2018, that figure was $696 billion. The new trillion-dollar cost
estimate is equivalent to nearly half of America's economic growth
in 2021.

287   *teenage overdose deaths:* Joseph Friedman, "Trends in Drug Overdose
Deaths Among U.S. Adolescents, January 2010 to June 2021, JAMA
Network, April 12, 2022.

288   *"Just like Congress did":* Author interview, Dr. Andrew Kolodny, May
2, 2022.

288   *"a huge gin and tonic":* Laura van Dernoot Lipsky, author interview,
August 20, 2021.

289   *left "to the whims of crazy people":* Nikki King, author interview,
November 27, 2021.

289 *the national average is only eleven:* David Axelson, "Meeting the Demand for Pediatric Mental Health Care," *Pediatrics* 144, no. 6 (December 2019).

290 *a worrisome paradox:* Ellen Barry, "The 'Nation's Psychiatrist' Takes Stock, with Frustration," *New York Times,* February 22, 2022.

290 *one and four:* Dr. Stefan Kertesz and Dr. Joshua Sharfstein, author interviews, September 1 and 2, 2021, for Dr. Kertesz, and April 6, and August 17, 2021, for Dr. Sharfstein.

290 *most are still:* Drs. Joshua Sharfstein and Yngvild Olsen, author interview, August 17, 2021. The addiction specialists believe that medical accreditation boards, while they now require doctors to recognize the signs of addiction, should go a step further and mandate that physicians know how to treat it. Although "taxpayers spend more than $10 billion a year through the Medicare program to support graduate medical training, about two-thirds of training programs do not support training in prescribing buprenorphine," Sharfstein and Olsen wrote in "Making Amends for the Opioid Epidemic," *JAMA Forum,* April 16, 2019.

290 *federal funding of syringes:* Alex Ruoff, "Record Overdose Deaths Prompt Congress to Reconsider Needle Aid," *Bloomberg Government,* July 22, 2021.

291 *"the decades of doom":* Dr. Arthur Robin Williams, author interview, October 1, 2021.

292 *a handful of walk-in:* Suzanne V. Jarvis et al., "Public Intoxication: Sobering Centers as an Alternative to Incarceration, Houston, 2010–2017," *American Journal of Public Health* (April 2019).

292 *"right now we have":* Greg Williams, author interview, August 2, 2021. Williams outlines his fixes for the opioid crisis in "What Would Dr. Kirk Do with This Moment?: An Open Letter to SAMHSA Single State Authorities," Third Horizon Strategies, April 1, 2021, https://third horizonstrategies.com/what-would-dr-kirk-do-with-this-moment/.

AUTHOR'S NOTE AND GLOSSARY

295 *"Call it medicine":* Dr. Sharon Walsh, March 21, 2019. Walsh interrupted me from the audience during a speech I was giving for a Fulbright Visiting Scholar Enrichment Seminar at the University of Kentucky.

Index

Note: Italic page numbers refer to photographs.

Index

Index

Index

About the Author

BETH MACY is the author of the widely acclaimed and bestselling books *Dopesick, Truevine,* and *Factory Man.* Based in Roanoke, Virginia, for three decades, Macy has won more than two dozen national awards for her reporting, including an L.A. Times Book Prize, a Lukas Prize, and a Nieman Fellowship for Journalism at Harvard. The creator of the Audible Original documentary *Finding Tess: A Mother's Search for Answers in a Dopesick America,* she has also been published in the *New York Times,* the *Washington Post, The Atlantic, Oxford American,* and *The Wall Street Journal.* Macy was a co-writer and executive producer of Hulu's television adaptation of *Dopesick,* which stars Michael Keaton.

BethMacyWriter.com
Facebook.com/AuthorBethMacy